S0-BJF-670

A TREPID AVIATOR

BOMBAY TO BANGKOK

*To Chuck Ross –
Hope you'll enjoy your
visit to India –
Wally Frazer*

W.W. FRAZER

Published by

GENERAL STORE
PUBLISHING HOUSE

1 Main Street Burnstown, Ontario, Canada K0J 1G0
Telephone (613) 432-7697 or 1-800-465-6072

Layout and cover design by Robert Hoselton

Copyright © 1995
General Store Publishing House
Burnstown, Ontario, Canada

No part of this book may be reproduced, stored in a retrieval system or transmitted in any form or by any means electronic, mechanical, photocopying, recording or otherwise, except for purposes of review, without the prior permission of the publisher.

General Store Publishing House gratefully acknowledges the assistance of the Ontario Arts Council and the Canada Council.

Canadian Cataloguing in Publication Data

Frazer, Wm Wallace
    Trepid aviator

ISBN 1-896182-01-1

        1.   Frazer, Wm Wallace   2. World War, 1939-1945—Personal narratives, Canadian.   3. Canada.   Royal Canadian Air Force—Biography.   4. Air pilots, Military—Canada—Biography.   I. Title.

D607.C2F73 1994   940.54´4971´092   C94-900878-B

First Printing 1995

This book is dedicated to the memory of
Steve, Chota, Murray, Ken,
And there was Eddie and Smokey... and Mac... and Phil
And, of course, Joe
And... oh... so many others!

A TREPID AVIATOR
BOMBAY TO BANGKOK

Chapters

Maps

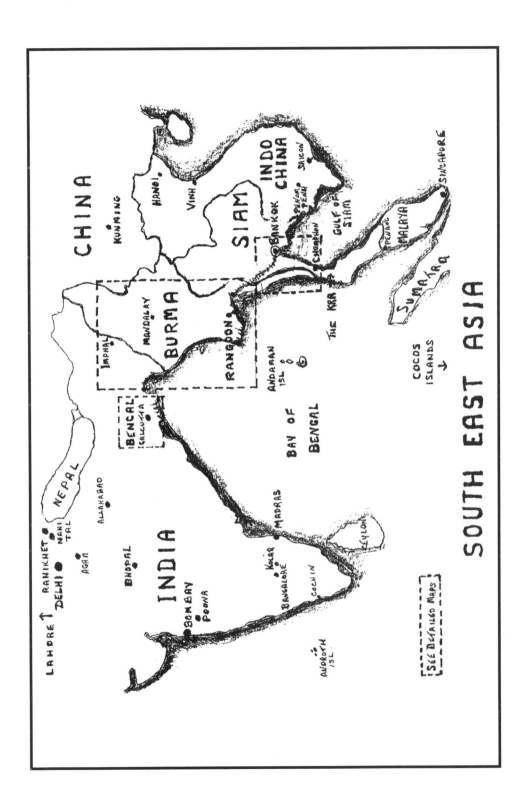

SOUTH EAST ASIA

MAIN PLAYERS

FRAZER CREW

Barlow, Joe	RAF	Wireless/Op
Cooper. Arthur	RAF	Flt/Engineer
Done, Bob	RAF	Navigator
Frazer, Wally	RCAF	Captain
Govan, "Jock"	RAF	Co-Pilot
Hill, Eddie	RAF	Top Gunner
Howse, Phil	RAF	Nose Gunner
Jones, Stan	RAF	Ball Gunner
McIlwaine, Mac	RAF	Wireless/Op
Reid, Joe	RCAF	Bomb-aimer, 356 Squad
Slight, Jim	RAF	Tail Gunner
Smith, Alan	RAF	Bomb-aimer, 215 Squad

OTHER SQDN

Beadon, C.V.	RAF	215	Flt/Commander
Brodie, Steve	RCAF	215	Captain
Brown, Art	RCAF	356	Flt/Commander
Cloutier, Phil	RCAF	358	`Blackpool Four,' Captain
Cox, Ken	RCAF	215	Navigator, Brodie crew

Gardner, Mac	RCAF	215	Captain
Gilbert, Eddie	RCAF	215	Captain
Harris, Art (Chota)	RCAF	215	Wireless/Op, Brodie crew
Insull, Jack	RCAF	356	Co-pilot, Brown crew
Jackson, Bill	RAF	355	`Blackpool Four,' Captain
Johnson, Johnny	RCAF	159	Captain
King, John	RCAF	358	Poona tent-mate
McMaster, Phil	RCAF	356	Captain
O'Connor, Percy	SAAF	215	Flt/Commander
Potts, Murray	RCAF	215	Co-pilot, Brodie crew
Robertson, Robbie	RAF	-	Railway Expert
Scriver, Russ	RCAF	356	Bomb-aimer, Brown crew
Shannon, Cec	RCAF	356	Bomb-aimer, McMaster crew
Sindall, James	RAF	215	C.O.
Sparks, G.B.	RCAF	356	C.O.
Waddington, Bill	RCAF	215	Captain
Watters, `Windy'	RCAF	356	Navigator, Brown crew
Williams, Roy	RAAF	215	Flt/Commander
Williams, `Smokey'	RCAF	215	Navigator, Gilbert crew
Willing, Ted	RAAF	159	`Blackpool Four,' Captain

CHAPTER 1

EAST OF SUEZ

MAR. 15, 1944

"Somewhere East of Suez." What an address to put atop a letter!

Doesn't it flash up pictures of elephants, snake-charmers, coolies, pagodas... and dark-haired girls with flashing black eyes?

But not yet. So far, just water — the Indian Ocean — the part that's called the Arabian Sea. From England, we've come through the Mediterranean, the Suez Canal, have just cleared the Red Sea. For a fellow who until he joined the RCAF — the Royal Canadian Air Force — was not exactly a world traveller... heady stuff! And next stop, straight ahead now —India!

Our ship is the *Stratheden* of the P & O line. I thought the letters stood for "Pacific and Orient" but a British Colonel straightened me out on that.

"Peninsular and Oriental!" he snorted. "Malayan Peninsula. Been making the run to the Med and the Far East for years. World famous, don't y'know?"

In some places, maybe, but not where I come from. Of course, in central Canada — in Ottawa — we just have rivers and lakes, no ocean liners at all.

The *Stratheden* is a nice little ship, not half the size of the old *Louis Pasteur* that brought us from Halifax to England nine months ago. In wartime, the *Pasteur* was strictly a troopship, men jammed in like matches in a box. But, hey, this *Stratheden* is like one of those cruise ships you see in the movies. Pre-war, our little cabin had just two single beds; upper bunks have been added. For four, it's not too crowded; we're quite comfortable sleeping, or even all sitting on the lower bunks if we space our knees right.

Yeah, it was disconcerting to find I'd be bunking with three RAF ground-staff blokes, but we've been a congenial group. Two have just

1

After Wings Parade
Author, March '43

finished training as Intelligence Officers. Robbie, the fourth, is older than the rest and carries 270 pounds of railroad expertise. He always has a quip: "wasn't it Will Rogers who said, `I never met a calorie I didn't like'?"

But one of his remarks to me — which I now think was a classic — could have earned him a bent nose if you didn't see the good humour in his eyes.

"Is it true, Wal... why a Canadian eats only with his right hand... he has to keep the left hand free to hold the can of beans?"

Leaving England in February, the first leg to Gibraltar was cold. But in the sunny Med we went shirtless, apparently shocking one passenger, a Russian colonel, who said our lack of military decorum was scandalous. Then, coming through the Red Sea, we sweltered! Said to be the hottest place in the world, we panted and mopped our faces for the entire 1,200 miles. Especially if the ship was moving in the same direction as any slight breeze, it was like no air at all, everyone gasping for breath.

"And this is only March," one chap said. "In peacetime, the captain in mid-summer would sometimes turn the ship around, sail into the wind for a few hours, just to give the passengers some relief."

Hah! Turn the ship around? That's crazy. There are always a few smart-ass guys in any crowd who think it's great sport to talk a simpleton into believing something stupid; you have to stay on your guard for that. Trouble is, sometimes it's not that easy to tell when your leg is being pulled. But reverse directions? It's true I never was so hot...

I've now been told a dozen times where the word "posh" originated, that the Red Sea had a lot to do with it. When travellers booked passage between Britain and India, to make the trip as comfortable as possible — to be on the shady side of the ship in either direction — they always stipulated that their cabins had to be P.O.S.H.... "Port Out, Starboard Home."

Robbie says our cabin is P.L.E.W. — "Port-Less Either Way."

Right now we're in the Main Lounge playing a little bridge. Lots of big windows and glass doors wide open. With a nice breeze, a lemon drink in one hand and an occasional ace in the other, the trip is going very well. Meals have been fabulous. And I can afford to put some weight back on. At five foot eight, I'm just average height; losing ten pounds in England dropped me to a scrawny 140 pounds.

But the best thing about the voyage are the girls — fifty nurses and Navy WRENs on their way to India, baring arms and legs to get some tan on skin ultra-white after an English winter. We even have dances on deck; only old records for music but with a full moon and all those smashing girls, you could think this wasn't such a useless war after all.

Port Said was our only stop. Nobody got ashore; they'd never get everyone back in the morning. But we could see people, houses, and my first palm trees.

Someone accused me of being a `touristy' kind of person, meaning I get a kick out of seeing new things, new places. I suppose that's true. Sure, the Suez Canal's just a big ditch dug in the sand, but now, when I see it on a map, I'll know what it looks like.

And that's where we learned a big secret. Where the canal widened into a lake — a whole fleet of warships! Battleships, cruisers, destroyers. I've never seen a naval force before, except in movies, but I'm sure there's not a more majestic sight anywhere.

"Has to be the Italian fleet," we decided. "Ships that surrendered at Taranto six months ago. This is where we're hiding them."

But at roll call, our Deck Officer said, "What ships? You didn't see any warships back there. If you think you did, forget it. And that's an order!"

"Your deal, Wal," Robbie is saying. He's my partner and we're not doing very well. I'm just learning the game and he's not much better. But I hear someone at the next table say, "Aden, on the port bow right now."

Hey, I've heard of Aden — the Gulf of Aden — it's on lots of maps. We've got to see it, right? The others follow me outside, though without enthusiasm. And nobody else in the lounge has left his seat. Yeah, I've heard of that... people taking a world cruise but never leaving their bridge tables.

Oh oh, I've boobed again. There's nothing to see but haze. That dark smudge might be Aden but you couldn't be sure. What I am sure of, looking back into the lounge... another foursome has grabbed our table.

The others go back to the cabin but I stay topside. I like the open deck, especially at the pointy end. It's mesmerizing to watch the prow slice into the water — up and down, up and down. The agitated ocean tumbles to either side, fuming and hissing, furious to be disturbed. It takes several minutes — a quarter mile — until the turbulence subsides to mere annoyance, until the sea behind us is calm again and we've apparently been forgiven.

Porpoises are escorting us, fifty feet to the left and running parallel.

Something else I've never seen before are flying fish. The tiny, silvery things come streaking out of the water by the hundreds, skim just inches above the surface, moving so fast it's hard to get a focus on them. Maximum range seems about sixty feet, their tails swishing like crazy.

"They're not really flying, you know," says an RAF fellow leaning over the rail beside me. "They have strong tails, build up tremendous speed in the water, then break the surface and glide on spread-out fins — pectoral fins which are unusually large. Waggling their tails in the air might add a bit of propulsion but I think it's more sailing than flying. But ratha' remarkable, wouldn't you say? The theory is they're trying to escape predators."

Yeah, that would explain it. I could wiggle my tail that fast, too, if I had a shark gaining on me!

MAR. 18

"How come you got sent to India?" That's usually the first question when people meet here. "Have you still got your crew?" is next.

I'm with two New Zealanders; in this business, you never lack guys to talk to. One wears pilot wings, the other is a navigator and, yes, they crewed up together at an OTU —Operational Training Unit — in England.

"Yes, our wireless operator and both gunners are with us," they tell me. "We understand we're to fly American B24 Liberators in India. You were told that too? Then we'll need more than the five-man crew we had on Wellingtons. Libs take about ten men. At least we've kept our original five as a nucleus; most crews got split up coming out here. Did that happen to you?"

"Yeah, just kept the wireless op from my original gang. Also a replacement gunner, but I've only met him once."

The first question? I'm not sure why I'm on this ship. Finishing up OTU at Harwell, near Oxford, we were waiting for the usual posting to Bomber Command in Britain. Then the three South African crews on the course were listed for India instead. But, in Cape Town, it seems brown faces aren't liked any better than black ones. India didn't suit them at all; they refused to go.

Flatly rejecting an order just isn't done, of course, and we had to admire their audacity as the SAAF guys took on the whole Royal Air Force. But sympathies changed when they threatened to have their government back them up. Why should South Africans be able to dodge a duty the rest of us couldn't? But they managed it. The postings were cancelled and a notice went on the board asking for "three crews to volunteer for an overseas posting."

That's when I suggested to my two buddies at Harwell that we at least consider the offer. Sure, India is too hot, uncivilized and distant. On the other hand, you don't need a PhD in math to figure out that doing thirty missions over Germany when the Jerries are knocking down five to ten percent each night sounds unhealthy. But Chris and Ed said they weren't worried, were certainly not interested in going out East, and so we agreed to stay together in England.

"Two days later," I tell the Kiwi guys, "I see that Flying Officer Frazer, which is me, is on the new list of crews posted abroad. I don't know if the Adjutant heard I'd at least thought about volunteering, or just picked my name out of a hat, but here I am. I'm not even sure if I'm sorry or glad."

But I shouldn't have said that. Nobody ever admits he volunteered for India, or even thought about it. The standard answer is, "Just my bad luck."

That's the reply which will show you're not concerned about personal safety, that you wish you'd stayed in the UK, stayed to fight it out with the Messerschmits. But when you've said something you wish you hadn't, you can't just scratch it out, like in a letter.

It's lunch time. The three fellows I know best on the ship, pilots on the same course at OTU, just went by the door and beckoned. The "Blackpool Four" we call ourselves because we were billeted at the same boarding house in that resort city waiting for this ship.

I suppose we're a strange mix. Bill Jackson is a veteran, an RAF Flight-Lieutenant with a DFM — Distinguished Flying Medal — and has already done a tour of ops. Bill can be a dour chap, but we usually let him act as our leader, partly because he knows more than we do about flying stuff, but also because he prefers it that way.

The rest of us are rookies. Phil Cloutier is an RCAF-er from Montreal. Not a hundred percent confident of his English, he doesn't say much. Tall and straight-backed, a little black moustache on a solemn face, he's the handsome one in the group. You wouldn't say that of Ted Willing. What you might say of Ted is that he's all Aussie. I've never known anyone so certain that if we'll all just relax, everything will work out fine. He also thinks that if you aim to become a battle-scarred veteran, you might as well start looking the part right away. His officer's flat hat looks so battered, the result of being stomped on, it could have gone through the Crusades.

"Parlay somet'ing in Urdu, Wallee," is Cloutier's greeting.

I've been going to a little language class each morning, mostly just to put in time though it wouldn't be a bad idea to know some of the local lingo.

"Teek hai," I tell him. "That means `okay.' We're not learning the grammar, just a few words. I can now count up to twelve....ec, doh, tin... char, paunch, chay...sawt, awt..."

"Nonsense?" Jackson interrupts. "We don't even know where we're going. There are hundreds of dialects in India. Besides which, when I was in the Middle East, we didn't learn *their* language, we made the natives learn *ours*."

Bill may be right. The old Colonel who's teaching us says Urdu is a Moslem language; Hindus in northern India might know it, but it'd be useless in Ceylon. But Bill's anger seems mostly aimed at the idea that an Englishman should ever have to learn another language, and that's a bit snotty.

Or are we all getting crotchety? Even with ship's concerts and other entertainment laid on, after three weeks you're completely bored at being cooped up on such a small piece of real estate, wish you could just get off and go for a long, solitary walk.

Mostly British Army, the passenger list also includes a few Navy types, the miscellany of nurses, some Yanks, and RAF or the colonial equivalent. Not many RCAF though, maybe twenty. Of course that's only the officers. Sergeants and other ranks have their own deck, their own eating and sleeping areas; this is very definitely a segregated society.

Hey, there's Keele and Johnson. I'll go talk to them.

Most of the Air Force here were at the same OTU in England, but Bill and Johnny I hadn't seen since Canada. Enlisting November '41, I reported to Toronto in January. That's where you got a blue serge uniform, a vicious haircut and an armful of needles. We met there, all lowly AC2s — Aircraftsmen 2nd Class — at the very bottom of the ladder.

After some guard duty at the Trenton air base on Lake Ontario, Bill and John were sent to one Initial Training School and I went to another. When you finished ground school there, about half were picked to train as navigators; others were sent to an Elementary Flying School. If you didn't wash out at that stage, you'd go on to advanced flying. But your gang would be split up again, some going on twin-engine planes, others on fighters. At the new station, you'd be re-joining guys you'd known months before.

If you traced on graph paper all the comings and goings of your original group, the maze of lines would diverge, criss-cross, come together for a time and then split off again. You'd also need wide, wide paper on the right-hand side of your graph if you tried to show the variety of jobs those guys are now doing, and just about anywhere in the world.

I wonder what history books will call this war. The 1918 affair was called the Great War, but this one's even bigger. Maybe the "Gigantic War?"

At the prow again, I see two men a deck below painting an air duct. From their dark complexions, they must be Indian seamen —'Lascars.' I guess I never saw anyone from India before.

"Mac! Hey, Mac," I shout. That's Bernie McIlwaine down there, my wireless operator. And the little guy with him is Stan Jones, our new gunner.

They're shouting back but the wind erases the words. Another big wave and they retreat out of sight. But I'm glad I saw them — only the second time on the whole trip. There's just no place we can meet.

Tom and Dave, the Intelligence chaps, are in the cabin. Hey, I've wanted to ask them about the fighting here in SEAC — South East Asia Command. It's crazy to be getting involved in a war you know so little about.

"Yes, we try to catch the BBC broadcasts on the ship's wireless," Tom says. "At this moment, a major battle is taking place at Imphal."

"Imphal," Dave repeats; he can see I've never heard of the place. "In Assam, the north-east corner of the country, right next to Burma."

"You mean the Japs are already in India?"

"On the border, anyway. They've taken most of Burma, are trying to push right into India. Yes, they've moved very quickly. After Pearl Harbor — then crippling the British Pacific fleet in a single bombing attack — the impossible happened. They took Singapore, as bad a shock to us Brits as Pearl Harbor was to the Yanks. When the Philippines fell a few weeks later, there wasn't much to stop them from flooding through the entire area."

"Yes, I remember that. But what about Burma?"

"Burma was invaded from Siam. Six weeks after Pearl. They took Moulmein, then Pegu, cut off Rangoon. It fell by mid-March. Then they headed north; it was a debacle for our side."

"There were British troops, of course, but any Americans?"

"A few. General Chennault had twenty of his Flying Tiger fighter planes in Rangoon to help the RAF defend the city. And General Stilwell's group was in northern Burma leading Chinese troops who were there to defend the Burma Road. Protecting the supply route into China was the Americans' main interest in Burma, of course.

"Even with RAF Buffaloes and Blenheims flying with the US fighters, our side had only about sixty so-called front-line aircraft against the Japs' four hundred. The Chinese Army was routed and many of the survivors headed home. What was left of the Flying Tigers went back to China. The Japs were moving so fast there was panic and confusion on our side. Our military people admit... the Japanese campaign was brilliantly planned, expertly executed.

"They reached Lashio to cut the Burma Road, took Mandalay about May 1st. Then it became a rout. Some Americans escaped into China, but Stilwell's party and the British troops walked all the way back to India — tough going through jungles and over mountains. And they had a lot of company. I saw estimates that about a million refugees — Indians and some Burmese — tried to escape back to India over that route, and half died on the way. Of the three Chinese divisions under Stilwell — 100,000 men — barely 10,000 reached India. It was a shambles.

"But the monsoon weather arrived to slow the Japs down. Tojo's troops in northern Burma are now based at a place three hundred miles north of Mandalay. It's Myitkyina on a map, but we pronounce it `Mitchenaw.' Yes, we still have a few men in Burma — mostly diversionary tactics to pester them. General Wingate's `Chindits' are in the jungles around Mandalay; some Yanks leading native troops are doing a good job of harassing the Japs in the north.

"That winter, we tried to re-take Akyab to the south. The Japs stopped us but it maybe postponed their invasion until this year. The British army plus the Chinese troops are at Imphal now. It'll be a major battle. I saw an estimate that the Japs have a quarter million men in Burma.

"Their immediate aim? Just cut our supply lines. But long-term plans are more ambitious. Have you heard what Tokyo Radio has been saying... that they're going to break into India and march all the way to Delhi? If the Japs win at Imphal, there's no telling what might happen."

"What do you mean?"

"Well, as soon as the Japs arrived in Burma, a lot of Burmese decided to join them. And we British aren't any better liked in India."

"The same thing could happen here?"

"I don't know what the thinking is in Delhi. I'd just guess the top brass must be plenty worried. Gandhi and the Congress Party are trying to get rid of us already. If the Japs break through at Imphal, there has to be some chance the whole country will welcome them. If that happens, anybody here with a white skin better keep his running shoes handy."

Cheez! And I thought I was coming out here mostly just to see what the country looked like.

MAR. 21

Land ahoy! The first shout just went up.

The deck's jammed, everyone anxious for a first look at our home for the next... who knows? We're going into Bombay and I have a spot right on the rail. There's a jumble of buildings, two to six stories high. Not skyscrapers, but not mud huts either; I guess I didn't know what to expect.

Now the tugs are pushing us in toward a quay with a big structure on it, looking a bit like the Arc de Triomphe — maybe sixty feet high, four small towers above that. And flying even higher — a flashy reminder as to just who owns this country — the Union Jack!

"It's called the Gateway of India," says an RAF guy standing beside me.

The tugs are grunting and shoving. Lascar sailors on the prow are holding coils of huge hawsers, other dark-faced men waiting on the dock. Some orders are given in a loud voice, the hawsers are thrown onto the dock and quickly wound around steel posts. Then a slight scraping noise, a small bump, and we come to a complete stop.

I think, indisputably, we have arrived in India!

"Attention," the ship's Tannoy crackles. "Disembarkation will commence shortly. All personnel will go to their quarters. When your name is called..."

I go to the cabin, the others already there. "Been waiting for you,Wal," Robbie says. "Got this Scotch from the steward for some small favours."

Already, he's pouring very generous portions into four glasses.

"A dab of water? I know you barbarians from America like ice, but we don't have that. Cheers! I understand when you run out of Ballantines and Beefeaters out here, there's only Indian gin; three jiggers and a toenail flakes off. Anything wrong with your drink, Wal? Want more Scotch in it?"

"No no, quite.. uh.. enough. Very.. ah.. good Scotch, Robbie."

I get that much out though the whisky just burned a hole in my lungs big enough all the air leaked out; it's hard work to re-fill them. Each sip makes me more certain that Scotch is the foulest drink ever invented. Why would any man in his right mind choose it, especially when it's as warm as bath-water, and tastes worse?

Damn. Robbie's raising his glass; it's another bloody toast.

"Here's to our long voyage together. We did get along very well. So wherever we go from here... good luck to everyone."

They all drained their glasses; what could I do but the same?

All this time the Tannoy has been barking out names. Hey, that's me! How many times have I met fellows, liked them, been good friends for a few days or weeks, and then had to say "so long"? With all the practice, I should be getting better at it. All I've learned is not to drag it out.

Up the stairs, out on the deck, lugging my loose gear. Lord, it's hot. And I'm feeling that damn drink. There's our crowd ahead. I pass some of the ship's officers looking cool and neat in white shorts and shirts. But there's no sense in what Air Force guys are wearing — full uniforms, even to black ties. And in this hundred degree temperature, what am I carrying but my winter greatcoat! It was useful in the Atlantic, then wouldn't squeeze into my trunk.

There's a rough line-up and I dump my stuff beside Phil Cloutier. A chap with a splendid tan is standing in front with a clip-board. He's in khaki shorts and shirt with the two blue stripes on the shoulder straps showing his Flight Lieutenant rank.

"All right, chaps," he says. "Welcome to our fair land. My name is Wooding. My job, my only interest in life, is to see to your every comfort and whim while you remain our honoured guests in Bombay."

Hah! Another David Niven type you meet so often in the RAF; a light-hearted manner that says, "Alright, men, a few minor chores to look after, but we won't take them too seriously, shall we?"

"I'll call your names. When we're certain no one has toppled overboard during your arduous voyage, we'll march you off the ship in jig time, find you some shade. Good Lord, from the way you're dressed, you must've thought you were going to the North Pole. Lorries will then whisk you to the RAF Reception Depot at Worli — a suburb of Bombay a half hour from here."

After a month aboard, those first steps on the solid dock feel marvellous. A ship always does a certain amount of pitching and rolling; you're never absolutely certain your next step will find the deck exactly where your head estimates it should be. Maybe our bodies don't like that. Right now, my legs want to stride up and down the concrete to savour its perfect stability. "Terra firma" the old Romans called it. The firmness of the terra is certainly one of its best characteristics.

Here come the trucks. Grab a seat on a bench; already we're starting to move. The canvas top wards off the sun and the sides are rolled up enough to allow some breeze. Now let's see this Worli place.

CHAPTER 2

JUST OFF THE BOAT

MAR. 22, 1944

First stop yesterday, the Stores Section, like similar units everywhere except that the Corporal's assistants were three young Indians, trim and neat in khaki uniforms. "Enrolled Followers," someone said. "Not full-fledged members of the RAF, but almost... help out in a lot of areas."

When we'd all crowded inside, a door opened and an officer appeared — an old gentleman with a moustache gone snow white on him.

"Gentlemen," he said, "welcome to India." Though he called it `Injaw.' "You are no doubt aware that, in Injaw, commissioned ranks must provide their own bed, bedding, other personal effects. At this depot, some such items are indeed available to you as a matter of convenience, but normally they are your own responsibility."

What's that? Provide our own beds? I didn't know that. From the buzz around me, others didn't either.

"However..."

Hah! When you hear that word, you listen very carefully. It's one of the most important in the English language, a key word that warns when the bomb is about to go off. But this time it was a dud.

"However," he repeated, "through the generosity of the Maharajah of Mahjanipore, you are being presented with a kit that will cover your basic needs. This is his personal gift to thank you for coming to Injaw's aid in her time of peril."

The big cardboard boxes could be manhandled back to the barracks building where we'd dumped our bags. It was like Christmas all over.

First, a rickety contraption of hinged poles and green canvas that made a camp bed. Next, a fold-up chair. More interesting was a gizmo of poles you arranged into two `X' shapes three feet high, on top of which you plopped a bowl-shaped piece of canvas to form a wash basin. But the bath tub on the same principle is laughable. Three feet square and just an inch off the ground... how could you bathe in anything as tiny, as flimsy, as that?

Last night, my first mosquito net. Pulled out of its package, it was just a big pile of netting, like a fish net only finer.

"Here, m'ite, you have to sh'ike it open," Ted Willing told me. "See, it's the sh'ipe of a corn fl'ikes box, open at the bottom. You tie the closed end to those wires up there, let the netting hang down all around the bed. When you crawl in and tuck the bottom under your sheet, you're enclosed in a sort of box, s'ife and sound for the night."

I slept okay. You can see out — like peering through cheesecloth — not that there's much to see anyway except another hundred beds. The net does cut down on the flow of air from the ceiling fans, but you have to use them, could be court-martialled if you didn't, because mosquitoes here can give you more than an itch.

On the ship, the Medical Officer lectured us that malaria kills a million people a year in India. You get the infection from a mosquito bite; not any mosquito, just a female of the Anopheles type. The insect makes its dinner on the blood from an infected animal, such as a cow, the parasite develops in her body and, if she can then get her proboscis into you, the alternating chills and high fever will start in about ten days.

Big posters on walls warn, "Beware the Lady Anopheles."

Fortunately, her lust to impregnate you is a night time thing. During the day, you can wear shorts and short-sleeved shirts; after sundown, it's slacks to the ankle, shirts to the wrist, swat anything that buzzes.

There was a roll-call at 9 a.m. so that Wooding could tick off his list. No, he didn't know how long we'd be here. Yes, except for morning `parade,' our time was entirely our own. "The bazaar — the local market — is just a ten minute walk. You can check out the latest in khaki fashions, guaranteed cooler than what you're wearing."

Noel Coward sang that "only mad dogs and Englishmen go out in the mid-day sun." But with the heat seeming to add twenty pounds to your weight, I joined several heading for the market in a sort of slow convoy. We'd stop under a tree, wipe our faces, eye the distance to the next shady spot. Luckily, there were a lot of trees. This Worli seems a high-class neighbourhood with wide, shady streets and big homes; many have been taken over by the military, such as the one we use as our Officers' Mess.

The native bazaar... I've never seen anything so colourful. Shops sell everything from shoelaces to emeralds. And such haggling!

"A khaki shirt," Wooding said. "Don't pay more than three

rupees." At three rupees to the dollar, that's just a buck.

Three rupees? Hah! The asking price started at ten. The merchants could see us coming, suckers swathed in hot, heavy uniforms. Standing in the sun, it took us a half hour to get the price to five. Nevertheless, I invested heavily in khaki. Even with long Boy Scout stockings, the lightness of the shorts and improved air circulation feel wonderful. And, after wearing nothing but blue for two years, it's a change to be neck to ankle in brown.

The people of this country seem a handsome lot. Most have good features, and the black hair, dark eyes and white teeth go nicely with the well-tanned faces... make you realize how washed-out the white race can look in comparison.

The waiters in the Mess are all men. Costumed in white pants, white jacket to the knees and a bright red sash that goes around the waist, they make the dining room a colourful place. They're called "bearers" — originally a porter who carries things, but the term now refers to any personal servant. At meals, several work each table, standing straight and solemn and silent behind each chair, quick to refill your water glass or whatever.

But I had one young lad badly perplexed. Lunch was a chicken-and-rice concoction; delicious, but too rich, too much, for a stomach shrivelled by British wartime rations. I told the lad to remove the plate but he didn't understand. I tried sign language, pointing to the dish and then the kitchen door. But his face showed utter bewilderment, maybe even fright.

"You're confusing him," an English fellow said. "You've left your knife and fork criss-crossed on the dish. The signal that you're finished is to set them side-by-side. Try it. Place them parallel on your plate."

I did that; the kid broke into a big grin, picked up the dish and headed for the kitchen.

Tonight we're taking it easy, sitting on the wide second-storey balcony that runs across the front of the Mess. It must have belonged to someone very rich because it's an elegant big home with a lot of cool grey marble, both inside and out. I'm with Cloutier and Willing and a dozen others, sipping lemon-limes and enjoying the breeze.

Yes, there's a breeze. It comes off the Arabian Sea where the surf is beating against rocks on the other side of that boulevard a hundred yards away. With long shadows stretching over the landscape, a pretty sight.

I heard a remark today about people being "just off the boat." It's definitely not a compliment, means you're very much a newcomer, still with "no brown on your knees." Our gang certainly fits that

Just off the boat
Author, Ted Willing

description. But we're at least starting to look like old India hands. We're all in tropical attire: tan slacks and open-necked khaki 'bush jackets,' a combination jacket and shirt which can be worn without a tie or anything underneath.

Tomorrow, four of us are going to have a look at Bombay. A few days here should be okay.

MAR. 23

It's a traffic jam. The four of us — the Blackpool Four — are sitting in a 'gharry,' a horse-drawn buggy. For a time we were clip-clopping along in high style, sitting in facing seats and feeling quite regal as we rolled through a fairly good section of Bombay. Our driver, a wizened little guy in tattered rags, is perched on a tiny ledge up front.

Now the traffic is heavier, and we're stalled. A brown-faced policeman is standing on a box at the intersection ahead, a gaudy sight in blue pantaloons, red jacket, a tam secured by a chin strap. With his right hand, he's holding up traffic; with his left, he's holding a parasol.

Now I spot the problem. It's a bullock cart crossing in front of us, a two-wheeled wagon powered by ugly animals with ridiculously long horns.

"Water buffalo," Bill informs us.

"Look at the wheels," Ted notices. "M'ide of wood... not even very round."

The driver, sitting cross-legged on the tongue, is in no hurry at all, the cart hardly moving; everything else is motionless. Eventually he inches out of the way. The cop blows his whistle... and bicycles, lorries, autos, ancient buses and other gharries start moving. It's as if the break in the film has been repaired and the movie has started again.

The men on the sidewalk wear a variety of costumes. Most are swathed in some sort of billowing white cotton, either a loose shirt or a jacket that drops to the hips or goes right to the ground like a skirt. Underneath, they wear pyjamas — an Indian word

Stratheden Shipmates
Jackson, Robbie, Author
Cloutier, — , Willing

— usually six sizes too large. But a few wear nothing more than a bulky cloth between their legs like a baby's diaper.

The neighbourhood has deteriorated shockingly; the crowds have increased tenfold and spill off the sidewalks onto the street. Few white faces now.

Buildings are still several storeys high — shops at the bottom tight to the sidewalk, tenements above. Laundry hanging, stucco peeling, woodwork needing paint. But mostly you're aware of people, teeming thousands of them, filling the street.

"Ridiculous," Jackson says. "We're not moving. Let's walk."

Bill, a take-charge type, is already out of the buggy to argue the fare with the driver... in sign language, of course. The old geezer holds up one finger: one rupee, 33 cents. That doesn't sound too much. But Bill shakes his head. He hands over some coins; the driver scowls, but then shrugs.

"I gave him eight annas," Bill reports, pleased with himself. "Half a rupee, fifty percent of what he wanted. I know these natives; they're all the same, Tunis or Cairo or Bombay. Never give them more than half what they ask."

Walking isn't much faster. The streets get narrower, the sides crammed with shop after shop, many just three feet wide. The crowd is almost shoulder to shoulder, like the midway at the Fall Fair on Saturday night.

15

Royal Canadian Air Force

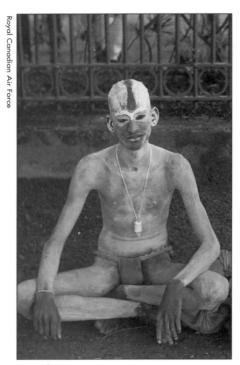

Street beggar

"Keep a hand on your wallet," Bill says, but I'm already doing that.

When I feel a gentle tug at my leg, I swing around, ready to punch. But it's a child — a girl, maybe 13 — a pretty little face if she ever washed it, but very solemn. She's holding a baby, a tiny thing draped across her hip.

"Baksheesh, sahib?" in a tiny voice, likely weak from hunger.

"Don't do that," Jackson shouts, seeing me reach for some coins. He says it more sharply than necessary. Dammit, he's not my boss.

"You can't feed the whole bloody country. She's just another professional beggar. When the others see you give her something, they'll figure you're a soft touch, hound us all day."

Well, maybe he knows about that. But when the kid sees I've changed my mind, there's a quick change in her expression... from hope to disappointment to despair in two seconds. A professional beggar? If she's that good an actress, she should be on the stage.

Over in an alcove off the sidewalk is another beggar holding a tin cup. This one's a young guy, my age but even skinnier, just a bag of bones, naked except for a loin cloth. He's sitting on a mat with his legs crossed under him, swami style. But closer up, I see that his legs aren't tucked underneath, but in front of him on the mat. They're deformed... twisted every which way... worse than a pretzel. Horrible.

"Sure," Bill says, "another professional beggar. They cripple themselves to get sympathy; that's what's needed to make a good living from alms. Maybe his parents did it for him when he was a baby — broke his legs, twisted them — got him set up in a career."

"Yecht, I t'ink I lose my breakfast," Phil grunts. I might join him.

A dignified Indian gentleman passes. He carries a briefcase so might be a businessman or a lawyer... although in my country such people don't go to appointments in bare feet or with shirt-tails flapping. I hear clunks as he drops some coins in the man's cup, then hurries on, not even slowing down to see the thank you gesture he gets. But do other

16

beggars rush to pester him? Hell, no; they completely ignore him. Does Jackson know as much as he thinks? I also wonder if that girl and her kid will eat today.

The sidewalks are now so badly blocked by vendors' carts that we're picking our way up the centre of the street. You want to be careful where you step because there's a lot of garbage on the road. Even the Indian pedestrians seem to be watching where they set their feet.

Yuck, I just stepped in something — a gooey, stinking cow-flop. The others chortle, think it's a great joke as I look for something to scrape my shoe. It's those damn water buffalo, I suppose.

"No, not buffalo," Phil says. "La culprit, dat's her ahead."

Yeah, maybe so. Up on the sidewalk, munching at some vegetables on a vendor's stand, is the scrawniest, saddest animal I've ever seen. It's a cow, a very skinny cow, loose folds of skin hanging down her sides.

"A holy cow," Jackson says. "To Hindus, a cow is sacred. But look at her eat those carrots. How can she look so starved when she eats like that?"

But I'm watching the vendor, who's watching the cow eat up his day's profits; he looks sick, disgusted, but resigned to his fate... certainly doesn't interfere. The animal finishes her chomping at that location, thinks a few thoughts, then starts a slow amble up the street to another booth.

"She par'ides like an old biddy Queen out for a stroll among her peasants," is Ted's description. But the people don't seem in awe of her; if they see they're on a collision course, they'll turn aside to pass. But they don't change expression; it doesn't seem that big a deal to them.

It's now noon and very hot. Wearing shorts, my legs aren't uncomfortable but my shirt is sweat-stuck to my back. The perpetual din — arguments, shouts and harangues — is very tiresome. From all the garbage and animal droppings on the street, the stink is terrible. We have horses on the roads at home too, but we also have street cleaners. Without those, and in this heat, the place can't smell like a rose garden.

"Omigawd, look at that!" The exclamation comes from Jackson, and Bill doesn't often allow himself to sound surprised.

Yeah, across the road... that old man, squatting on the edge of the sidewalk, right at the curb; he's dropped his diaper to his ankles and he's having a... he's defecating, right onto the street!

Other pedestrians pay no attention, just detour past. The old fellow stands up, wriggles back into his diaper, disappears into the crowd.

And here's something else to remind you that customs and standards vary from one society to another. It's another bullock cart, but this one is moving along fairly smartly. The driver crouched just behind his water buffalo is pushing a sharp, pointed stick right into the animal's backside. Pushing hard, and I mean right in! I think the M.O. calls it the anus. It certainly keeps the beast moving briskly, but must hurt like hell. Is there no SPCA in this country, or is cruelty to animals okay here? Or are we just getting too squeamish at home?

Ted says, "I've seen enough. Here's a taxi; let's get out of here."

Nobody disagrees. I'm goggle-eyed at what I've seen today. This country's going to be interesting, maybe not always pleasant.

MAR. 27

I'm on the balcony this morning, pretty well recovered from the bug which gave me the `runs' — chills, weak knees, a lot of forty-yard dashes.

"Quite common," the Doc said. "Take this castor oil; you'll feel chipper in no time. The problem comes from sudden changes in climate and diet. D'you want the medical term? It's called the `Delly Belly.'"

Hah, I like that. I've heard of Montezuma's Revenge, the Cairo Capers, the Tunis Trots and a few others, but Delhi Belly — that's a new one!

Most guys went off to swim but I'm still too weak for that. Last night, though, I got to the camp cinema, our usual after-dark diversion; it's a big open-air place with a roof but no walls in case a breeze should happen by. Just benches — the first twenty rows for officers — and no popcorn, it's primitive but fun as we cheer the hero and hiss the villain.

Afterwards, a good chat with Bernie McIlwaine, also Stan Jones who's an older guy. "Hope we'll all stay in the same crew," they say. I hope so too but had to tell them I've no idea what's going to happen.

After missing some roll-calls, I got there this morning. The greeting from Wooding? "A touch of Bombay Bum, was it, Frazer?"

One nice surprise; we get extra pay here. RAF-ers were aware of the India Allowance but I didn't know we were included. A worthwhile 220 rupees per month, there's a question as to whether it represents `danger pay' or a `hardship allowance.' Not that I like the sound of either.

"It's neither," Bill Jackson says. "It's to help RAF people pay the higher mess fees out here where we have to buy our own food, maybe recompense us a bit for being away from home. But you RCAF are already well paid."

Bill is bitter that the British pay scale is much below that of other countries. I agree it's not fair, but I don't know what I'm supposed to do about it. And what's that about Mess fees?

"You didn't know that? In Britain, an RAF station is provided with basic rations. A Mess may then charge a little more to cover extras. But in India, nothing is supplied. Each Mess is on its own, buys what it needs, charges the members enough to cover its costs. How much? Well, it'll vary but I hear they can be a hundred rupees a month."

Okay, I can afford that. With the India Allowance, I must be up to... cheez, $280 a month, likely more than Dad makes. Compared with my $12 a week before I enlisted, it's a fortune. Not that I was so hard-up then.

After paying half for my board and $3 on my car loan, I got by, was having a ball.

The RCAF pay for an aircrew cadet starts at $1.3O a day. Even with room and board, that's not a lot. But you kept getting increases until — surprise — you find you're damn well paid. But anytime they want to send me home, I'll gladly go back to my twelve bucks a week.

Several guys have had `the Belly' and we're all recuperating on the balcony. Johnny Johnson just handed me the local English-language newspaper. It's mostly war news — headlines about heavy fighting on the Burma border. The Japs have surrounded Kohima, and that's serious.

Johnson seems to want to talk. "Are you married, Wal? No? Engaged?"

"Well...sort of. But no ring, nothing like that."

"Yeah, same with us. Some guys got married right after they got their wings... had a few weeks together. You must have thought of doing that? Yes? Then why didn't you?" Johnny's a direct, blustery kind of guy.

"Well... we knew this'd be a... a risky line of work. I thought... I suppose I thought if I get through this, there'll be time after the war. If I don't... well, would she be better off as my widow or... well, I think it'd be easier for her to pick up the pieces if she was still Miss Jeffrey."

"Yeah," Johnny says. "That's about what I thought, too."

Finally some mail, just one letter each from Jean and Dad, and writ-

Jean

ten seven weeks ago, but at least the Postal Gods know where I am. Getting mail is terribly important. Important enough in England, doubly so away out here.

I'm feeling a very long way from home.

APR. 5

"Camel Rides — Four Annas." Yeah, let's try that.

Phil and I draw one, Bill and Ted take another. Not that there's much to choose; they all look cantankerous. They're ridden `dual,' one behind the other as in a Tiger Moth or Finch. The despatcher gets our animal, a big one, down on its haunches, and we climb up into the double saddle. The camel turns its head to look; never have I seen an unfriendlier face.

But getting camel-borne is as tricky as getting airborne. The attendant shouts something and the animal struggles to its feet, the manoeuver done in two stages and so clumsily you wonder if the brute has never tried it before.

First it extends its rear legs. With its front knees still on the ground, the rear section points at the sky; sitting up front, I'm looking straight down, big Cloutier spread-eagled across my back. Then the front end comes scrambling up. The animal levels out, staggering on unsteady feet until it gets its legs organized... like my grandfather when he stands up after sitting too long.

Starting out on the assigned course, I have the reins but can tell right off that this beast isn't going to let any stranger tell him where to go, especially some guy just off the boat!

What a strange pitching gait, like a ship in rough seas. After just one circuit, Phil says, "Let me off. I t'ink I get seasick."

So all four of us are now riding this elephant. It's lumbering and solid and slow — more appropriate, I suppose, for bomber pilots.

We're in town for the day. The trip to the Victoria Gardens was in a ramshackle '32 Packard, topless and missing a door. Our driver, a swarthy over-fed fellow in flowing robes, had a heavy foot. The ends of his turban got loose, blew straight back in horizontal streaks like flags in a gale.

A screeching halt in front of some big gates. The driver grunts "Vittario Goddins," we say "teek hai," and he replies with a guttural "hokay."

We walked the gardens, had our camel safari. Then it was shoes off for a tour of a mosque, climbing up the narrow stairway in one of the minarets for a good view of the city. A little sign, in broken English and other languages, got its message across: persons having any interest whatsoever in living till sun-down would not take it upon themselves to call the faithful to prayer.

We're in another cab and I'm checking the pamphlets I picked up at the Museum. "Bombay, first inhabited two thousand years ago by the Koli people," I read. "That's where the word `coolie' comes from."

"Aw, who cares about that," the others say. "Here's the Taj Mahal."

Wow! As far from a little mud hut as you could imagine — seven stories high with little bulbous towers above that. Ornate but spectacular. So that's the great Taj Mahal!

"No, no, no," Jackson jumps on me. "The real Taj is away up north, in Agra. This is a hotel; they just borrowed the name."

The doorman, eight feet tall in his turban, looks us over carefully. In the lobby, triple wow! This is the ritziest place I've ever seen.

To find the bar, you just follow the crowd. We spot some guys from Worli at a table that has empty chairs. Most customers are in uniform, but I notice some older white men in civvies, even a few ladies, even a few Indians.

The two fellows sitting beside me are arguing. The Aussie says, "I understand you Brits don't allow n'itives into a lot of your clubs, pl'ices like the Royal Yacht Club, the Gymkhana, the Byculla Club... but there are Indians here. Does it mean you're getting more democr'itic?"

"This isn't a private club," the Englishman says. "It's an hotel. And it's owned by an Indian... Mr Tata, a wealthy Parsis. The Parsis? They're a different race, originally from Persia, but that was centuries ago... settled around Bombay. Supposed to be very smart people... prosperous anyway.

"Here's the waiter," he continues. "You want a real India drink? Order a 'toddy.' No, it's not a 'hot toddy' though the Scots got the name from here. Made from the fermented sap of the coconut palm. You'll like it."

A lie! It's the sourest drink I ever tasted; castor oil, even Scotch, would taste better. I wish I would stop trying new things.

The bar tab — the 'chitti' — brings a chorus of whistles.

"We're going to the Cricket Club," says a fellow with a NZ badge on his shirt. "You could join us. And it's just for tiffin... not too expensive. You know the word 'tiffin' — a light meal at noon? Well, do you know where the word comes from? When men met for lunch and had a few drinks, they often got into little arguments... 'tiffs.' So the noon meal became 'tiffin.'"

Ahh, that's crazy. Is he kidding me? Yeah, I think so.

Twelve of us are on a veranda — another Indian word — overlooking the cricket pitch. Most of the guys get well into the gin before lunch, but I keep ordering lemon-limes to get rid of the taste of sour sap.

Returning to camp, pelting along Marine Drive beside the ocean, Ted suggests, "Let's go up Malabar Hill, see where those millionaire Parsis live."

Which we do. What mansions! Such wealth beside such terrible poverty!

"No, Parsis aren't Hindus," Bill says. "Brought their own religion from Persia... Zoroastrianism. I read about it. I say, there's a place near here you should see. Driver, take us up to the Towers of Silence."

Our chauffeur shakes his head. "No, no, sahib, never to going there."

"Of course you can. A taxi took me last week."

Jackson is enjoying his little mystery, won't tell us what it's all about. When the taxi stops in a parking area, the driver wants his fare, but Bill says if we pay him off he won't wait for us. We leave him muttering, and start up a steep path. After climbing two hundred yards, we come to a big iron gate.

"We can't go in," Bill says, "but see that wall over there? You can just spot it through the trees... a stone wall, twelve feet high. There are seven of them. Each is a circular wall with nothing inside except a concrete pad... and a pit. This is where the Parsis dispose of their dead, the Towers of Silence."

I think I've guessed what's coming, something to do with that bunch of vultures circling above.

"This isn't a regular cemetery," Bill is explaining, enjoying himself. "The Parsis don't bury their dead. Their religion believes that earth, water and fire are the three sacred elements... never to be defiled as by burying or cremating a dead body. That doesn't leave many alternatives. So they let the vultures do the job. Instead of burying a corpse, it's just left out, naked, on the concrete pad. Everyone leaves — except the vultures. See them sitting along that wall? They're waiting for the next funeral, the next feast."

Bill is saying how efficient the system is, the attendants coming in afterwards to shovel the bones down into the big pit. But what I'm noticing is a lot of small bones in the grass; maybe the birds drop some.

Omigosh, there's one with meat still on it! I've seen enough for today.

APR. 13

The Willingdon Sports Club accepts Allied officers as temporary members. Beautiful gardens and grounds, also a golf course. We skipped roll call today, got here at the same time as the sun. We rent golf clubs and tell the young Indian clerk we also need balls.

"Most sad, sahibs. No golf balls. Since war, ver' ver' scarce."

That's ridiculous! What good are golf courses without golf balls!

The clerk finally acknowledges he could let us have, strictly on a loan basis, one ball each. Unlocking a cabinet, he carefully brings out four badly abused 'nuts.' But only one each! With my slice, I can lose two balls a hole.

"Oh, no, sir," the lad smiles. "Never to lose; never to be possible."

What does that mean? Especially keen-eyed caddies?

Ted and Phil hit respectable drives; Jackson really catches one. With no rain for months, the fairway's as hard as an airport runway; the ball rolls nearly a quarter-mile, clear out of sight, but on the fairway.

My drive is also a beauty, straight down the centre... for the first fifty yards. Then it jack-knifes to the right, past some white stakes, over a road and into thick bushes. Damn! Just one swing — ball gone, game over!

But, hey, what's the commotion over there? Flashes of white, some scurrying around? And someone's racing this way. It's a kid, just a little lad of five or six. He's got something in his hand, held high over his head. Yes, it's a golf ball. Very excited, he's shouting something.

"Doh anna, sahib, doh anna. Baksheesh!"

Yes, it's my beat-up old ball and I'm more than happy to give him his four-cent tip. The kid seems overjoyed, puts the coins in his pocket, then scampers back to where he came from. I now see about twenty of these young ball-hawks spread out along the perimeter.

I slice several more off the course with the same result and the same finder's fee. Then Phil hooks one into deep fairway rough and we all head in that direction to look. But the kids get there first.

"Ec anna, ec anna, sahib," is the cry this time.

We get it figured out that the tariff is one anna for a ball found on the course, but double that for out-of-bounds. Which seems fair enough.

The kids stay with us the whole game. Mostly they just sit, watching and waiting. Only when it comes my turn to hit do they all stand up.

Wouldn't anybody get a little miffed at that!

APR. 19

War news isn't all bad these days; most people now think we can win this thing eventually. Russians have stopped the Germans at Stalingrad, the Japs are being beaten back in New Guinea, our troops are getting close to Rome.

And Britain? No sign of any 'second front' yet but the bombers are busy, the USAAF and the RAF hitting Germany hard. Here's the item about last night's raid; to check what the losses were, skip right to the end. Jeez! "Ninety-five of our aircraft are missing." Damn. How many men I knew — including guys I trained with at Harwell — would be in that total?

As for Imphal, the headline says, "Heavy fighting continues. Jap forces threatening to cut our supply lines but our men resisting with great courage."

Jeez! "Fighting with great courage" usually means we're losing.

"I have gen for you," Wooding told us this morning. "Most of you will shortly be going to Kolar in southern India to start training on Liberators."

I finally got some mail — five great letters from Jean and three from the folks. However, as Jean numbers hers, I can tell that two more are missing; maybe the rumours about a mail plane crashing in Persia are true.

"C'mon, m'ite, time to go." We thought of trying our luck at the races, but a shortage of cash decided us to settle for a movie downtown.

En route, we've stopped at a department store where Ted has heard they have merchandise from Aussie-land. I nip over to Sporting Goods. "Sorry, sir. Since war, no golf balls."

The sales clerks are men — Indians — some not as dark as others. But, wait, they aren't all males. I see three women standing behind counters over in the Ladies' Department, all very good-looking. I think they're Indian, though I've never seen any in European dress before. One is really smashing —slim, sort of an ivory skin, wavy black hair. Quite lovely.

"Anglo-Indian," murmurs a chap in British Army garb standing beside me. "Indian mother and British father, usually. Yes, that one's a beauty."

"Let's go," from Ted. "They only hold reserv'itions till eight-thirty."

The cinemas are so busy we booked seats in advance. Not a `continuous show' as at home, but screenings several times a day. Ted got us in the best seats — about 80 cents — up in the balcony in the British style.

We get a taxi, but the traffic is fierce. And each time the cab has to stop, a dozen beggars charge the vehicle, their arms reaching into the cab, palms in our faces, all shouting, "Baksheesh, sahib, baksheesh."

We're shouting back, "Imshee! imshee!" which translates roughly as "beat it, scram," but it has no effect. When your taxi starts to move, you're free of the nuisance, but only until you have to stop again.

It's a treat to go into the theatre, a fancy big place with the new cooling system they call "air conditioning." The movie is a comedy, "Miracle of Morgan's Creek," and for two hours you can feel untroubled, amused, and deliciously cool. But leaving the cinema, brace yourself or that first blast of sweltering hot air can bowl you over.

There are no cabs, but someone points the direction to find a taxi stand. The street quickly becomes much darker, not inappropriate because people are sleeping on it. They're not really on the street — there's still a lot of traffic — but they're on the sidewalks, in doorways or alcoves, up dark alleys, in any vacant spot big enough for a horizontal figure. We just passed a traffic circle where a hundred were camping out.

There are men and women of all ages, usually lying on a mat or a piece of rug but sometimes right on the pavement. Some are fully dressed, others in a loin cloth, sometimes with a sheet or rag over their bodies, but usually not. They may have started the night spaced more or less parallel but now they're sprawled in all directions, arms and legs tangled with a neighbour's, a head on somebody's ankle, a foot on somebody's neck.

And we have to walk through that? Through that tangled mess of bodies and appendages? You pick your way very, very carefully, setting your shoe between two sprawled legs, your next step close to a man's head, the next between the bodies of a mother and her kid.

But you can't avoid accidents. If there isn't quite enough room to set your shoe between two torsos, your toe goes into somebody's ribs. In the dark, you can miss seeing an outstretched hand on the ground. Or somebody rolls over and his leg slides right into the spot your foot is aiming for. Then a groan or a curse, and eyes open to peer up at you, aggrieved or furious.

"Let's go on t'e road," Phil suggests. We do that, trying not to get hit by passing vehicles, but also careful to stay out of gutters.

Here's a taxi. We flag him down and retreat to Worli, non-stop.

MAY 1

"Hey, been here six weeks now. How much longer?" we ask Wooding. We're fed up doing nothing except hunt for ways to amuse ourselves.

What isn't amusing me are ugly sores on the back of my legs. India must be Insect Heaven. Ants, for example, come in red or white or black, and they come in the millions. In the dining room, I'd been trying to eat more two-handed in the English style. I gave it up; it's a useless system when you need one hand free to swish flies off your plate.

Cockroaches, spiders and lizards are everywhere. The most vicious insects you don't even see; they lie in wait beneath the surface of wood... and wicker is what chairs in the lounge are made of. You're okay wearing slacks, but sit in shorts and the back of your knees — or any place your skin touches the wood — will soon be a mass of red welts. During the day, guys sit very strangely, almost out of the chair, all bare back-side off the wood.

Life here has settled into a routine. A card game most mornings. After lunch: Siesta time — a most marvellous institution. Most evenings we're at the camp cinema, no matter how bad the movie. At least you can munch walnuts and watch the big-eyed excitement on the faces of the piccaninnies looking through the fence when the Comanches attack the covered wagons. In this country, the `Indians' cheer for the `whites.'

Late afternoons are usually for swimming either at the Willingdon Club or the Breach Candy Baths, an acre-sized pool right beside the ocean. You can't swim in the sea here; it's reserved for sharks. But you can borrow some of their salt water.

"Originally you had to be `British Empire' to come here," someone said. "Now it's open to anyone at all, just so your skin is white."

At least rank doesn't matter and I've gone twice this week with Mac and Jonesy. It's a nice spot with big umbrellas to sit under after your swim.

One sight seems to epitomize Hungry India. Waiters all carry their trays at shoulder level on an upturned palm. Very professional. But why are the ones carrying food always preceded by a uniformed boy waving a long stick with streamers flapping? Of course... it's not ceremonial, it's those birds circling up there. The guard is trying to ward them off. But every few moments another hawk peels off and dive-bombs through the anti-bird defences, levelling out just as it reaches the tray. Sometimes a clear miss, but usually the bird snatches a morsel off the tray and escapes unscratched, the entire manoeuvre carried out at full throttle. The unhappy waiter heads back to the kitchen; Air Force types cheer. We haven't seen decent flying like that in months.

I enjoy the chats with Jones and Bernie McIlwaine. Mac and I have been together six months now and shared plenty of misadventures in the UK. Somewhat frail in stature, he's about my age, sports a little moustache, is a quiet, gentlemanly chap.

"You could cast him in the flicks as a country parson," one of our crew in England said. "Not only would he look the part, but if I had a problem, wanted to talk to somebody, Mac's the one I'd go to."

Stan Jones is a bubbly chap, a small face with a little black moustache, curly dark hair that's getting a bit skimpy, eyes that dance with enthusiasm.

"Home's Blackpool." It comes flooding out like a water faucet turned on full. "Photographer in civvie street... I'm married, two daughters, both young... lost my crew in England... hope I can stay with you... maybe ball turret gunner... could I get a crew picture to send home?"

Cheez, a three-man crew picture! But having a photographer in the crew might be handy; the film I took in for developing was all stuck together.

We're all getting restless. There's more bad temper, more complaining about petty things, an increase in what I call `the great white sahib complex' where guys give servants hell over some trivial mistake. A waiter brings a gin-and-lemon instead of a gin-lime so gets a tongue-lashing.

The crazy part is that the lad won't even understand the insults thrown at him, his English just good enough to know they aren't compliments. Needing the job, he has to stand there, chin on his chest, and take it. I'm ashamed it's one of my own friends who explodes more than anyone. John's a good guy, is just venting his loneliness and frustrations. But using a defenceless kid as a whipping boy is an ugly way to do it.

Or am I getting restless and cranky too? Things are starting to irk me. One irritation is hearing a native — any Indian from a coolie to a Maharajah — referred to as a `wog.' An ignorant term, and I'm trying not to use it.

Yeah, it's time we got out of here, did something.

CHAPTER 3

DECCAN DELIGHTS

MAY 8, 1944

We're on our way, destination Poona. A hundred miles inland, it's a major British Army base. But most guys left for Kolar, the Liberator place, three days ago. Why Poona? Could we be going to a different job, getting separated from our buddies? You get to know how a pawn on a chess board must feel.

I nipped over to the sergeant's barracks before leaving.

"Yes, skipper, all packed," Mac said. "Jonesy? Didn't you hear? The gunners all left for a course on American gun turrets... some place called Bhopal. No guarantee they'd ever get reunited with their friends. Jonesy was very upset, wants to be in your crew."

From Victoria Station, it's an hour to get out of Bombay. Then farm country, the villages as close together here as farm houses at home. Now it's a desert, like Arizona in a Tom Mix movie.

These First Class compartments are great. With no outside corridor as in Britain, the compartments go right from window to window. It means you can't leave your room while the train's moving, but you get privacy. In this heat, we can strip to almost Garden of Eden standards for most of the trip — just keep khaki shorts handy for station stops.

The compartment is 12 feet long with benches down each side; the leather cushions would be fine to sleep on. Above each bench is a substantial shelf with more cushions. Our bags are piled up there now, but stack them on the floor at night and you'd have two more bunks. Strangely, the engine is soundless; I thought only toy trains ran on electricity.

That door at the end opens into our own private toilet and shower, tiny but sufficient. The accommodations would be quite okay for four people on an overnight journey, are more than adequate for six on a one-day trip.

I'm with a Canadian navigator, Johnny King, plus Bill Jackson and three RAF men I don't know. The English guys have a trunk on the floor, using it as a bridge table, but there's a lot of cursing as the wind blows the cards around. I'm enjoying my first look at the India countryside passing by the window, a desolate scene.

"Just before the monsoon season, no rain for months." King has put down his book and joined me. "We're coming to the Western Ghats, the mountains along the coast. The rail line climbs eighteen hundred feet in fifteen miles. That should be worth seeing."

We're into the hills now. The locomotive has to be working very hard — the engineer pouring the volts to her — because the inclines are steep, with tunnels, bridges across gorges, tracks hanging onto the sides of steep hills. Even the bridge players are at the windows now.

The terrain's levelled off and the Englishmen go back to their game.

"We're on the Deccan now, which means `the south,'" one of them says. "Most of central India — the big `V' jutting into the Indian Ocean — is a plateau, two thousand feet above sea level. Cooler and drier than down on the coast."

But I question that. We've stopped at a station and the Indian conductor comes along the platform, very self-important, striding along as if he might own the train. But he stops to answer my question.

"Temperater now one oh two, soon to becoming one oh fiver."

Wow! The little fan on the ceiling can't handle that. We're moving again and there's a breeze, but like out of a blast furnace. It's back to under-shorts and lots of towelling down.

Again we've stopped, right in a shabby little town; lunch break. There are street vendors hawking food, a row of poor-looking cafes down the street, but in this country you don't just eat anywhere; our briefing was to trust only this one place right beside the station.

"But don't drink the water! Get something in a bottle."

It's a terrible crush, but I grab a made-up chicken sandwich and some mangoes. I see McIlwaine but there's only time for a wave.

We're rolling again, an hour to go. King has gone back to his book.

Wondering what's coming up next is a permanent condition in the Services. I've now made about twenty `career moves' to a new stage of training or a new location. Each time it's like opening another door, stepping through it to see what's in the next room. In another hour, it'll be the door marked "Poona."

The bridge game is over. Three of the players are trying to sleep but the one who knew about the Deccan has joined me.

"Did you hear them? Three cards blew out the window but they wanted to play anyway. That's crazy! Bridge is complicated enough already."

"Yes," he answers me. "I've done ops. North Africa. Navigator on Wimps. Yeah, bombed Rommel... targets like that."

Hey, this gets my attention. Almost always I'm with guys still training, who've never yet been shot at. And he's done a whole tour of ops! The door marked "combat flying" is the big one we've yet to go through. He already knows what's on the other side.

"After Africa, I instructed in England, stood in a classroom all day. So I agreed to come to India. Experienced navigators are apparently considered quite important out here... a lot of ocean and practically nothing in the way of navigational aids. For a radio signal to take a bearing on, just the one station, Calcutta, and only for five minutes an hour. Otherwise, all you've got is dead-reckoning and whatever star shots you can get with your sextant."

Hey, I guess there really is a lot of water out here —Himalayas to the north and oceans on the other three sides. And nothing but star shots?

MAY 16

We're still at Poona, waiting for the next course at Kolar. Why shipped out of Bombay? Another boat was arriving and they needed our bunks.

It's crowded here, too. Bill Jackson's two stripes got him into the permanent quarters; Johnny King and I share a tent. This means an oil lamp, latrines a quarter-mile away, sleeping in temperatures that would bake a cake. The tent is staked right to the ground so I spoke to the corporal.

"You want ventilation, sir, you raise the flaps. You want to keep snakes out, you leave them down."

I just woke from a long siesta. I'll have a shower and then see who's in the Mess, join one of the groups sitting around to curse this damn war. But Johnny King comes in, stands at the opening to the tent. "Say, Wal, did you notice that big house up there?"

It's not often John sounds that excited, except maybe when he's had a few, which I don't think is now. He pulls back the tent flaps and points at a building on the top of a hill a mile away, surrounded by a high wall, lots of gables and spires.

"Yeah, I saw it. Looks like a small castle. What about it?"

"Right. It's the Aga Khan's palace; the Adjutant just told me. Do you know who's living there now? Mahatma Gandhi! You've heard of him?"

Sure, the skinny little guy in the newsreels a lot, usually sitting cross-legged on the ground, wearing something minimal. "He lives there?"

"Locked up there. Gandhi leads the Congress Party that wants to kick the Brits out of India, and I say `hurrah' for that. But not yet. The people will be better off if Gandhi chases the British home rather than the Japs."

John's an older guy, knows about politics, stuff like that. Someone said he was a Socialist, whatever that is. He sure has strange ideas, such as about Ghandi and freedom for India. Any newspaper I've read speaks of the Mahatma as a rabble-rouser who'll have to be sat on hard, and yet a story in an American magazine made him sound like a hero. Some things are hard to figure out.

Johnny's still muttering in his slow Western drawl, almost a whisper. "I'd sure like to meet this Mahatma chap. Maybe you and I'll just wander up there tomorrow, see if the guards will let us in."

But I'm pretty sure he's just kidding.

John's famous in camp now. The night we arrived, I hit the sack early but John wanted a nightcap. He's a little 12O-pounder, usually very quiet, but the heat or the gin must've got to him. At midnight, I heard a skirmish outside the tent; two military police came in, my feisty pal still putting up a struggle. But pushed down onto his cot, John went right off to sleep.

The word next day was he'd been into some kind of political argument with a Squadron Leader whose face and opinions he didn't much like. During the discussion, the RAF man's nose got in the way of some knuckles. John was next day marched in front of the C.O.

His penance? Pretty severe! He got `dis-barred.'

What that means is, for two weeks he can't go into the bar. Luckily, he has lots of friends here, all smuggling enough drinks out to him he'll never get dehydrated.

A big party Saturday. The main attraction? A dozen English nurses from the local hospital. Despite the competition, I had some dances. And I got letters from Jean, two of the envelopes singed around the edges. It doesn't take a Sherlock Holmes to figure out they salvaged some bundles out of that mail plane that crashed.

Tomorrow we leave for this Kolar place, everyone except Johnny King. Surely that little altercation with the RAF officer wouldn't be the reason he's being kept back. But he thinks it is, looks ready to erupt again, to `vesuviate' and `lavate' all over Poona.

Kolar is near Bangalore, near the southern tip of India. We'll report to #1673 Heavy Conversion Unit, which means Liberators. It'll be a long trip — three days on the train — but I'm glad to be going.

Last night, a big surprise! Who came into the Mess but Ernie Green, one of the gang when we were training on Harvards back in Canada!

"Just got in. Quite a dump, eh? Came through Suez, a week at Worli. Boy, is it jammed! So they sent six of us here, just for a few days, then over to the east coast. Know anything about a Spitfire squadron near Madras?"

"You're going on Spits? You lucky bugger, how did you wangle that?"

At the Uplands Service Flying Training School, that's what we all wanted.

"Going on Spits? Hell, I've done a tour on them. Straight to England after Wings Parade in March, operational training right away, got to the Squadron in July, finished in November."

"Cheez, a whole tour, and I haven't done a damn thing. Tell me about it."

"The Spits? Great. We mostly did sweeps into France. Good fun. Losses? Yeah, we lost a few planes, but not too bad; I didn't get a scratch."

When I push him for details, he has several good stories. Guys will talk about their adventures if you press them. Of course it's bad form to do it without being invited. You have to be asked, even coaxed. Even then you can't be emotional. Especially if there was danger involved, you must tell your story in a matter-of-fact way as if risking your neck is a natural thing to do, a routine matter as boring to your listeners as it was to you. To make a joke about a foul-up or predicament is permitted; any mention of fright or excitement is `verboten.'

But I enjoy such stories, am fascinated by guys who have faced the enemy. What were they thinking while being shot at? Were they terrified? Did their minds go blank, frozen with fear, or did they find themselves thinking very quickly, clearly? Do you get used to being in danger... numbed to it... or what? But nobody's ever been able to describe these things to me very well.

"Well, I dunno," they'll say. "You're there, and they're firing at you and... well, there isn't much you can do about it... so you just go ahead and do whatever has to be done."

Maybe it really is what everyone has to find out for himself.

"Three months at RCAF HQ in London," Ernie says. "Lousy desk job. Then got this chance to come out here. You don't know anything about Madras? Are the Japs sending many bombers into India?"

When he sees I know nothing, we head for the bar to talk about Uplands.

"Moving up from a Tiger Moth to a Harvard... 125 horse-power to 55O... that was tough," Ernie says. "Worse than jumping from there to Spits. The Harvard is a lot of airplane for a beginner. Americans train on them too... call them the AT6... but they don't go straight from an elementary trainer. They do some hours in a Vultee first. Makes sense. But I hear they're switching to our system; figure if we can do it in one jump, so can they. But what do you know of the Uplands gang?"

I can tell him of Jim Savage flying Mosquitoes in Britain; the American Harvard man, Howard Nemerov, on Beaufighters; Nobby Norton on Catalinas in the Caribbean. And of my French-Canadian buddy, Louis Bisson, killed in Canada.

Ernie has more news... a lot of the guys are dead now. Then we get the idea of having a little drink in memory of each of them, one by one by one.

I'm back in the tent, packing for tomorrow's trip. Hope I'm not forgetting anything, but I'm pretty damn tipsy. It took a lot of gins.

We're at Kolar, waiting at the rail station for transport to camp.

A 55-hour train trip is too long, but with cloud shielding the sun, the little ceiling fan working 24 hours a day, and frequent showers, no great problem. Except for the dining car. "Lousy food, slow service and big prices," all agreed. So we switched to a different catering service.

At one station stop, a uniformed lad comes by to take your order — tea, biscuits, meat pies, omelettes, whatever. He then wires ahead; at the next station a man waits on the platform with your tray, exchanging it for rupees. A stop after that, another boy collects your empty plates.

The train stopped at every sleepy little town. But the empty platform within seconds became crowded with beggars peering up into the open windows, hands outstretched, wailing for alms. But do you get hardened to other peoples' misery, soon just ignore it?

I waded through the panhandlers and hucksters looking for McIlwaine. Several cars were jammed with natives, then one had passengers pale of skin. "Third Class," the sign said. Mac shouted at me to join him.

Hey, not a posh way to travel. Little more than an open-sided boxcar with high-backed benches, four long rows going end to end, two facing on the left, two on the right. With a surfeit of bodies to fill the seats, and the space between the rows littered with kit, it was a jumbled, crowded mess. And they have to sleep there at night! The Brits try to keep commissioned people reasonably comfortable; they don't seem to give a damn about anybody else.

"Sit down, skipper." Mac's companions squeezed to make space. And when the whistle blew, "There's enough room if you want to stay awhile."

They were interested in anything to break the monotony of the long day, if only just somebody different to talk to. Some faces were vaguely familiar; I maybe met them at Harwell. But in England they were in blue serge, wearing caps, even greatcoats. Here they're wearing almost nothing.

Also, without shirts, you don't know anybody's rank or what job he has in the crew. Sitting on those hard benches, the absolutely only thing that matters is whether you're a pleasant fellow to sit beside, to talk to, and whether you can "take it" —the heat, the miserable conditions, the boredom — without losing your sense of humour. Mac's friends would score high on that.

There's boredom in First Class too. You can play cards or read. And we talk a lot, moving from one compartment to another at station stops.

Some were discussing the war. Of course, most RAF guys feel closer to it than we do — the one with Germany anyway. Many have had homes smashed, family or friends killed by Hitler's bombers. You can understand their wanting to smash back. But I think many RCAF-ers were just as un-heroic as I was, having too much fun to put on a uniform before they had to. So we enlisted just before turning 21, when we could still choose which service we wanted. After that, it could be the Infantry or whatever.

"But why the Air Force?" someone asked. "And why volunteer for aircrew? You could have enlisted as a clerk or a cook."

You could say it was because nearly everyone was doing it, but that's not a good reason. Partly it's because flying is still a romantic thing to do... still so very new, the Wright Brothers' first flight barely forty years ago. Until the war, I knew no one who'd even had a ride in an airplane.

But another reason — a good reason — was those parades of war veterans each November 11th, so many short an arm or leg or otherwise banged-up.

"Join the Air Force," was the wisdom of the day, "that won't happen. You won't end up a cripple, will either come home all in one piece or not at all."

But wasn't there another reason to try for pilot?   If you fancied yourself a bit of an athlete — hockey player, that sort of thing — could you volunteer for mail clerk? How would that look? Could you settle for being a dishwasher? So nearly everyone I know, who could pass the medicals, is in air crew.

In Bangalore, a two hour stop. I took a taxi into the city with two RCAF guys — Potts and Brodie — for breakfast at a fancy hotel. The city might be a place to come on leave. We hear there's nothing in Kolar.

Cheez, it's hot. Where are those lorries? And why's everybody looking up? Ah, a plane crossing above us, undercart down for landing. A big four-engine job. Yes, a Lib. Lordie, it's big. Will I really be flying one of those?

Here come four lorries with the RAF roundels. I'm impatient to see the new station. And to have a look at those Libs!

CHAPTER 4

CREWING UP

MAY 21, 1944

Wow, this Kolar place looks like a South Sea Island village. My idea of one, anyway. No blue lagoon, but big palm trees shading a cluster of brown buildings close to the ground with thatched roofs. Our billet has four rooms side by side. Each unit sits on a concrete slab providing a solid floor, and extending behind the back door for a place to set up canvas tubs and basins.

I drew Bill Jackson as room-mate. That's okay; he knows more than I do about flying, and I take all the help I can get.

"Look at this construction," Bill says. "Simple, ingenious, all local materials. Instead of two-by-fours, just these heavy bamboo poles."

Both the outside walls and room partitions are just flat strips of palm leaves about four inches wide interwoven to make a tight matting.

"It's called `rattan,'" Jackson informs me. Bill likes to inform people. "And look at this. No nails or screws. The matting is just tied to the bamboo studs with twine. A building like this is called a `basha.'"

Our room is empty except for two `charpoys' — India-style rope beds. A solid wooden frame has coarse hemp rope stretched from side to side; that's what you lie on. Trouble is, even atop two blankets, the raspy hemp leaves welts on your back. War is really hell.

"We need furniture," Bill says. "A course is finishing this week. We find out who has the things we want, go to their rooms Saturday morning, early... help them pack... be on the spot to get what they leave behind."

Don't you have to admire a guy who knows all the angles!

Today, another first; I hired an employee. The thing to do is have a servant, a `bearer,' to do household chores. On a new station, they're scarce, so when this Dulla came to the door, I grabbed him. About 14 with a small monkey face and tired eyes, it turns out he's never been a bearer before, doesn't speak a word of English, and is neither bright nor

Basha

ambitious. You should have heard Jackson! Next time *he* can hire the damn staff.

Dulla's face goes blank when I try my Urdu on him, which leaves only sign language. So far he's learned to wake us up, bring tea after siesta and hot water for shaving after that, see the room's kept fairly clean and keep our water jug full. For this, three dollars a month.

No jobs have been assigned yet. "You're here early," the Adj told us. "Next course starts in a week. Just stay out of the way until then."

Haven't seen a Lib yet. They're flying overhead, but the `domestic site' is three miles from the airdrome. In this heat, you wouldn't walk that far.

At the Officers' Mess last night, a get-together-again party with Keele, Cloutier, Willing and others. They're all taking ground school lectures now, two weeks of that before they start flying.

"Plenty to learn," they all say.

The lounge is another big `basha' structure. Cocoa matting covers the floor, scatter-rugs over most of that. Yellow shades on electric lamps, bright curtains and gaudy cushions make it colourful. In this country, of course, the Mess is where you spend your time; there are no pubs down the road to go to.

The only liquor — Indian gin — can get you loosened up in a hurry. Somebody started to pound the piano and soon more than fifty voices were belting out songs. I like that. It was boozy and slurry, but loud — a

35

Basha — back door

great way to spend an evening, especially of course when there's nothing else.

But we've got to have a look at a Lib.

MAY 23

"There's one," shouts Murray Potts. The aircraft is parked just off the taxi strip on a big concrete pad, men working around it. The area has a sheltered look, surrounded on three sides by a mound of earth ten feet high.

"Must be one of the `Dispersals' they talk about," from Steve Brodie.

"Compared with England, lots of space in the countryside here," Jackson says. "Aircraft can be parked a hundred yards apart and the Japs couldn't smash the fleet in one bomb run. The berm around each site would help too."

We've hitched a ride on a lorry going to the drome. Another two hundred yards and we pass the next Dispersal, but it's empty. But here's another one; we're turning in. Yeah! A Liberator, a huge mottled-grey bird, sitting all by itself on its concrete perch out in the middle of nowhere, nobody around her... just sitting, very quiet, very still. Looking a bit pensive, maybe lonely.

Cheez, I've heard of "love at first sight"... but for an airplane?

The lorry stops, we jump out. Gosh, it's big! It doesn't have the nose-

36

in-the-air look of an RAF Lancaster sitting back on its tail. Because of its nose-wheel, the Lib has a hunkered-down, close to the ground look. But what really staggers me is the wing span. Standing at the nose, the wings look to stretch half-way to the horizon.

"Longest wing span of any plane anywhere," Jackson says. "One hundred and ten feet."

The four big radial engines look powerful. Bill sees me staring up and says, "Pratt and Whitneys, twelve hundred horsepower each."

"Where you getting all this?" Murray Potts asks him.

"Pilots' Manual," Jackson tells him. Bill can sound quite smug. "Got it from the Engineering Office. Lots of gen about the plane, just like the handbook you get with a new automobile."

We walk out under the wing to get a side view. What hits you from there is the size of the tails, two of them. They must be four feet wide, six high, the top higher than a small house. From this angle, the body of the plane — the fuselage — looks a bit... well, short. Maybe out of proportion with the wing span and the big tails.

"Length... sixty-six feet," from Bill. "British bombers are longer than that."

"But the fuselage looks larger than RAF planes," I say. "Must be lots of room inside. That's why it looks... uh... well, a bit stubby."

Cheez, I'm defending a plane I haven't even been in yet.

"You could say stubby," from Brodie. "You could just as well say `fat.'"

I resent that but can't think of a good answer. The plane does look just a trifle over-fed, its belly sagging close to the ground.

"Sirs, going now, leaving these boxes... be back in an hour. You want to look through the kite, have a `dekko'? Best way in is through the bomb-bay."

The driver goes to the right-hand side; we hear the whine of a motor, a rumble of casters moving on rollers, and the bomb doors open. Instead of hinges, they slide up on tracks along the outside of the airframe, flush with the body, one half to either side. Very neat.

You bend over to get under the plane — into the bomb-bay — but then can see right to the top. Mostly what you see are metal posts going straight up. Two rows run fore and aft dividing the bomb compartment into two halves. The posts are about ten inches apart, a metal grill connecting them at the bottom.

"Catwalk," Bill says. "To go to the back, you tip-toe along that catwalk, squeezing between the posts, between the bombs hanging on either side."

From the bomb-bay, you can also climb forward, up into an open area.

"Flight deck," Bill explains. "Radio operator's station on the right. Those switches must be for the Flight Engineer to change fuel tanks; that opening is to the mid-upper gun turret."

But what I want to see is the pilots' cabin just ahead of the Flight Deck.

And there they are, two big seats side by side. Squeeze forward for a closer look. Omigosh! What a confusion of switches and levers and knobs and handles... beside the seats, between the seats, above the seats, and on the instrument panel across the front. Such a mess of gauges and dials, most in groups of four. How could anyone learn all that?

Jackson is already in the seat on the left and I take the other. Great, almost like easy chairs! The B24 is said to be Number One for pilot comfort. But Bill is sitting where the first-pilot sits. My seat, on the right, is for the co-pilot. I don't know which I'm going to be, but I'm thinking I'd like to try for captain. Of course, that depends on a lot of things... including whether I'll be able to learn what all those knobs and switches are for.

"Hey, going to spend all day there?" It's Brodie.

Jackson leaves, but there's something I have to do first. Something important. On the instrument panel is a box with 12 levers sticking out of grooves. The ones in the centre are throttles controlling those 4800 horses; you have to grab all four in one hand. The knobs at the end of each lever are close together but each is an inch wide. I have a small hand. Is it big enough? I'm trying it now.

Yes... okay, okay... I can handle it. By using my thumb too.

Back in the bomb-bay, I crawl down into the navigator's work-station, directly under the flight deck. Not much to see: a small seat, pull-down shelf for a table, shelves for maps and protractors and other tools of the trade. The adjustable light would be important because it's dark here.

Right in the nose is the bomb-sight. For a view, that's where to be, nothing underneath except window. Above that is the front turret.

Back in the bomb-bay again, Jackson leads me across the catwalk towards the rear. Darn flimsy; you hold onto the bomb racks for support. Miles up on a bumpy day, I think you'd hang on very, very tightly. But no bombs today, just a mess of hooks and electrical wires.

We're now in the rear section. It's huge. Quite bare, floor boards under your feet and the ribs of the fuselage going up the sides and meeting at the top. You could imagine you were inside a big fat, grey cigar.

But what's that? With my eyes adjusting to the dark, I see a bulbous steel and plexiglass contraption half embedded in the floor.

"Ball turret," Bill says. "The gunner crawls in there, then the whole thing is lowered by hydraulics so it sticks out the bottom of the plane, gives you two more guns to protect the belly of the aircraft. Cramped quarters for the gunner? Well, yes. Just room for a small chap strapped into his harness with the machine gun between his legs."

And that's what little Jonesy wants to be! I'll have a job for him.

Further back are machine guns set on tripods, one on each side of the aircraft. Jackson is removing a panel; it uncovers a window, fairly big. No glass though; you can't have glass when you're going to shoot through it.

Bill is at the gun, swivelling it up and down, maybe shooting down Zeros because he's shouting "rat-a-tat-tat." That makes me smile; Jackson is usually a no-foolishness kind of guy. It's my turn next and I also rat-a-tat a few. Further back is the rear turret, but even Bill knows nothing about American gun turrets so we don't touch it.

Brodie and Potts have arrived, are lifting something off the floor. It's a door, hinged at one end. Open, it leaves a hole in the bottom of the plane about three feet by two feet. "Escape hatch," Bill explains, unnecessarily. "Big enough you could jump through with your parachute on."

The lorry just pulled in and the driver shouts "haloo." His timing is perfect. Jackson lets himself out through the escape hatch and the other two follow. Damn. That leaves me the job of closing it and going out through the bomb-bay. But the catwalk doesn't feel as flimsy this time.

Yeah, I'm going to like this aircraft.

MAY 28

Jackson isn't so smart; his scheme to get us furniture was a flop. A draft did leave yesterday, and we were at their bashas at sun-up.

"Sorry," they said, "you've been a big help, but old Pete was my drinking buddy here and I promised him my table and lamp a week ago."

We did pick up a four-drawer bureau, only two drawers missing. A table, with three legs, came with two boxes; one atop the other, they're almost perfect for the fourth corner. We also nabbed a chair, have strengthened its legs with rope. Our room is starting to look quite elegant.

I'm thinking a lot about picking a crew, something I really messed up in England. The result of my procrastination and indecision was that I didn't get around to picking a crew at all, was just given the bods left over, that no one else had chosen. Some, like Mac, turned out to be good men anyway; others didn't. I must never be that stupid again.

But many guys here are refugees from crews that were broken up, are unattached. Most navigators arrived straight from Navigation School. Bombardiers aren't even here yet. I can have another crack at building my crew.

My crew? How do I know it'll be *my* crew? Sitting in the Lib the other day, I liked the idea of being captain of the ship. But would that be smart? I've had fair ratings on my flying, but never figured I was any super pilot. If I could fly second dickey with an experienced guy, somebody with bags of air time, wouldn't that be the best thing to do? But, except for Jackson, I don't know anybody on our course with more hours than I have. Join Bill? No, I don't think so.

There's Ted Willing at the bar. I'll ask him. He has his own crew, and they've started flying.

"Don't be a stupid ass, Wal. If I can be captain, so can you. What's the matter with you? Hell, you've tr'ined for two years. D'you want to fly second dickey to some dumb bugger who knows less than you do, have to take orders from somebody you find out is bloody stupid? Anyway, what's the big deal? Your crew will all know their jobs. All you have to do is land the plane, make a decision once in a while."

Ted's full of Australian gung-ho. And he's telling me what I want to hear; nothing holds your attention better than that. But to try for first pilot, how do you go about it?

"Nothing to it, m'ite. Just ask lads to fly with you. The RAF is very democr'itic about crewing up. A course will turn out, say, fifteen crews. That means there'll be thirty pilots, either officers or sergeants. You have to put two pilots in each crew. Except for that, the RAF doesn't give a damn how you pair up. If you want to be captain, you find guys who'll fly with you. If you want second pilot, you get somebody to take you into his crew. Simple."

But it doesn't sound simple at all... might require delicate negotiations. The simple, easy way would be to draw names out of a hat... though I can see that wouldn't always work out either.

"But what happens if there are more sergeants than officers?"

"Doesn't matter. You could have two officers teamed up in one crew, two NCO's in another. If one of each, either could be the captain. On the last course there was a Pilot Officer flying second dickey to an NCO, and the navigator was a Flight-Looey. But the Sergeant in that case had done a tour on Wimpys, had bags of experience."

In the US Air Forces, I understand that gunners, engineers and radio men almost never get to be officers. Pilots, navigators and bombardiers always are. But in the Air Force of the supposedly class-ridden society of Britain, you could conceivably have a sergeant as the captain of a crew in which everyone else was commissioned. That amuses me. I don't know how it rates as military policy but it sure as hell is democratic.

But if I try for captain, another big question: What kind of crew would I want? Some RCAF-ers, guys you could talk hockey with? But there are few Canadians on our course. A couple of navigators I wouldn't want; wrong chemistry or something. But one possibility might be Ken Cox from Vancouver. A college man, seems sensible and likable. Yes, I think we could get along.

But my first choice would be Art Harris, a chubby little guy from Nova Scotia. Everyone calls him "Chota" — Urdu for `small.' He's very bright, never without a big grin and a joke. Wouldn't somebody like that be great to have in the crew, and as your room-mate. But he's another radio man; we'll carry two wireless operators but I couldn't ask Harris to come in as 2nd W/Op. And would it be fair to ask Mac to drop back to number two?

Another question: Would NCOs be easier to lead than officers?

Eleven-man crews. Cheez, that's a lot of guys to control. Could I do it? That's my biggest concern. A lot of men here are older than I am, some nearly forty. If I had to order someone that old to do something, would the age difference increase the danger that he might say, "To hell with you, laddie."

If that ever happened, I guess you'd be finished as a captain.

All these questions are important. Or do I worry too much? Maybe I should be like Ted Willing and just assume everything will work out fine. He's right, you know. I should be able to handle it.

I'm 23 now. I'm not just a kid any more.

MAY 31

More lectures! Since enlisting, I've spent more hours in classrooms than in the air. But just one more week.

Here, even classrooms

Royal Canadian Air Force

Art "Chota" Harris

are dispersed so it's a bouncy two-mile run before dawn. Lorries are disgorging their loads, 150 men milling about, a variety of ranks and trades. A thought: Among them are the men I'm going to be flying missions with. Isn't it weird I don't yet know which ones they'll be? Except for two; the gunners did get back from Bhopal.

"Keeping ourselves available," Jonesy and Mac assure me.

At 6:30, a whistle blows; each trade heads off to a separate classroom. Of the thirty pilots in our group, over half are from the Officers' Mess so I at least know their names. Some NCOs, such as Mazengarb and Brooks, were on the same course at Harwell but others I haven't met before.

Buildings are the usual basha construction. We sit three to a table, not so different from school at home. One big change: we're all concentrating like crazy. What we pick up here could be the difference between life and... well, you try not to think of alternatives.

We've had brush-ups on navigation, radio and armament, but mostly we've been studying the B24, a very complex piece of equipment. For a guy who's no mechanical genius — who usually needed help even to get the rear wheel back on his bike — all this talk about manifold pressure, relief valves and turbo superchargers is terribly befuddling. Each crew will carry a Flight Engineer but pilots should know as much as possible.

Recess time, and my head is glad of the break. Dispensing his brew from a big metal container is the `char-wallah' — the tea fellow. At home we'd be drinking coffee, but when you're attached to the RAF you'd better learn to like tea. You can also buy peanuts, bananas, mangoes, cakes.

A fat black-faced gent, sitting on his haunches amongst his wares, is the vendor; you'd take a snap-shot if you had film. His large round face is grave and dignified as he grunts a perfunctory "sahib" each time he pockets another two annas for your `cuppa.' Altogether, he's quite the perfect picture of a prosperous turbaned businessman. And at four cents a cup, no overhead, and this volume of trade, he'll retire early.

But char-break is the chance to circulate, cup in hand, and meet other pilots, wireless ops, gunners, engineers and navigators. You talk to the ones whose looks you like, try to guess if you'd be compatible, whether you'd want to spend the next months together — even face some danger together. And it's not just a popularity contest to find the nicest guys. Isn't it more a question whether they're capable bods, people who can cope? Surely it's better to have a navigator who's a real sonnabitch but can find his way home in the dark, rather than a swell chap who'll leave you lost and out of petrol over the Indian Ocean.

So how to choose? The Nav Section might give you the marks each navigator got on his courses, but does that tell you how he'll perform under pressure?

Our Flight Commander at Harwell, an old bomber pilot, told us, "If you don't have trouble, it doesn't matter who you fly with. It's only when you run into a spot of bother that it matters. Then you need the man who can still function when the panic button is going beep-beep-beep."

But how pick out people like that after just a few moments of conversation? Hell, I've no idea how I'll react myself!

Another concern. You might ask someone to join you, only to have him look you up and down and say, "Thanks, old chap, but I think not."

Back in class, the topic is Astral Navigation — finding where you are on the earth's surface by taking readings on the stars. Interesting stuff. But I'm not concentrating. Maybe I should ask Ken Cox and Chota Harris if they'd like to join up with me.

I'm also thinking of a chat with Howie Sweet, an RCAF navigator in a course ahead of ours.

"You're worried about getting a good crew?" he scoffed. "Hah, you should think how others feel... all the other trades. I have to admit it; the pilot is the most important man in a crew. Whether he can fly, whether he has any common sense... those are the major factors in whether the crew survives. I've been lucky but I can tell you some of my friends are worried. You can be sure a lot of navigators and others are looking you over right now."

Maybe so. I've noticed guys looking at me out of the corner of an eye... just as I've been trying to study them without being too obvious about it. This is being a very strange business...not simple at all.

It's one p.m. and we're finished for the day. Another lorry ride, lunch, and I'm back to my room. Off with the dripping shirt and peel down to bare essentials. After siesta I'll have another go at figuring out the Lib's fuel system. Or...is it more important that I come to some decisions about picking a crew?

I'm also thinking of Howie Sweet's other comment. "I don't think it's fair, but always it's the pilot chooses the crew. Why is that? For everyone else, it's like a girl going alone to a dance. She has to stand around, try to look attractive, wait for some pilot to come up, ask her for the next waltz."

Yeah, gotta find some people to dance with. Right away!

JUNE 1

I feel sick to my stomach, completely disgusted. The business of finding a crew... I've fouled it up again. Didn't do anything about it yesterday, or again this morning. Oh, I thought about it... just didn't come to any final decisions as to who I wanted, how I'd go about asking them.

Jackson wasn't in the room after lunch but came in later, informed me he now has his crew all lined up. Already! Cheez, we won't be flying for a week! I thought there was still lots of time. But Bill rattled off all their names... how the engineer led his class, the gunners are crackerjacks, the navigator a winner of some kind of award. Why does Bill have to sound so self-satisfied all the time?

"You haven't started yet? Haven't got anybody?" His face is close to a smirk. "Just like at OTU. You'll end up with the men nobody else wants!"

That does it. That gets me off my fanny. I pull on shoes and shorts and head for the room Ken Cox and Chota Harris share. I'll ask them right away, get them signed up, not put it off another damn minute.

Strange, nobody's there. Not 15 minutes later, nor a quarter hour after that. Maybe doing something at the Mess. I dress and go to check. And that's where they are, sitting with a couple more at the back. When I get closer, the extra two are Steve Brodie and Murray Potts.

Steve waves. "Come here, Wal. Want to talk to you. What'll you have?"

When I'm settled in, he continues, his drawl slow and deliberate. "Having a little celebration... like you to join us. We thought there should be at least one Canadian crew here, mostly RCAF anyway; we've just decided. Murray has agreed to fly co-pilot with me, Ken and Chota make four. And we've talked the two Canadian sergeants, Washbrook and Irvine, into joining us. Mighty pleased about it; wanted to share it with you."

If Joe Louis, the heavyweight champ, came up and smashed his fist into my gut, I couldn't hurt more. Suddenly I feel very alone. And a great disgust — at myself — for being so stupid, for blowing it again. The disappointment... you try not to show it but I'm not sure I manage. But when I congratulate them, that's sincere. They really are four good guys. So I buy a round, everybody else does too, and we're having a nice little party even before dinner.

But tomorrow, I've got to... just got to... do something about a crew, stop putting things off, make up my mind. Tomorrow morning. Without fail!

JUNE 2

Recess time, at last! First out of the classroom, I collect my tea from the char-wallah as guys come streaming from the buildings.

The very first thing: find a pilot to team up with! And I've definitely decided who my first choice will be — if he hasn't picked his own crew, is still uncommitted. We're in the same class, but that was no place to talk.

The fellow's a Scot — a Sgt Govan. We've shared a desk, talked several times. He's one of those people who have bones one size too large for their skin. Raw-boned, I think it's called. A pleasant, honest face with a mop of unruly brown hair sticking straight up. A solid down-to-earth fellow without any airs if my intuition is any good. A calm and sensible gent... also likable. Dammit, that's important too.

Okay, so what am I waiting for? Well, I have to find him, don't I? Okay, there he is. Talking to some fellows wearing gunner's wings. I'll just march right over and ask him, that's what I'll do. What am I waiting for? Why the hell am I so hesitant about asking another man to fly with me? Isn't that the biggest compliment you could ever give anybody?

I order my feet to start heading that way, walking slowly, trying to look as casual as I can. Why the hell am I feeling so nervous?

"Hi!" I say, wishing I had something more brilliant to start with.

"Hello... Hi... Hello." All three answer. Dammit, this is business, not social; I think Govan and I should stroll to one side for a little privacy. But he stolidly holds his ground, his henchmen sticking close beside him. There's no turning back now.

"The name's Govan, isn't it? `Jock' Govan?"

"Aye." Just a trace of a chuckle, then, "That's what I'm called heerre."

It's time to take the plunge. "I was wondering, uh, if you are crewed up yet. If you aren't... well, I'm trying to get a crew together and I... um... wanted to ask if... if you'd be interested in... ah... joining up with me?"

No reply. Not a "yes" nor a "no." All three look very serious. Govan's cool eyes are looking straight into mine, in no hurry to answer. And yet... I get the impression he knows very well what his answer will be, just wants to word it carefully. Damn! He's going to say, "Thanks, but no thanks."

Here's the answer coming now. "Aye... that would be just grrrand... I'd be verrry happy to join you. But one verrry imporrrtant condition."

Great! Fantastic! But, hey, what's this? What about a condition?

"These gunners are frrriends of mine. They'd have to come too."

"That's it? That's all? Sure, that's okay. Hell, yes, that's great! I already have one gunner; now we have three."

There are introductions and handshakes all around, everyone smiling. Not that the new men are jumping up and down in any frenzy of excitement. My guess is they all keep a lot of themselves in reserve, and I like that.

The two gunners are Jim Slight and Phil Howse; Slight is another Scot. The way Jock Govan can roll the R's off his tongue is phenomenal enough but Jim's come off his lower jaw like a troop of Bulgarian tumblers making their big entrance on stage. When he said my name just now, it sounded like a machine gun reverberating.

He's a short barrel-chested lad of about twenty, shy, doesn't say much, but a small, pleasant grin to go with a squarish face, a strong jaw and eyes that look right at you. No mama's boy this. You wouldn't push him very far in any direction he didn't want to go.

"Beforrr the war? Aw, I didna' do much. My fatherrr's a shepherrrd; I helped him some. Was in a Whitley crrrew in Scotland, just towing bloody gliderrrs, so volunteerrred for India. Met Stan Govan two days agohh."

He says he wants to be the rear gunner. When you need someone willing to put up with long, lonely hours in the rear end, he might just do.

Phil Howse is a very different type: a short, slim chap with slicked-down black hair and a small Hitler moustache. Older than me.

"Twenty-nine," he volunteers. "Salesman in civvy street. Batteries, radios. Now I'm a nose gunner. In Jock's crew since England."

These details are tossed out in a breezy fashion. What he's really concentrating on is me. I'm being studied with cool and watchful eyes that don't miss much; he hasn't made up his mind yet, but will give me the benefit of the doubt for now. We might even get along okay as long as I don't make any dumb mistakes. My impression is that he's both cool and capable.

So I'm well satisfied with the gunners I've inherited, part of the package deal. And standing here with Jock, I have the warm feeling that I was lucky there too. He's a calm, relaxed sort of fellow with a nice chuckly sense of humour; some people you just feel comfortable with right off. And also... but here come Mac and Jonesy; their timing is perfect.

"Got news for you. We've just teamed up with Jock Govan's crew here."

Which brings another round of introductions. The amalgamation appears to be going well. But maybe not pleasing everyone. With a frown, Jonesy pipes up in his high, thin voice. "I hope nobody else wants to be ball gunner."

Hah! That anybody else'd want that job is the joke of the day.

I manage to get Jock off to one side; we've got to talk about finding a navigator. Especially after the troubles I had in the UK, I'm desperate to find someone to handle the maps for my crew who knows what he's doing.

Did I say "my crew?" Although we've agreed to fly together, we haven't mentioned the other question... which of us is to be the aircraft commander. Clearly, Jock would make a good one. But what's this he's saying?

"... had my own crrrew in Britain; except for Phil, it was all broken up. Expected I would want my own grroup here too. Been giving it a lot of thought, but decided everrryone has a betterrr chance if the skipperrr is commissioned. Being arrround the Officerrs' Mess would imprrrove his chances of knowing what was going on, maybe get a wee advantage now and then."

Cheez, that was unexpected. I'm glad to know I can try my hand at leading the crew, but I feel for Jock — wrestling with the same questions I have — his answer something he's been agonizing over, rehearsing in his mind, setting out the rationale for his decision. It had to be placed on the record.

He's just standing there, waiting for some kind of answer.

All I can do is mumble something about "... a tough decision, Jock, but if that's what you've decided, I'm glad we're together. With a crew this big, running it could be a two-man job."

He nods. There's no need to say more.

I break the quiet. "We have to find a navigator. Right away. Any ideas?"

"No one in particularrr. Don't know how you'd find who'd be a good one."

"Yeah. We'll just have to rely on our intuition. But there's one chap I like... like his looks anyway. That's all we have to go on. There he is... the RAF sergeant... slim, dark brown hair. I've talked to him... liked him. Don't know anything more, but he'd be my first choice."

"Aye, I know him," Jock says. "Pleasant chap... seems smart. His name's Bob. Yes, I think that's rrright... Bob Done, spelled D-O-N-E but pronounced like `bone.' He might be a good man."

That satisfies me. Let's ask him. I'm often slow to move on things, but other times I surprise myself by being `juldi, juldi'... which in this country means quick, quick. Now I've got over my inertia, my shyness, whatever it was, I feel gung-ho to push ahead, get more things settled.

"Okay, Jock, let's go. Talk to him before somebody else does. Other crews are looking for navigators too. Let's grab him."

Because he's the fellow I want. No question. He's the one to navigate us around the Indian Ocean, someone we can depend on. Call it a hunch, based on nothing but chit-chat and the fact I like his looks; don't people get married on little more? So let's go. Already, my eyes are darting right and left to see if any other pilots are heading in Done's direction.

But Stan Govan is still ruminating. "Well, pairrhaps. I rreckon he could be a good man. There are navigatorrrs I wouldn't want, and he's not one of those. I can't think of anybody else I expect would be betterrr."

"Okay, okay... let's go. Find out if he's in a crew yet."

We're strolling over to where the three are standing. As we get closer, I'm looking straight at Done, ignoring the others. Seeing us approach, he looks up, and our eyes meet; his two friends move off a little to one side.

Cheez, it really is! Just like going up to a girl at a school dance.

What I say is, "Hi, I'm Wally Frazer. This is Jock Govan. We're getting a crew together... looking for a good navigator, wondered if you were available."

He has a little half-smile on his face. "That's a coincidence. I was just looking for a good crew."

Hey, a neat answer. About my age or a bit younger, he's good-looking without quite being movie star calibre, which I think is about right for most guys. English accent, of course, and a pleasant one; I don't like them all. And do I detect a touch of `upper class' in it?

We chat. Bob has an easy, casual manner that suggests to me he'd remain unflustered in an emergency. His remarks show common sense as well as a touch of humour. I think I've been lucky again.

Back with our group, there are now seven of us standing in a sort of circle. Another round of handshakes as Bob doesn't know the others.

Looking around the field, there are little groups all about. Some are embryo crews like ourselves. That's Brodie's gang over there and it's great to realize that the pangs of envy have left me. But there are other groupings. Unpicked navigators with other navigators, gunners with other gunners, maybe half the original total still waiting to be asked. By now they must be getting concerned, starting to wonder if they'll be picked for any crew, asking themselves, "What's wrong with me?"

In another group are unattached pilots. Hah, I now feel quite superior. Why don't they get cracking? Once you get started, it's not that difficult.

Though I still think the system of throwing 150 men into a pot, then standing back to see what crew combinations come out of it, is a harrowing process.

I'm standing with Jock when I notice Mac at my elbow with a face that says he's waiting to say something.

"Skipper, I'm the only wireless operator yet. If you're looking for another radio man, I'd recommend Joe Barlow. At our course in England, I came second, Joe came first." After a short pause, "If you wanted to make him First Wop, I'd be satisfied to be the number two man."

Three thoughts. First, that's a generous offer by Mac. Two, I'm sorry to learn too late I might have invited Chota Harris into the crew without Mac's feelings being scratched. And, three, wouldn't it be a joy to inform Bill Jackson that my two radio men came first and second in their class!

I don't like agreeing to someone I've never even met, but I look to Jock and he gives me a definite nod.

"Sounds good, Mac. Can we meet him?"

"He's right here. Joe!" he shouts.

He could have whispered. Barlow must have been standing right at my ear. In one second flat he's in front of me, pumping my hand. With that kind of alacrity, no wonder he came first in his class.

He's about five feet high and two feet wide, most of it muscle. Squarish face on top of that, right now with a grin that stretches nearly 180 degrees. With an accent that is obviously north-country, he's saying, "I'm Joe Barlow. Know most of the lads in your crew. Sure like to join you."

Not many introductions required this time. I turn to speak to Bob but glance back for another look at Barlow. He and Mac and Jonesy are pummelling each other in great glee. I'm not unhappy about that, maybe just bothered a bit that some of the guys seem to have picked Barlow before I did, that introducing him was just a formality.

Now Jock is saying, "If you want to go ahead, settle on a flight engineerrr, I know a good man."

"Yeah? What's his name? Another Scot?"

But I shouldn't have said that; it slipped out. Sometimes my tongue is faster than my brain. Am I suspicious that the crew is being chosen for me?

"Noo," with a little chuckle. Jock guessed what I was thinking. "He's a Londoner. I bunked beside him on the Stratheden, expect he'd be a capable laddie. Name's Arthur Cooperrr. As of yestairrday, he didn't have a crr-rew. If you'd like to meet him...make up your own mind... I could find him."

With all those complicated fuel and electrical and hydraulic systems, one of my biggest prayers was for a first-class engineer. And I don't know any here at all. Here's Jock coming back with a husky fellow in tow. Hey, this is no kid. Older than me, well into his thirties, he looks a very serious fellow, likely quite good-looking before he got middle-aged.

P-Peter Crew:
Done, Govan, Author, Cooper,
Howse, Jones, Slight,
Hill, McIlwaine, Barlow

"Arthur Cooper," he says, looking right at me. "Glad to join you."

Hey, you're not with us yet; this is just a job interview. But he does look capable, a big, dependable workmanlike gentleman, dignified and calm. On a long trip, he'd switch petrol tanks carefully and correctly; somebody else would have to supply the jokes.

Okay, I'm sold. "Welcome aboard, Arthur; glad you're joining us."

There goes the bell; just time for a word with Jock and the gunners.

"We did well. Except for the bomb-aimers yet to come, we just need a gunner for the top turret. Why don't you check around, see who's available?"

Jock and I head for our class. What a morning! More successful than I could have hoped at breakfast. Not only do I have a crew, I think I was lucky as hell in who I got. And I don`t feel alone any more!

JUNE 3

Another Saturday night. This week, the Sergeants' Mess in the middle of nowhere at a place called Kolar which nobody at home even heard of.

Home! I remember it well. If it weren't for this damn war, the whole gang would be at Lakeside tonight, a nice breeze off the water, great music from the orchestra and room on the big dance floor to swing. All the girls would be in summer dresses, and Jean would look best of all.

How often these days do I think, "Life was so great then, before this stupid war messed up our lives!" Did we realize how lucky we were, appreciate how much freedom we had then to live much as we chose?

But no point thinking that. It's 1944, there really is a war on, there's no cool breeze, and there sure as hell are no girls. What this place does have is an over-abundance of guys, a big mixture of heights and widths though too much sameness otherwise. You get tired of the khaki colour very `juldi.'

The building is another basha, maybe not as fancy as the Officers' lounge, but bigger. Must be two hundred men here tonight.

Bernie McIlwaine came to tell me the crew were planning a party, and I was glad to come. Things happened fast yesterday. I came home elated, only afterwards wondered what I'd done. Can you truly judge a man by the look in his eye, the way he talks? If not, I've committed myself to go flying into Burma with strangers. I want to know them better, and soon, starting tonight.

"Welcome, skipper," Mac greets me at the door. "Follow me; we have a table at the back. And now, I present the latest addition to the Frazer crew ... raw-da-da-daw... Eddie `top gunner' Hill!"

Wasn't it the Agatha Christie mystery, "Ten Little Indians," where the cast kept getting smaller. We're just the opposite; our number keeps growing. Tonight we could say, "and now there are ten."

"Skip," this Eddie Hill says, "this is a good crew. I'm glad to join it."

At least that's what I think he said. The way those Lancashire vowels came `ow'-ing out, I wasn't sure. It's their language; they're entitled to pronounce it any way they wish but, omigawd, will we need an interpreter?

A handsome lad, Eddie's main feature would be his very blond hair; he'd be popular with the girls. I don't expect you'd rate him as a particularly serious lad, as a very studious type, but more a brash fellow who'd be a good man in a scrap. Exactly what you want in a gunner.

"I'm twenty-one," he says. "Worked in a mill; a `bump and grinder.' Why does everybody laugh at that? It's one of the trades in a cotton mill."

The party's been going a couple of hours now. A beer shipment just arrived but as the ration is only four bottles per month — small pint bottles at that — nobody's getting stinko. You don't ever drink somebody else's beer, even when invited, so I've been sipping lime juice with a little Bombay gin added because there's always plenty of that.

We've been comparing backgrounds. Of the four oldest, Jonesy, Arthur and Joe Barlow are married. Mac has his pencil out. "Average

age... twenty-six," he says.

That's fairly high although I don't know it proves anything. The main reason it's high is Stan Jones. Wee Jonesy, the one busting with enthusiasm, whose excited words come in a torrent, the fellow who wants to hang upside down in a ball turret, is 39. Old enough to be my father!

At that age, he needn't be in uniform at all, could be at home tonight in Blackpool with wife and daughters, his job to go to on Monday morning. But he's sitting across the table from me, perspiration dripping from his face, shirt soggy with sweat. He joins the others in complaints about the shortage of beer or whatever, is involved in every discussion or argument. I think he's actually enjoying himself. Was photography not that exciting?

Arthur Cooper, our engineer, is just his opposite in both temperament and size. He seldom says anything. Jock mentioned he lived just outside London, was a strong union man. What would a flight engineer have done pre-war? Maybe a mechanic in a garage, something in that line?

"No... nothing like that," he says, "a cabinet maker."

"A carrpenterr, only betterrr," Jock adds, seeing I don't understand.

"Oh... sure." But it's hard not to show disappointment. A carpenter as our engineer? They only know hammers and saws and lumber. Even if they did take a special course on B24s, wouldn't a mechanic be better?

Then I remember that my own job resume wouldn't impress anybody. Maybe they won't ask. If they do, I'll have to say I've piled a lot of cement blocks in my day, then for a year was sort of a book-keeper. It wouldn't be fair to expect that all the others have college degrees.

Phil, from London, is the salesman. Joe Barlow, 28, was a real estate agent. A Yorkshireman, he lives with his Welsh wife in Wales.

At 23, I guess I'd be next in age.

Earlier, before the noise in here got so bad, we compared notes on a lot of things. Most had gone through Harwell or similar training in Britain but Bob Done has never been to an OTU, did all his courses in South Africa.

"Rhodesia, actually. Oh, yes, many RAF trained there. Got my Navigator wings last January. Expected we might be coming to India, were afraid we might be sent here directly, but they shipped us back to Blighty, gave us a fortnight's leave, then put us on the Stratheden. In the last year, I've spent more time on the ocean than in the air."

"Did the RAF know you'd be coming to India?" I want to know.

"Well, no one actually said that, but there were hints we'd have to get used to hot weather. We did a lot more Astral Navigation work than you'd ever use in Britain. Most of us guessed India."

So that's why the navigators were pulled out of our crews at Harwell: the RAF knew they had replacements doing special training in South Africa coming to meet us in India. Maybe the RAF plans further ahead than I thought.

Jock Govan is listening to this. "Early on, the RAF trrained all its airrcrews in Britain. Then some were sent to South Africa, thousands went to Canada, but I did my flying trrraining in Amerrrica."

"You did! I didn't know any RAF trained in the States."

"Oh, yes. We had to solo on Tigerrr Moths in Brritain fairrst to prove we could fly. Went to Canada in Aprril of `42, then to Georrgia on Stearrmans, and to Alabama on Vultees and Harrvarrds. Got my wings at Selma in Alabama, finished at Eglin in Florrida forr tarrget shooting. Back to Brrritain and did some hourrs on twin-engined Oxfords and Wellingtons therre."

My mouth is wide open. "You trained on Harvards too! How in hell could two single-engine fighter pilots end up flying a four-engine bomber?"

"B24s were a surrprrise to me too."

Two fighter pilots to fly a bomber! The RAF must be crazy.

Jock was a student in Scotland, half way to becoming a chartered accountant. "D'ye ken that rrresidents of Invairrness are considerrred to speak the purrrest English of anywherrre in the worrrrld."

Jock's drinks are making him talkative. "Ye' might call me Stan Smith; Stanley is my real name and Govan is the Gaelic for Smith."

Bernie McIlwaine had been in a clerical job before enlisting. Bob Done's answer seemed a bit imprecise. "My family's in the textile business; I worked there before I enlisted."

It's getting terribly loud in here. I can barely hear Jim Slight saying he comes from Jedburgh, south of Edinburgh. "At gunnerry school, my buddies wairr Ivan Small and Dicky Shorrt. At rrroll call, our names were called out in alphabetical orrrder. The Officerrr said he'd never hearrrd anything like it; the names went "Shorrrt... Slight... Small.""

What a mix of guys. Different in sizes, ages and nationalities. Various pre-war jobs, and then trained in different parts of the world. Maybe some diversity in family backgrounds too. And here we are in India, thrown together by a variety of happenstances to form one aircrew. With me as their captain! But I know nothing of that. Being the lousy quarterback of a terrible high school football team didn't teach me anything. Isn't there a quick course to take, a pamphlet to read, something to teach me in a hurry how to be a leader?

It sure is getting hot in here. Trouble is, you get so sweaty you're thirsty, and then you take another wee sip and the gin just makes you hotter. I'll just finish what's left here and then, bingo, that'll be it.

Another thing I'm finding out tonight... I'm enjoying myself. These are a good bunch of guys. I still think, underneath the laughter and the banter, they're really a pretty mature and serious group. But tonight... hey! We're having a li'l party, eh?

Something amusing me is that here I seem something of a minor celerb... celebrity. Maybe just a curiosity. Gunners leave, bring back other gunners to meet their new skipper. Or Bob's navigator pals come by to introduce themselves, make their own assessment as to how lucky or unlucky he's been.

The crew are curious about me too. Unner... understandable, I suppose. Some have maybe never met a Canadian before, not to sit and talk to close up anyway. Which is another reason to be studying me almost as if I were a visitor from another planet. Not unfriendly; just interested to find out what I'm like, in what ways the same as they are, in what ways different. Maybe the way you'd touch and poke at a traveller from Mars to see what he was made of, to ask how cold the winters are on that far-off planet.

Now that they're getting used to me, lots of quoss... quizzical little comments are being floated in front of me. Not hard, flat-out personal questions because they're really quite a well-mannered binch... bunch. I'm only being invited to answer the ones I think are appop... appropriate.

Cheez, my glass is full again. I thought I'd emptied it.

Now they're talking about pilots. Joe's saying a captain in the course ahead was an instructor, 1,900 hours in the air. Phil's talking about a Transport pilot who had 3,000 hours.

Hah! I know what they're hunting at... hinting at. I'm not that... hic... dumb. They want to find out how much flying I've did... hic. Jock could tell 'em, maybe even Mac, but they're just smilin'. What should I say? Don't wanna disappoint 'em, worry 'em. Could I tell them I was an old bush pilot, born in a cockpit? That'd make 'em happy. No, don't think I could pull it off. They're all waitin' for an answer. What the hell, I'll tell 'em the truth.

I think it's the gin makes me do it.

"I know what you guys wanna know... you wanna know what kinda pilot you picked." The noise is so bad in here I havta shout.

"Well, I'll tell ya'. You guys picked one of the potench... potentially great fighter pilots of this damn war. That's what I am... a fighter pilot. Spitfires, Mosquitoes... wouldn't matter. And so's Jock. Didja all know that? You got two fighter pilots to fly your big old Lib."

Jeez, it's got stinkin' hot in here. And I'm just a wee bit woozy. I look aroun' the table; what I can see is, I certainly got their attention.

"You want flying experience? Okay, I'll tell ya'. You wanta count time in trainers... Harvards, Oxfords? No? How about passenger time, link trainer time? No, just bombers? Then you havta mean Wellingtons. Good old Wimpys, only airplane ever named after a character in the... hic... comic strips. Didja know that... named after this fat old guy who's Popeye's pal, this J. Wellington Wimpy, Esquire? And so that's why they call the good ole Wellington a Wimpy. D'ja know that? Oh... ya' did."

"Yeah, flying hours. My total... grand total, just big planes? Okay, I'll tell ya'... it's not three thousand and it's not two thousand. What it is... it's ninety-six. With no instructor in the plane, it's sixty-five. That what you wanta know?"

Cheez, that's put a damper on the party. The room is still very loud but at our table it's quiet. Did I go too far? Maybe honesty is the best policy only when you can't think of anything better.

"However," I better try to patch things up, "there's only one pilot with more hours than Jock and I have. We'll learn our jobs the same as you will."

But, as an audience, I'd lost them. I'm heading back to my billet now. Our li'l party seemed to break up fast back there. But it was a damn good bash, ever'body enjoying themselves... till right near the end, anyway.

CHAPTER 5

INTO THE AIR

JUNE 7, 1944

D-Day! Invasion of Europe! We heard Churchill's speech on the BBC. Jeez, I hope the landings are successful. If not, this war could go on for years.

At Meteorology class today, the topic: monsoons. I thought the word meant rain. Wrong... they're winds. Out of the north-east and dry during winter, they reverse direction in summer and blow in from the sea with spectacular cloud formations, electrical storms, and rain too.

The Met man is a typical Cloudy Joe, loves to warn about bad weather.

"In this area, we will get a taste of it. But many of you will be flying out of bases in Bengal. I must warn you that monsoon conditions in that region of India are exceedingly severe. You have no doubt had some experience with the turbulence associated with large cumulus clouds. That was true in the UK. But with the extreme climactic conditions in this country, the cumulus spawned here are even more dangerous. Loaded with tremendous up-drafts and down-drafts, they must be avoided like the plague."

Back to our room, we've siesta'd, and here comes Dulla with our tea, his manner penitent; he was late again this morning. Bill gave him a tongue lashing; I got in a few licks too. Missing breakfast is a serious matter.

"Next time he's late, we fire him," Bill says.

Jackson is pretty tough. In the RAF since 1940, he was a sergeant-pilot with a tour of ops and a medal before he got his commission. He has little patience with bearers who sleep late, airmen who don't measure up or, for that matter, sprog officers with shiny new wings. I wonder what he's like with his crew. Very strict, I'll bet; there'd be no question in his crew as to who was boss. Is that what makes a good leader?

The whole matter of leadership and discipline is on my mind a lot.

Some captains stay on a formal basis with their men. Lots of "Yes, sir!

No, sir!" stuff. But our crew is mostly on a first-name basis now... the way you'd be on a football team. But is it a mistake to be too informal?

"Military discipline... baloney!"

Johnny King, my Poona pal, had ideas on everything. "Do you know why they keep enlisted men separated from their officers? Partly it's to keep them from seeing how much better the officer class is treated... meals and such. But the main reason is so the troops won't get to know their officers too well, won't find out too soon what dumb buggers many of them are."

Dulla will be back in an hour with hot water for shaving. I could finish that Nero Wolfe mystery. But that pamphlet on the turbo-super-chargers is on the table. I better go over it again. I'm certainly a lot more conscientious than I ever was at school. I guess I have responsibilities now.

JUNE 10

"Buhar kee chandni rat hi."

Another Saturday. After midnight now, we're bouncing along a country road, six of us on an RAF lorry getting a ride back to camp after a short weekend in Bangalore. With nothing to do except sit, we pooled our scanty Urdu in an attempt to say, "It's a moonlit spring night."

But everyone's tired now, just sitting and looking straight ahead.

What a beautiful night! The big round moon is almost overhead and very bright. But it's not the harsh brightness of a midday sun that produces black shadows behind anything that gets in its way. A moon is much kinder to the landscape, emitting a gentle light that softens hard edges, can transform ugliness into a pale, pastel, mystic beauty.

Every pond — a mud puddle by day — becomes in the moonlight a shimmering, silvery jewel. That shabby village on the right — a jumble of squalid huts in the sunshine — is tonight a shadowy, mysterious hamlet fit for the Queen of the Fairies. Now the road is passing under big trees, a row on either side meeting at the top to form a sort of roof; it's like driving through an empty cathedral. It's darker in here, but the spaces between the tree trunks could be huge windows; lights can be seen flickering outside.

But we're in open country again, passing ghostly half-seen shapes with patches of half-dark and fully-dark penumbras behind them. With no lights to be seen now, and not a sound except the engine of the lorry, it must be like driving down some lonely highway on the moon.

Bangalore wasn't great. But we had free days after finishing ground school and took the train into the city. Yanks and British army filled the hotels, but we found a rooming house run by an Anglo-Indian woman.

Last night, a dance. At least, that's what the Notice Board called it.

Two hundred guys and, not hard to count them, four girls — two white and two ivory. A bit of competition I don't mind, but that's ridiculous.

"Let's blow this place," Brodie suggested. "Try the night club, watch a show." But it was a crummy spot, noisy, crowded and hot, and we left early.

At dinner, Brodie asked, "Well, a movie, or back to that Club?"

"Anything else?" we wondered.

"According to the Yanks at lunch, not unless you know someone to get you into the Country Club. Or, I have another suggestion."

I'm getting a lot of respect for Steve as a guy who always has ideas worth listening to. Is that a big part of being a leader?

"We could go back to camp... take it easy for a day before we start flying. There's a truck going to Kolar tonight; I checked with Motor Transport before we left. It leaves at eleven; I know where to catch it."

Here's the turn-off to the Station. It'll be good to hit the sack.

JUNE 14

The `B' Flight office is a shack just big enough to hold a desk, a filing cabinet and two chairs. Luckily, it's in a grove of palms. If this week is any example, we'll be spending a lot of time just sitting around.

"No flying for you today," Flt/Lt Mathews told us again. "The graduating class has trips to finish; we need the aircraft for that."

There are no hangars here, just the open-air Dispersals, and we've spent some hours clambering through a Lib parked near the Flight Shack. But we did have one flight, our first time off the ground in months. Just a ferry job to pick up chemicals at Bhopal, seven hundred miles to the north. An instructor, P/O Palmer, was the pilot; our crew filled the other spots. Jock and I took turns in the right-hand seat. Yeah, we actually flew the big Lib!

Compared to the beat-up old Wimpys we had at OTU, the aircraft flies beautifully, the controls delicate and responsive — at least in the smooth morning sky. Returning in the afternoon heat, the air had gone all bumpy.

The landscape below was unlike anything I've seen from the air, nothing but parched earth. Bob came on the intercom, sounding worried. "I'm not sure where we are. There's a town on our left, a rail line on our right, should be a river between them but it's not there. I must have the wrong town."

Palmer's answer: "In dry months, rivers disappear. Then, during the rainy season, there are lakes and streams the cartographers never dreamed of. Makes map-reading interesting. But to find your river bed, look for a bridge."

"Nose gunner here. Bridge ahead, no water under it." And Bob could relax.

As a familiarization exercise with the Lib, it was useful. A nice plus: the temperature a mile off the ground is a helluva lot more comfortable.

JUNE 16

"Frazer! Your crew all here?" It's Flt/Lt Mathews. "C-Charlie needs an air-test. We'll go in the lorry, pick up parachutes on the way."

We've reached the Dispersal. The crew chief, a Sgt McEvoy, is saying, "Routine check, sir. We replaced gaskets in #4; should be okay now."

In the cockpit, Mathews takes the right-hand seat. Hey! I'll be flying!

"Do your pre-flight check," he says.

Concentrating hard, I start checking item after item, 21 in all, making damn sure I don't forget anything. Altimeter reading at zero, gyro compass on and set for compass heading, hydraulic booster pump on, etc. etc. Finished, I glance at the man beside me; he's been watching closely.

"Do it again," he says.

Damn, what did I forget? Yeah, lock the brakes for start-up. Do I have to go through it all again? I do. This time, Jock and Arthur count too. Mathews nods, curtly, and gives a flick of his wrist forward and up. I'm to carry on, find out how much I remember of what I've read and been told.

Sgt McEvoy is standing in front of the nose, very patient. I guess he's seen first-time Lib pilots before. I show him three fingers; he replies with three of his own. You start #3 first because the hydraulic system is operated by a pump on that engine. I remember to flick my intercom switch to `on' and say, "Ready to start engines."

I'm wondering how nervous I sound.

I instruct my co-pilot to turn on the ignition switches, set the throttle to one-quarter open, mixture control to `Idle Cut-off,' then give a thumbs-up to McEvoy. I can't see the #3 engine, the inboard one on the starboard side, but the Sergeant passes the order to the airman manning the portable generator on a trolley. There's a humming sound as #3 is energized. Counting out the stipulated 12 seconds, I flick the `mesh' switch.

Wow! What a coughing and spitting and snorting. Like an animal in its death throes, in agony. But the engine catches, comes alive.

Mathews flicked on the fuel booster pump as the engine started. I move the mixture control to `auto-lean' and check that the oil pressure comes up to normal. The engine is making a gawdawful racket which reminds me to throttle back to 1,000 rpm.

Hey, I can relax a little, even feel a bit proud of myself, like a cowboy who's just broken his first bronco. The big #3 has been tamed, is now purring smoothly. But Mathews has his mike off to shout in my ear. "Aren't you going to tell me to turn off the fuel booster pump?"

Dammit, I forgot that. Too much to remember. But now he's staring straight ahead, head-set back on. I have to flip my intercom switch and say, "Pilot to second pilot. Turn off fuel pump."

The ground crew are waiting again so I hold up four fingers. Energize, wait, mesh. This time I don't forget the booster pump.

When all four engines are running nicely, and the hydraulic pressure, fuel pressure and oil pressure gauges all give okay readings, Mathews comes on the blower to say, "If you're ready, let's go."

An AC2 `erk' - aircraftsman Class 2 - is holding a rope. I put my hands to my chin, then tug them apart, the signal to pull the chocks away from the wheels. Engines idling, I release the brakes. Nothing happens. Okay, we need some juice; I advance the throttles for the outside engines, #1 and #4. Still nothing, so give the throttles another nudge...then just a bit more. Hey, now we're moving, and very nicely.

What the hell, we're picking up speed. Haul back on the throttles! But we've too much momentum, are out on the taxi strip, rolling across it towards the soft sand on the other side. At this speed, will a B24 turn on a dime? No, it could crash over onto a wing. I'm trying to stay calm and think fast but there's no bloody time for that. If I slam on the brakes, won't the Lib flip up on its nose? Like a Harvard? No, the Lib has a nose wheel! Praise the Lord and whoever invented the nose wheel. Brakes! Both brakes — hard!

But the pedals are already pushed right down; Mathews got there first. There's a horrible "wump" sound as the nose wheel tries to go right through the concrete. But I don't think it did because now there's a sickening "crack" from behind, the little tail wheel smashing into the pavement back there. Now another "wump" and another "crack"...a few more of each. Not as loud, though. The pitching motion is finally slowing down. Now it's stopped.

I'm still pulling on the throttles to make sure they don't slide forward. A peek towards Mathews shows him sitting bolt upright, legs still pushing on the brakes. Now he's trying to say something. When I pull off my earphones, he's shouting, "I'll take it; there may still be room to turn."

And he does it, a ninety degree turn with an inch of concrete to spare. We're moving again. I'm watching very carefully; you need a fair shot of juice to get started, very little after that to keep moving.

But even at this modest pace, the slightest touch to a brake sets up a yawing motion, starts the nose undulating. The wing tips, 55 feet out on either side, wobble as they dip up and down. I have to admit it; while taxiing, a Liberator does look like a fat man in a congo line.

Mathews is leaning towards me again. "I think the nose wheel still seems serviceable. Take over, but for God's sake, take it easy until you get the hang of it."

That's the only blast he gives me. I like this fellow; he didn't get that excited, and the little roasting he gave me was done privately when he could have done it over the intercom...easier for him, more embarrassing for me.

We're moving forward again, but carefully, very slowly. What I don't need is another bollux like that one. Makes sense to be extra cautious, right? After several minutes, we've gone about one hundred yards. But here's the click of the mike again. It's Mathews, his voice gone all snarky.

"Very good, Frazer. But could we move a little faster now? If we don't, the war may be over before we even get to the damn runway."

More proof: never let yourself think an instruc-tor could be a nice guy.

Morning Huddle
Author,
Cooper, Govan, Done

But we're moving better now. Coasting up to the runway, I give a touch of star-board brake which brings us to a stop at a 45 degree angle to the taxi strip - in perfect position for engine run-up, just the way Palmer did it at Bhopal. But Mathews, checking with Arthur that everybody's ready for take-off, didn't notice this neat man-oeuver. Now he's say-ing, "OK, Frazer. Do your final check. Then call the Tower for permission to take her up."

Starting with #4, I set the mixture to `auto-rich' and advance throttles to 2,000 revs to check the magnetos. What a helluva racket! But it gets worse when I increase to 2,700 so Arthur can check temperature and pressure. Then I throttle back to 1,200 rpm and return to `auto-lean.' So far, so good. The other engines check out too.

A few more things to see to. Booster pumps on, generators on, mixture back to `auto-rich,' increase prop pitch, check free movement of the ailerons, elevators and rudders, set trim tabs...and a few others. We're ready to go.

But Arthur's banging my shoulder. "Flaps," he's shouting in my ear.

Cheez! I grab the lever, hear the hydraulics extending the wing flaps to provide extra lift. At least if you're heavy-loaded, forget the flaps and you're dead. But Mathews is busy watching an aircraft coming in to land... maybe didn't even notice.

The Tower answers me. "C-Charlie. You have permission to take off."

We wiggle out onto the runway, get lined up, looking down the long, straight ribbon of concrete. Both brakes are on, and locked. It's time to go, time to find out whether I can handle one of these babes.

A deep breath. Push all four throttles forward to the `stops,' the brakes still on. The din is awesome; the aircraft shivers and shakes as if going to disintegrate. Kick the brake release and we start moving forward. Very slowly at first. Now we're picking up speed. Mathews is calling out the airspeed.

"Fifty. . . sixty. . . seventy."

I'm keeping an eye on the runway. We're drifting a bit to the left edge, but a touch of right rudder straightens us out.

"Eighty." I remember to ease the control column back, but cautiously. We don't have enough speed for take-off yet. The nose comes up a bit; the nose-wheel's supposed to come off the ground now. I think it has.

Hey, this is exciting. Nothing like it. The adrenalin must be flowing because I feel wonderful...alive...every nerve tingling. Not that there's much time to think about it. I've got to stay centred on the concrete.

"Ninety-five . . . one hundred."

Mathews' voice is surprisingly calm. Very reassuring. "One-twenty, Ease back on the stick and take her up."

Here we go! I draw the wheel toward me, into my gut. But gently. No more rash moves today. But nothing happens. Pull the stick back some more. But we're still stuck to the runway. Omigawd, there's not much of it left. Ease the nose up still more. But then I feel the wheel coming back to my chest. Mathews has taken control, has hauled the control column right back. The nose comes up, away up. But won't the kite stall at this angle? I still have my hands on the wheel, but just touching it. Mathews is doing the flying. I peek out my side window. No runway below, just grass and bushes.

The intercom squawks again. "Alright, Frazer, old chap...you take it."

I acknowledge, take a grab on the wheel, try to get re-oriented fast. The wings look level enough, and the angle of the nose above the horizon seems okay. Maybe I should check the rate-of-climb; damn, I can't find it. No time to hunt now. The port wing is low but a smidgen of aileron brings it up. Ah, there it is - the rate-of-climb gauge - right under the Artificial Horizon.

"Speed one-thirty," says Mathews. "You should raise the undercart."

Yeah, the captain decides when the wheels are to come up.

"Undercarriage up," I say, feeling dumb to repeat back what he just told me. But now we're climbing okay. At 600 feet, safely off the ground, reduce manifold pressure and ease off on the throttles. A few moments later, I direct Mathews to raise the flaps. Everything's going very, very nicely.

The instructor again. "Height's one thousand. Level off, start your turn to port and do a full circuit. Don't forget the hill."

Yeah, the countryside is flat for miles except for a big hill beside the main runway. Whoever chose the location must've bought it from his brother.

Next step: level off, adjust engine settings. A touch of aileron and rudder and we're doing a gentle turn to port. Another turn and we're on the down-wind leg. I can relax for a moment.

At cruising speed, it's not as noisy now. When Mathews leans toward me and pulls off his head-set, I do the same and can hear his shouts.

"That was almost a good take-off. You kept straight on the runway. When we got airborne, you climbed smoothly enough. But be more decisive at the moment of lift-off; you have to get the wheels unglued, force the aircraft to come off the deck, show her who's boss."

We've gone around a second time while I practise some shallow turns. On the downwind leg, Mathews makes a big, momentous announcement.

"Okay, let's see you land her."

Hey, adrenalin time again. Flaps down, wheels down and locked, brake pressure okay, fuel booster pumps on, fuel mixture and propeller pitch set, reduce speed. I glance over my shoulder and see Arthur nod.

I've turned cross-wind, wondering when to start the next turn, the one to bring us into alignment with the runway. I think we should turn...now!

Oh, oh! Left it too late. We're two hundred yards to the right. Gotta get lined up. Okay, a zig to the left, straighten out, and the ribbon of concrete is directly ahead. No big problem. Except...damn, I'm almost up to the runway and still at nine hundred feet.

"Flaps, forty degrees," I holler, and pull back on the throttles.

"Height seven hundred," I hear Mathews say. "Throttle back some more... you're still too fast. I'm giving you full flaps."

I pull the throttles back, but I don't like it. These crates surely won't glide without power. To keep some airspeed, I push the nose even further forward; we must look from the Tower as if we're dive-bombing the field.

"Height three hundred, speed one-thirty. Still too fast. The runway's just ahead. Height one-fifty...you're still at one-thirty; we're already over the damn field."

Mathews doesn't sound calm and reassuring any more. But, dammit, all he's got to worry about is the height and airspeed. I've also got to keep the plane flying, wings level, stay in line with that strip of concrete.

"Height fifty feet, speed one-fifteen. Start to level off and hit the deck. We're running out of runway!

"Speed one-ten. Cut the engines!" He really does sound scared.

But I'm still twenty feet over the runway. Cut the engines here? We'll stall; one wing will drop, catch the ground, we'll crash. That's what would happen in a Harvard. But he said to pull the throttles back, so I do. Except

I can feel his big hand over mine, over the four levers, and he yanks them right back to the `off' position. Much too roughly, I'm certain.

Not that I'm doing much thinking; mostly I'm just waiting for the crash. Instead, two loud "plops" as first one wheel and then the other finds the runway...hit hard! We seem okay...racing down the runway, what's left of it, at a hundred miles an hour, but the plane seems in one piece. As we lose some speed, the nose drops down and there's a squeal as nose-wheel meets concrete.

"Brakes!" shouts my co-pilot. I hit the pedals immediately, but Mathews again beats me to it. The screeching of the tyres and the stink of burning rubber are fierce. With the brakes on full, we're still thundering along at sixty miles an hour. Can we stop before end of pavement?

There's nothing to do but push brake pedals and hope. One thought: the nose of the plane is so low I've never had such a clear view over it...likely because the braking is putting all the weight and pressure on the tiny nose-wheel trying to dig a trench in the concrete. From the side, the Lib must look like a hound dog hot on a scent, nose to the ground, tail straight up.

But it's working. We're slowing down. The wheels don't screech as badly ...though the stench may be worse. Now, finally, the aircraft has come to a dead stop. We've made it! I have mixed feelings: joyful we're down and safe, but disgusted with myself, a strange combination. At least I remember to adjust the fuel mix, prop pitch and all that stuff.

But we're just sitting at the end of the runway. We can't stay here. I look over at Mathews but he's sitting like a statue, staring straight ahead, looking tired out. Maybe thinking it'd be safer to go back on ops.

I suppose the awkward silence only lasts seconds. I break it by asking, "Should I try again? Or back to the Dispersal?"

Still staring straight ahead, he says, "Dispersal. Turn right on the perimeter track."

Then his backbone seems to relax and he pulls off his head-set to talk more privately. "This aircraft can't fly again till they've checked the brakes and the undercarriage. Nose-wheel, too."

I'm taxi-ing to the end of the pavement, a very, very short distance. Mostly to make light conversation, I say, "We had fifty yards to spare."

"At a hundred miles an hour, that's one second. Check it out."

Which ends the chit-chat. We reach `C's' parking spot. I roll the air-craft on to the dispersal pad, hit the left brake, give #4 a shot of juice, and we do a neat 180 degree turn so the plane is pointing out towards the taxi strip again, ready for its next flight.

But Mathews isn't impressed, just says, "Cut the engines." When the props have stopped ticking over, he shouts, "Alright, chaps, everybody out."

Outside, Arthur, Jock and I follow him around to look at the tires. Sgt

McEvoy is already there to find out what I've done to his Charlie; even if blind and deaf, he would have smelled us coming.

"Needed a little brake, did we, sir?" he asks. He touches one of the tyres, but snatches his hand away. "Still seems a bit warm, sir."

"Yes, a fairly hot touch-down," Mathews tells him. "Had to use the brakes. But that's what they're for, wouldn't you say, Sergeant?"

McEvoy has no reply to that. Just how Andrews planned it, I expect.

"I'll report to the Engineering Section that we had a hard landing," he says. "Don't let anybody take her up until she's inspected."

To the rest of us, but mostly to me, Mathews says, "She's a real tough old bird. Can take a lot of punishment."

After a moment, he adds, "Not too bad for a first attempt. As I said, the take-off was almost very good. You messed up the landing approach when you misjudged when to turn, but that just takes practice. The big mistake...you should have gone around the circuit and come in again.

"But when you continued with the landing, you were too tentative, too slow in cutting your speed and height. Be more decisive. Of course, you have to know when to be decisive and when to be cautious, and that only comes with experience. I'd say you did passably well for your first try."

Hah! If that was passably good, a pilot would kill himself if he did passably average! I know I did lousy. Mathews is maybe trying to make it sound better for the crew's benefit; it must cause additional hassle and paperwork for the whole staff here if an entire crew mutinies against it's skipper.

But nobody in the crew is saying anything. Here's our lorry; it's a silent ride back to camp.

CHAPTER 6

DICING WITH DEATH

JUNE 24, 1944

We solo'd today. A few `dual' circuits, then Mathews said, "Away you go." No problem. A little practice, then Libs almost fly themselves.

It's siesta time and we have a newspaper. War news is good; our troops in Normandy are hanging on to their beach-heads. And compared with two years ago when the Japs went through Burma like beer through a drunk, we've finally won a big battle. Nip-and-tuck for a time, but we sent reinforcements into Imphal by the thousands — men and supplies ferried in by aircraft to break the siege. The paper says the Japs are now retreating.

Here comes Hassim with our tea. We had to sack Dulla. Rather, I had to do it. "You hired him... you have to fire him," Bill said.

That's a crock. Then Jackson admitted he didn't have the heart for the job. Hah! So Bill's not as tough as he pretends. But I didn't like it either. When I told the kid he was fired, he burst out bawling that his whole family would now starve to death. Cheez! I ended up giving him three months' extra pay. But I'd never tell Bill that; I'll have to pay it myself.

Six apprentice bearers were at our door next day. But Hassim, about 15, sparkling eyes and a big grin that flashes white teeth, was an easy choice. He's a sharp kid. When Bill asked if he spoke English, his reply was, "Yes, sahib, ver' good." And then with a peek at my shoulder tabs, and a big grin, he added, "and Canajian too."

There's a party on tonight, the class ahead of us just finished here. The guys already have their postings: Ted and Johnny to something called 159 Squadron, Phil Cloutier to 357, others to 2OO, 355, 356. Newcomers from 215, a Wimpy outfit, have just arrived to convert to Libs. The RAF must have more B24 units out here than I thought.

"Let's make a run for it." A jim-dandy thunderstorm but the party will be starting. Also, I'm starving. It'll be more bully beef, though. That's been the meat dish every meal for three weeks. We've had it fried, curried, as a shepherd's pie, sauteed in a batter, boiled with onions... disguised in any number of ways. But it still tastes like bully beef.

Yeah, war really is hell!

JULY 2

We've done two cross-country trips. P/O Palmer came along on the first, mainly for a nap. But first he introduced us to `George,' the automatic pilot.

"Get the plane straight and level, flick the `on' switch, let George take over. No, he doesn't like bumpy air but if it's reasonably smooth he'll fly the plane without help for minutes at a time. When a wing dips, just twiddle the knobs to get the plane level again. On long flights, a big help."

Next, a five-hour trip. Solo. Just the crew, me, and the big Lib... all on our own! From Cochin on the coast, we flew west — two hundred miles out over the ocean to some tiny specks called the Androth Islands. Out of sight of the mainland for three hours!

As soon as we got over open water, the gunners clamoured to test-fire their guns. Four turrets and the two beam guns. What a bloody racket, the stench even worse! But ten .5 machine guns in each plane! A lot of fire-power. We won't be going into action defenceless.

We also released smoke flares for the first time. Jim Slight drops one down a chute; when it hits the water and starts to smoke, he takes a reading on it from a scale in his rear turret.

You can't map-read over water. If the navigator doesn't know the speed and direction of the wind, he won't know where it's blown us. A drift reading will tell him something. But for more information, we do a jog right, left and then back on track, Jim taking a reading on all three headings. Using a little geometry, Bob can then make a fair estimate of the breeze.

And we've been `moonlight dicing' — which means night flying. `Dicing' is of course short-hand for `dicing with death,' which is the RAF's jolly description of any flying at all.

After five circuits with P/O Palmer, he unstrapped his harness. "Do three solo landings," he said. "With the bonfire burning on the hill tonight, you shouldn't hit it. Good luck."

JULY 5

Tonight we finish our flying at Kolar, a `passing-out' test before we get sent to a squadron. Seven crews went last night and five tonight.

"Get sent to a squadron." Hey, a reminder that after all this training, we're finally getting to the real thing. In just days we'll go to an outfit using real bullets, real bombs... where war is not just an abstract concept.

At briefing, the CFI — Chief Flying Instructor — says, "Take-off will be in five minute intervals; flying heights are allotted in five hundred foot increments so you won't get entangled." Jeez, all that for just five aircraft!

When the Nav Leader pulls the curtain aside, the red ribbon has a lot of blue under it, the kind of blue you can't parachute onto without getting wet. The last tack is away out in the Indian Ocean, half-way to Burma!

"No, not the Indian Ocean, only the part of it called the Bay of Bengal. Your turning point is a map reference over the sea; you'll then return to India at Madras where a Spit squadron will meet you, and simulate an attack."

Then the Met man. "Just as I accurately predicted for last night, the weather will be clear with a large moon. There's a weather system to the north, severe but stationary, not due in the area for twenty-four hours. Of course, should you perchance stumble upon a stray cu-nim drifted into your path, you will give it a wide berth."

Now he's into another long dissertation on the turbulence in such clouds, about aircraft that have blundered into one at, say, 5,000 feet, been tossed out at 15,000, or 100 feet. But we're tired of those stories.

Then the C.O. wishes us good luck. Hey, it's only a practice flip. Back at the billet, Bill is just waking up; he was on last night's trip. "Nothing to it," he says. "Don't know what all the fuss is about."

Which matches my view. Not that I always trust Jackson's opinions. Some guys always describe things in superlatives; a task is either the toughest damn job in the world or it's the easiest, never in between. Is it coincidence that the choice to describe something in positive or negative terms is always the one that makes them look best?

But I'm beat. The Control Tower usually closes down at dusk. But in case some stray aircraft happens by, a Duty Officer has to stay around. I've had the job the last two nights. But Q-Queenie, our plane tonight, needed an air test today, the result being I've not had much sleep. And tonight it's a seven-and-a-half hour trip, seven hundred miles of it over the sea!

JULY 6

There's a nice serenity about flying at night, even in a big aircraft with a big crew. Not that the noise level of the pounding motors isn't high; they make a helluva racket, could give us ear trouble some day, the Doc says. And the steady "rrr... rrr... rrr" isn't at all musical. But it's a comforting sound... reassuring. You would not want it to stop. But, except for that, it's surprisingly quiet. Bob will ask for another drift reading, or give a course change, but minutes pass without a word spoken.

It's now 2:30 a.m. Bob says, "In thirty minutes, we'll reach those map co-ordinates, can turn for home."

I'll be glad to get back over land, even happier to get to bed. Jock is flying the plane, which means adjusting George's knobs as needed.   Our auto-pilot is doing fine, just letting Queenie's nose drop every few minutes, which is normal. We're at 6,000 feet, with two planes ahead of us, two behind, but some distance away. I can relax, have another cigarette.

What a beautiful night, moonlight dancing on the water. I'm thinking that the little glints reaching my eyes have come quite a distance, reflecting all the way from the sun to the moon to the water to me.

The sudden crackling of the squawk box is always startling; this time it's Phil. Is there a trace of concern in his voice?

"Skippah, a row of clouds. Big ones. Ahead and to the left."

"Ahead? Yes, Phil, I see them now." Still some distance away, in this half-light they aren't very distinct — just shadowy shapes, a different texture from the smooth greyness of the open sky.

"Are they a solid bank, or scattered?'

"Hard to tell. Might be spread out."

I motion to Jock and we pull off our ear phones. "What d'you think?" I shout. "Should we try to pick our way through?"

"We could cairry on for a bit, see if it's clearrr ahead."

We've come up to those shapes. Magnificent monsters —cumulus or cumulo-nimbus — gigantic. They start down at ocean level and billow straight up, two miles, maybe more. Thick and black in the shadows at the bottom, the middle section is a mixed bag of greys, but up near the top... where the moonlight hits them... they're pure white, like fresh-fallen snow. Beautiful, but scary. I'll be glad when we're past them.

I hear Bob asking Jim for another drift reading; that's about four in the last ten minutes. Unusual.

Jock taps my arm, points out his window, and I squint to see. What the hell! Cloud out there too, lots of cloud! On both sides of us!

I flick my switch. "Phil, see any gaps in those clouds ahead?"

"Well... it did look open; now I think it's closed up."

I think so too. A solid bank of big ones. We've got cloud on three sides... cloud that wasn't there ten minutes ago. Maybe we should get out of here. I wave my arm to get Jock's attention, draw a semi-circle in the air to signal a 180 degree turn. He nods — a definite nod.

I try to reach Bob to tell him we're turning back, but he's on the blower getting another drift from Jim. Strange. Now he's calling me.

"Skip, I don't know what's going on. In ten minutes, the wind's switched from north to east to south to west. Now it's north again; right around the clock! You can imagine what my chart looks like. What does it mean?"

I've never heard Bob sound perplexed or worried before.

"Hell, I don't know. Could we be in the middle of something, the eye of a hurricane, something like that?" I'm trying not to sound panicky, but it's hard to be nonchalant discussing that sort of thing.

"Well... maybe. With a three sixty degree wind shift, it has to be something weird... something we weren't taught at Nav School."

"Bob, I'm turning back. Give me a course soon as you can."

Now it's Jim Slight. "If ye want to go back the way we came, ye'd best hurrrry. Therrre's a lot of cloud behind us noo."

"That's right, skip." A Lancashire accent from the top turret. "Cloud all around us. Came from nowhere. A solid bank... like we were in a box."

What the hell! I don't understand this. And things you don't understand scare you more than anything.

"Pilot to crew." Keep the voice calm. "We're in a pocket of cloud. Could be bumpy to fly through so we'll circle here until we're high enough to go out over the top. Everybody stay alert; we might see an alley through them."

Not that I'm very confident... either about finding an alley, or getting over them. The brutes are towering high above us, maybe too high.

Damn, we're going to run into one; they're closer than I thought. Tighten the turn! Okay, we just skimmed through the corner of it. What a monster! Up that close, it looked to be seething, like a ravenous sea creature grasping at passing prey. But it missed us that time; we're out in the open again.

We better start climbing. The altimeter says 5,900 feet. I increase power, get the nose in the air, and the rate-of-climb needle is pointing up. It takes several minutes to reach 6,200; it'll be slow. I wish I knew how high those cloud tops are. Maybe too high already, maybe still growing. We aren't carrying oxygen... can't go much over 10,000 feet.

We've now circled for the fourth time, have had a good look at the wall surrounding us. What a sight! It's as if we were in the Alps, in a valley, maybe a mile across, towering peaks all around. With the moon almost overhead, it's like day. Wherever a piece of cloud sticks out into the moonlight, it looks like cotton candy — white instead of pink — airy and bubbly and soft. But the black spots in the shadows look hard as ice.

The altimeter reads 6,500. That's all. I need more throttle. But climbing is hard on gas; we couldn't keep this up for long.

Damn! A big cloud right in our path. Where'd he come from? Is our valley shrinking? Hard left, maybe squeeze by? No, we're in the stuff. We're still turning... should be out in a moment, but it's taking a long time. Dammit, it's bumpy in here; black and misty and unpleasant.

Okay... moon again... we're back in the clear. Better start climbing again. Check the altimeter. Omigawd! We're at 4,500. We dropped 2,000 feet... in seconds. Must have hit a down-draft. Jock is pointing at the gauge, making sure I've noticed. Okay, okay, but I've got to figure out what to do next.

We'll try to climb again, but keep a tighter circle.

In ten minutes we've gained back a thousand feet. It'll take too long to get to ten thou, and the cloud tops could be at 20,000. What should we do? I know in my heart we can't climb over the top. We can't fly into them. And it's absolutely certain we can't stay here. What does that leave?

I wave at Jock and we pull off our earphones; there's no sense scaring everybody. "I think we have to go under the clouds, Jock. Right down on the water; don't like it, but there's no choice. What do you think? Were we ever told what it's like under a cumulo-nimbus?"

"Don't think so. But you'rre rrright. Therre's no altairrnative."

"Pilot to crew. Time to head for home. We'll go down on the deck, make a run for it under the cloud. At a hundred feet, we shouldn't be affected by up-drafts or down-drafts but it could be bumpy and wet. We'll start letting down now. Bob, any thoughts? Do you have a course for us?"

"Wal, I think you're right. But a course? I've no idea where we are."

"Well, India's somewhere to the west. Within four hundred miles. Let's get out of here, then figure out where we are."

"Alright. Let's veer south for now, say two-forty."

I have the throttles pulled right back. We're dropping down fast, down to 3,OOO feet... 2,5OO. We're doing tight turns but still scraping some edges. Flying manually now, not using George. I wish I knew more about flying under big clouds. What would happen if you got caught in an up-draft?

It's Joe Barlow. "Skipper, should we radio a message to base?"

Yeah, if we have an accident, nobody'll know what happened to us.

"Good idea. Tell 'em, `Bad weather, returning base under cloud, position blah blah, heading two four oh.' Bob, give Joe a position... best you can."

We're down to 8OO feet... 6OO... still in bright moonlight.

"Pilot to crew. We're at five hundred feet. When we go into cloud, we'll have to fly by instruments. Knowing our height will be crucial. But air pressure in this stuff will be different from at base, so our altimeter reading is useless. When we get down to a hundred feet, before we go under the cloud, we'll try to gauge how high we are over the water, re-set it.

"Jonesy, you better come out. You might get splashed."

"It's fine, skipper... good place to judge height over the water."

Well... okay, I guess. We're dropping down, down, but still having to make steep turns to stay in the clear. The wing tip pointing at the water must be close to the surface. Jeez, that's no good. If it so much as touches, we'll somersault right in. I'll level off. We're low enough.

"Okay, crew, altimeter says a hundred twenty feet. Does that look right?"

"No, no," are the answers. "More like fifty, maybe seventy-five."

"Okay, set the gauge at fifty, Jock. I'm going up to a hundred."

"Wireless op to pilot. Message sent to base. No reply."

But I'm not interested in that right now. "Okay, here we go!"

In a second, we've gone from moonlight to total darkness. Just the little cockpit light and the gauges glowing green. And rain. Torrents, cascading down the windows as if under Niagara Falls. We couldn't see outside even if there was anything to look at. But my eyes aren't on anything except the instrument panel — mostly the airspeed, the artificial horizon, the altimeter —especially the altimeter.

But I can't keep it at a hundred feet because of the bumps. We're bouncing terribly, like a bus driving across rows of ditches. The nose goes up, the airspeed plummets, and I push the wheel forward, my heart at my ankles. Then the nose dips, we're plunging towards the water and I pull the stick back. The wing tips are jouncing up and down; I can't see them but can feel it. Jeez, that last bounce dropped us to sixty feet. We've got to go higher, allow more margin for error. Jam the throttles forward and we're up to one thirty. That's just an average; the altimeter's bobbing fifty feet above and below that.

But with the extra height, the turbulence gets worse. The aircraft is straining... shaking and shuddering. How long can it keep this up? And now there's lightning... damn close. We don't need that too.

How long have we been on this terrifying roller-coaster?

Fifteen minutes... half an hour? I've no idea. It seems forever I've been pushing and pulling and swearing and sweating, Jock sitting rigid and tense beside me, ready to grab throttles or control column if I need help. But strangely, I'm enjoying it. No, that's not true; not enjoying. But at least we're doing something. It's better than that dumb stumbling about we did back there, circling around without knowing what the hell to do next.

Hey, is it getting less bumpy? Maybe. Just as much rain and lightning but, except for the occasional jolt, Queenie is behaving much better, the little airplane symbol on the Artificial Horizon holding fairly level.

And what was that? Out the corner of my eye, out my window, did I catch a glimpse of something different, a different shade? A grey colour, not as dark as the solid black. Just a flash... now it's gone... but beautiful!

There it is again. Definitely! A lighter patch. Could some moonlight be getting through? Now more greys, lots of them, and brighter. Suddenly, in a flash that's hard on the eyes, we're out of the cloud. We're in full and gorgeous moonlight. The air is calm and smooth.

Even with earphones on, I hear big cheers from behind me, from the flight deck. I feel like joining them. But we're not finished yet. The first thing... put some distance between us and that water. Extra throttle gets us to 1,OOO feet in a hurry. Everyone agrees the cloud is behind us. It's perfectly clear ahead, and time to re-group.

"Pilot to ball gunner. Did you get splashed, Jonesy? I think you should come out now." For the first time ever, I don't get an argument.

"Bob, we're still on two-forty. Do you want to change that?"

"Working on it. But how do I chart what we've been doing... wind swinging around the compass. And circling for half an hour. How do I plot that?"

"Cheez... I dunno. Could you maybe ignore all the turns, assume they just cancel out? While we were circling, assume we were stopped over one point and the wind just blew us for thirty minutes? Would that do it?"

"Well... maybe. I don't know what else. I could use the same reasoning for the wind changing around the clock... ignore it. But it would help if I knew what the wind's doing now. Are you staying at one thousand?"

"The sky's clear. I think we should go back up to six thou."

"I'll wait til then to check the drifts; the wind will be different up there. Meanwhile, steer two-eighty now."

Jock is already at work on George's knobs. Arthur says he's checking the petrol situation but we started with over ten hours of gas, should be okay. Maybe I should be more worried we don't know where we are but, for now, I'm just satisfied to be out of that cloud.

I only wish I wasn't so tired; it's 22 hours since I slept.

We're at six thou now, Bob taking some star shots. Jim drops more flares — the ones that burn on the water — and Bob is getting his three-cornered drift readings. The gunners are taking turns coming out of the turrets, the wireless ops are changing again. Here's Bob.

"Navigator to pilot. I think the wind has picked up, blown us further south than I expected. Change course to two nine five. India... Madras if we're lucky... should show up in two hours, give or take an hour."

Everything seems under control. We can relax. Lord, I'm sleepy. That was hard work back there. Maybe terror wears you out. I'd sure like a nap for a few minutes but, no, Jock looks weary too; I better stay awake.

"Some light in the east, skip," from Eddie. Good, it's been a long night.

The four engines are still pounding away. In this smooth air, George is doing well. Now the nose is dropping. Jock hasn't noticed so I give the elevator knob a twist. Okay, we're level again. Cheez, I'm tired. And the engines are droning... droning... droning.

What the hell! Who's hitting me, banging me on the shoulder. I get my eyes open. It's Joe Barlow... excited, shouting hard.

"Wake up! Wake up! We're in a dive. Wake up!"

Omigawd, the nose away down, a diving turn. The speed's built up — too far gone to correct with George. Quick! Flick auto-pilot off, wheel back, left rudder, stop the dive. Speed is 240... far too high. But it's dropping. The nose is coming up, speed 200 now. But be careful... don't over-correct. We're levelling out, speed 180. Yeah, we're okay.

But another five seconds? We'd have been going straight down — too late to pull out. Right into the ocean... ten men... both pilots asleep! I'm in a lather. I look at Jock; he's curled up in his big seat, dead to the world.

Might as well let him sleep now.

When I twist my head, Joe's face is at my shoulder. Checking that I stay awake? And Arthur's right behind him. I give Joe a thumbs-up. He gives me a grin, but it's the nervous kind with no humour in it.

We're back on course. The sky is brighter now, but I'm still fighting to keep my eyes open. Maybe if I switch off George, fly manually? Yes, that's better. You have to concentrate more, keep your arms and legs moving.

Now there's stirring on my right. Jock is sitting up, rubbing his eyes. Boy, is he in for a surprise! I might as well tell him what happened; if I don't, the rest of the crew certainly will.

"Feeling better?" I shout in his ear. "We had some excitement. Both of us asleep. George was taking us into a dive, but Joe woke me up."

Which is a lot to absorb when you're only half awake.

But here's Phil. "Land ahead, Bob! Smokestacks. Looks like a big city."

"Right, Phil, has to be Madras. New course to Kolar... two seven five."

That proves it! Not only is our navigator good, he's also damn lucky. To hit Madras dead on after all that twisting and turning, he'd have to be.

"Top gunner to pilot. Spitfires... about ten... two o'clock."

Dammit, the fighter affiliation deal. I forgot that. But I'm exhausted. "Jock, you want to play with these guys? I've had it."

"I've had enough forrr tonight."

"Pilot to crew. Sorry, gunners. We're both worn out. I'll waggle our wings, warn them off." But I'm too late.

"Here they come... one o'clock high," shouts Phil. I get just a snatch of several shadows flashing by, screaming by... just overhead, damn close. But I'm rocking Queenie from side to side, wing tips going up and down.

From Eddie. "They've disengaged, think we're short of fuel or something."

The Spits pass in front. The leader is waggling his wings too. I guess he's saying "good luck" if he thinks we're in trouble. I don't know what he'd be saying if he knew the bomber boys were just too pooped to play.

We make it to Kolar. My charpoy is waiting; I'll sleep 'round the clock.

JULY 10

"Hey, Fraz, next trip, take an alarm clock, keep yourself awake."

That's what I've had to put up with. Everybody thinks it's a great joke.

But other pilots ask how bad the turbulence, the rain. Of course, we're the senior class now. It happens every time. On each new training base, you start by being the green rookies. A few weeks later, you're the veterans. Then you start again as bungling newcomers at the next stage of your training.

Won't it be the same when we go to a squadron?

So we've finished here, are just waiting around for a posting. And wondering where we'll be going, what duties we'll be assigned to.

CHAPTER 7

JUNKET TO JESSORE

JULY 15, 1944

A posting to 355 Squadron! Rush, pack... all excited... catch the train. Over to Madras, up the coast to Bengal. Five crews: Brodie's gang, three NCO captains, and us. Four long, hot days. Arrive here at Salbani, eighty miles west of Calcutta... and the Adjutant says there's been some mistake!

"Sorry, chaps, never heard of you. Must be a foul-up. Not the first time, ha,ha. But I'll call 231 Group in Calcutta, get it straightened out."

It took several calls. "This is quite droll," he tittered. "Someone really messed up. You should be at 215 Squadron... at Jessore, the other side of Calcutta. They were expecting you today. No big rush though."

"Tell you what..." He could see we didn't think the mistake was such a rib-tickler. "Rest up here, stay tonight, go into Cal for a couple of days, carry on to Jessore Tuesday. How would that suit you?"

So, for 24 hours, we're `on strength' at 355 Squadron.

"Started operations eight months ago," one chap said. "We've done seventy missions now. Burma and Siam. First trips were at night, but started daylight ops in May with crews increased from ten men to eleven.

"Tail markings on the planes? They're our Squadron markings, two vertical white stripes on a black rudder. We share the drome with 356 Squadron, you know. They're across the field, just some meteorological flights so far, but they'll fly their first mission any day now.

"Yes, we're the new bomber squadrons, on B24s from the beginning. The other three bombing outfits — 99, 159 and 215 — got here two years ago. There are more Lib outfits, some on coastal patrols, others doing secret stuff."

"Casualties?" I ask.

"Not sure what to expect on daytime ops, but not too much trouble at night; Japs aren't strong in night fighters. The weather's often hideous but the Nips haven't been too tough on us yet.

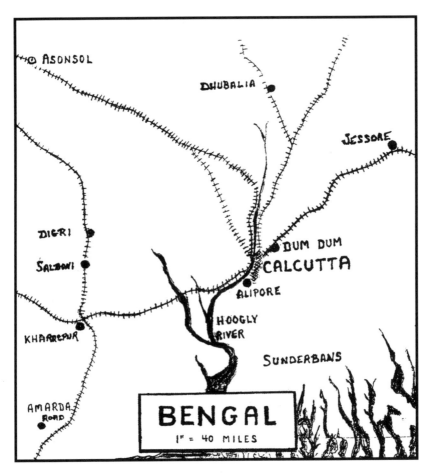

Map labels:
ASONSOL
DHUBALIA
JESSORE
DIGRI
SALBONI
DUM DUM
CALCUTTA
ALIPORE
HOOGLY RIVER
SUNDERBANS
KHARAGPUR
AMARDA ROAD

BENGAL
1" = 40 MILES

"Yes, we're mostly RAF, Aussies and Kiwis, only a few RCAF. Be glad to have more but I hear you're all going over to 215 at Jessore. No, can't tell you much about them. But you'll get all the gen when you get there."

JULY 19

Jessore, our home for the next few months! A helluva disappointment.

Kolar and Salboni were in open country, dry and dusty but quiet and uncrowded. But Jessore is a big city, a jungle city, trees everywhere. With one shower after another, dripping rain adds to the sweltering humidity. Miles from the airdrome, we're housed in a former school, a compound of brick buildings surrounded by a high fence. The streets around us blare the usual cacophony from native shops, hawkers and traffic jams.

We got here by train — two hours from Calcutta — are just finding our way around. But the Mess last night was almost empty.

"Yes, they're all down at Kolar converting from Wimpys to Liberators," was the answer.

Calcutta — Grand Hotel

Yeah, the group arriving at Kolar as we were leaving. Does that mean we'll have to wait for them to finish training?

We sampled Calcutta on the way through. There's a posh hotel for senior ranks but I was with Chota Harris at the Grand; the crew went to a billet for NCOs. Being the only officer in our gang, I can see I'm going to be alone a lot unless we're travelling with others.

The Grand Hotel is four stories high, covers a city block. Old-fashioned looking on the outside, it's quite modern inside. My first mattress in months, a huge overhead fan. Best of all, a real tub with high porcelain sides you can lean against without all the water spilling out.

The hotel is on Chowringee, a fine wide street but overloaded with traffic, pedestrians, sidewalk salesmen. The city's blacked out at night, but not like in England. Enough light seeps through open doorways that it's no problem to find your way about. But concrete blocks in front of shop windows?

"Air raid precaution. Yes, Japs bombed the city in `42, at Christmas. They could be back."

The crew got together for dinner and a movie; I also spent time right under the big fan in our room. Bengal is almost at sea level, hot and humid, so we didn't attempt any complete examination of Calcutta's delights. We'll be back; it's apparently the only possibility for a weekend leave.

Here at Jessore, I share a room with Chota, Ken Cox and a Newzie chap. It's a one-storey building with big, open windows, but fitted with iron bars. We got sweepers in to clear the cobwebs; paint and whitewash will help. If this is to be our home for several months, we better try to make it livable.

I woke this morning early and hungry, came to breakfast on my own, found the dining room empty. But here's someone coming; yes, I recognize him — the Adjutant. He takes the chair opposite me.

"Howard Johns," he says with a smile, extending his hand.

Hey, that's unexpected. As a trainee, both before being commissioned and after, I've been on a lot of air bases. Never did one of the permanent staff introduce himself when it wasn't necessary, or choose to sit with a transient unless no other seat was available. Understandable, I suppose. Regular staff would prefer to sit with friends, ignore the waves of students with anonymous faces and forgettable names who'd show up for a few weeks and then move on. But here's the Adjutant sitting at the table with me, and sounding friendly!

"You're Frazer, aren't you?" And then, with a chuckle, "I hear we almost lost you to 355 Squadron. Hah! Glad it got straightened out.

"I want to meet you new chaps. We'll be living together for a time... six months or so... want to make life as pleasant as we can."

Hey, that's right. We're no longer just passing through. We're still rookies but we've made the team, are permanent staff too, and the Adj comes to chat. I like the feeling that, finally, we belong somewhere.

"What do you think of the B24s?" he's saying. "We have two new aircraft to be picked up at Allahabad. That's west of here, half-way to Delhi. You and Brodie will be going to get them."

Wow, a brand new bomber, ultra modern, the very latest thing! But I'm also interested in finding out when we'll start ops against the Japs.

"Oh, a few weeks yet. You know that most crews are down at Kolar? Wing Commander Sindall will train right here, but he's away for a week. He was a Flight Commander on the Squadron when we had the Wimpys, just got promoted. Jim's a very good man, will make an excellent Commanding Officer.

"When will we start operations again? Well, not until the monsoons abate. And additional training is in the plans, formation flying for example."

Brodie and Potts come in and I do the intros. Johns seems genuinely pleased to meet them too. I like the old Adj; my father's age, he's tall and narrow with a soft English accent, lively eyes and a quick chuckle.

"How long've you been with the Squadron, Howard?" Steve asks.

"Oh, since Pearl Harbor; 215 was shut down in 1919, but re-formed in `41 to come to India. Air crews left Harwell, flew their Wimpys out here in March of `42. We arrived in April — a long sea trip around South Africa in those days — joined them at Asansol where the four Yank squadrons are now."

So 215 used to be at Harwell in England where I did my OTU! And the Americans have B24 Squadrons in India?

"Got here just as the Japs were storming into Burma... weren't sure they mightn't keep right on coming. The Squadron flew ops for a time and

Calcutta — Chowringee St.

dropped supplies to our army retreating out of Burma. After that, the worry was that the Japs might invade. We went to Madras, did coastal patrols for two months. Then up near the Khyber to practise with Ghurka parachute troops."

"Including Wimpys, there were three heavy bomber outfits in India in those days," Murray says. "Which was first?"

"Oh, 215 did the first ops; 99 brought their Wellingtons from England a bit later. Then 159 formed up in the UK as a Lib squadron, did some missions in the Middle East, came on to India in `42, started bombing ops in November.

"In March... that's 1943 now... we came to Jessore, got back to bombing work full time; 99 joined us there. The Jap invasion attempt kept us busy... patrolling roads to bomb lorry convoys, hit anything showing a light. Crews were then involved in ferrying reinforcements and supplies into the Imphal Valley. You've heard the news? The Japs are retreating."

"Many losses?" Why am I always the one to ask that?

"A few. Jap fighters are thick around Rangoon. But losses weren't too bad until last month; we lost several on that troop ferrying work. And that brings you up to date. Whatever history comes next, it'll be you chaps who make it."

Yeah.

AUG. 5

We picked up our new Lib! Model B VI, serial number EW 224, out of the Detroit plant. Except for being ferried out here, she's brand spanking new, without a scratch. Even in her camouflage colours — mottled greys with tinges of blues and browns — she could win a beauty contest.

We brought the plane back to Jessore very carefully, visit her every day. The rudders — the rear portion of the tail fins — have been painted black with two white horizontal stripes as 215's squadron markings. Yesterday, a big black `P' was painted on her sides. Our Lib will be `P for Peter.'

"Our Lib?" We certainly consider it our aircraft, have even discussed what logo to paint on its nose. But can we do that? We signed for her, brought her home; that should count for something. But the Adj didn't agree.

"We'll have sixteen Libs and twenty-three crews," he said. "No crew has exclusive rights to any one aircraft. You'll fly whatever kite is assigned for that mission."

But I've something else on my mind today. My ship, quite literally, must have come in. Fruit cakes and chocolates from Mom and an aunt; 3,200 cigarettes from Dad, his Lions Club, my uncle, and Jean. About half the cigs are from Jean, my MacDonalds Export brand in the green packs. For cartons mailed overseas, the tax-free price is only $1 but, as her pay is only $58 a month, I'm sure she's going without lunches to send them.

Chocolate, scarce in India, is also the occasion for a party in the crew's billet. Another reason: both Jock and Bob are now Flight-Sergeants, a crown to go with the three stripes.

It's another Saturday night. There are only so many in any lifetime and you shouldn't waste them, but that's what I'm doing again. All the guys have gone to the movie but I've already seen it twice. So I'm alone in the room, trying to finish some letters. I resolved to get at least one a week to my folks, and usually manage a couple to Jean.

It's sometimes good to be alone. There's little privacy in this life; almost always you're with guys... in a classroom, the dining room or bar, flying, in lorries, even at latrines. Not that you'd want to be alone much either; you couldn't take this country without friends.

Our single light bulb is bright enough that long, black shadows streak up the white-washed walls, jagged and sharp right to the top. It's a black and white scene, and eerie. But I can sit and watch fireflies trying to light up the darkness outside, dream a little that I'm somewhere else tonight.

Not that it's so quiet. A thumping concert is taking place —a choir, a chorus of thousands — in that pond outside the fence and the grass around it. Bullfrogs provide a steady beat and deep-down resonance with a persistent "burripp... burripp... burripp." Crickets, higher pitched, carry the melody. Not a great tune... repetitious and monotonous... but they're all right on key. Of course they should be pretty good. The same group, with occasional replacements, has been practising a long time... more than a million years?

But this letter. What to say? That it's hellish hot, my shirt stuck to my back, but I can't take it off because there are mosquitos in the room? That I did get punctured earlier, but won't know for ten days whether I get malaria? Naw, I'll tell them I'm just sitting around, doing nothing, hardly any flying at all. Yeah, they'll like that.

Voices outside; the movie must be over. I'm glad to hear them. Guess I'm feeling a bit `down' tonight. I'll meet the guys at the bar. Just one drink; we're flying to Amarda Road tomorrow. But maybe I'll hear some new jokes.

AUG. 10

I had brought Hassim from Kolar. His idea... he wants to see the world. And why leave him sitting in Jessore and polish my own shoes here at Amarda Road? His eyes opened wide when I suggested he fly with us; it took him two days to decide. Mac looked after him, said he seemed fascinated to see the landscape sliding by underneath. But he kept his hands over his eyes at the end.

"When land down, ver' scare, sahib." But he'll have lots to tell the other bearers around their cooking fires for a few nights.

The Mess here is one high-ceilinged room. There are no fans — called `punkas' here — but a good substitute. Six bamboo poles, each in a horizontal plane, one behind the other, are suspended by ropes from the roof so that they swing freely; large pieces of matting hang from each. The poles are then attached one to the other in sequence by a long rope which disappears out a hole in the end wall.

Standing outside, attached to the rope, is the `punka-wallah' whose one and only duty is to tug it in a regular fashion. Pull, let it go, pull again. The result of this is that the pieces of matting in the room swing to and fro, creating a most pleasant waft.

That's the theory. In practice, the matting will swing quite rapidly at first, but then the action gets progressively slower and slower until there's damn little wafting at all. When you notice that the breeze has disappeared, you let out a holler, will be joined by everybody in the room shouting, "Punka wallah... punk, dammit, punk!"

This will have the desired effect; for a few moments the mats flap at a great rate. Then the pace slackens from slow motion to a virtual dead stop. Everybody starts shouting again, the breeze picks up, and the process is repeated. This goes on all evening. It's not a bad system although one flaw is that, in this humidity, such heavy hollering brings perspiration to your face.

I liked Brodie's suggestion, though with Steve you're never sure when he's kidding. "Why don't we just hire more men to do the shouting?"

This morning we're off for some air-to-sea firing. Out over the ocean, the gunners will shoot at objects set to float on the water, their first opportunity to fire at an actual target from B24 turrets.

"Aircraft `P'. Take-off is on runway two-six-oh," the Tower says. "Turn left on the perimeter track and proceed anti-clockwise."

Damn, that's two miles, all around the field. I give the outer engines a shot, and we pull out of the Dispersal and swing onto the taxi strip. It's a fine morning; cloud will build up during the day but...

"Look out," Jock shouts. "We'rrre close to the edge!"

Cheez! Left brake, quick! Get back in the centre. I was going too fast... wasn't concentrating. We're almost off the concrete!

Omigawd! Too late. The plane — the entire aircraft — just tilted to the right, a terrible slant. The starboard wheel must be off the pavement, down in the mud. My wing... the port wing tip... is up in the air, several feet higher than normal. Gawdamighty, what about the starboard wing? Did it crack the ground? I feel sick. I un-snap my seat harness and twist around to look. There it is... about six inches above the mud.

"Did it hit?" I'm already in trouble enough, but if it hit hard, if the whole wing's been damaged, I'll be on bread and water for years.

"I dinna think so," Jock says. "Didna' hearr anything. But we're in verrr' deep... don't expect we can pull it out with the engines."

"Arthur," I yell. "Go have a look."

He's back in a minute. "In deep, mud over the axle... tyre's almost disappeared. With all the rain, it's just muck. We'll need help to get out."

Cheez! I'll have to call the Tower, tell them what I've managed to do. It'll be like a murderer calling the police to tell them what he's done, and where the damn body is... also where he is. But I give the Tower the news.

"Yes, yes... in deep. The taxi strip? Oh, sure, completely blocked. That's right, no one can squeeze past. Yes, sure... I'll wait here."

Damn, my first prang. But so dumb, so stupid. I'll really get a blast. What the hell made me think I wanted to be captain of an aircraft?

The crew have gone out on the tarmac. Jonesy shouts up, shows me how deep we're embedded by spreading his arms, stretching them as far as they'll go.

Thanks a bloody lot.

Should I get out too? The rule about a captain staying with his sinking ship likely doesn't apply in this case. But the Tower might call back.

Our ground crew guys arrive next. Sgt Frey, the crew chief, is under my window. "Pretty bad, sir, tyre's almost out of sight."

"Yeah, well let's get her out. Can you tow her?"

"Don't know. Never saw a wheel in so deep before."

Jeez, thanks a lot to him too.

Now a Jeep is pulling up. A Flight-Lieutenant gets out, an older fellow. He goes to the tilted-down side first, but re-appears at my window.

"I'm Potter... Engineering Officer. How'd you manage this, old chap? Bit of carelessness, wot? Righto, you might as well come down; it'll take time to get equipment here." And he roars off.

A crowd has gathered, mostly from the Libs lined up on the taxi strip, unable to move. Planes can't back up, will have to be towed. What a mess!

A few come over to offer condolences, but I'm not in the mood to chat. I've learned over the last couple of years that there are times when the smartest thing you can say is nothing. Offer no explanations, excuses or apologies; just keep your face blank and your mouth shut.

We've been waiting for an hour. Even huddled under a wing, it's bloody hot. Most of the crowd has gone, but Sgt Frey and his men are still with us. Of course, what they're here to maintain is P-Peter, and Peter's location at the moment is indubitably right here.

"Here's Potter," Frey says, as a Jeep skids to a stop.

"Equipment's on the way. Have you out in twenty minutes," he says.

And, by gosh, he's right. A crane lifts the wheel right out of the ooze; we all help carry a big metal sheet from the lorry, slide it under the tire. One end disappears in the muck; the other sits on the concrete with a chain attached. Peter's wheel is lowered back into the quagmire but the steel platform is underneath. A tractor hooks onto the tail and slowly pulls Peter up the ramp. There are lots of cheers, half of them mine.

Potter gets Sgt Frey and me together. "We'll just tow the kite to the Dispersal. I'll be back to look at the wing. But the undercarriage, Sergeant. You'll have to clean it up, check it out. Can you do that today?"

Frey winces; maybe he had other plans for the afternoon, perhaps even a nice siesta. But Potter chooses not to notice, and Frey says, "Yessir."

"Good. I'll be back later to see how it's going. And Frazer... we'll want an air test tomorrow morning. Be available. You might also wish to contemplate on the problems that can be caused by carelessness."

While I'm getting ticked off, Sgt Frey is looking at me with a look devoid of any brotherly love whatsoever. But I don't respond to either of them. My face is blank, my mouth shut tight.

AUG.25

It's called a 'box formation.' From underneath, I suppose it would look like that. A Sq/Ldr O'Connor is in the lead plane for some formation practice. We're in the #2 slot, on the left side of his aircraft, slightly behind and a little lower. Brodie is flying #3 position, level with us but on the other side. Sgt Brooks in #4 completes the square by tucking in behind O'Connor, further back and lower still.

We've been flying various alignments. 'Line astern' is just follow-the-leader; 'echelon right' is a lot like Canada Geese in flight. A 'Vic' is three planes in a 'box' without anyone in the #4 spot.

The box formation certainly concentrates your fire-power; four planes flying together... forty machine guns. A full squadron mission has 16 aircraft — four boxes of four planes each, the boxes also numbered #1 to #4.

"I wouldn't want to be a Jap pilot attacking a formation which has one hundred and sixty guns waiting to blast him," say the guys who like to keep good thoughts.

Flying a bomber soon gets boring, but formation work keeps you awake. Getting wing tips tangled would be fatal. "Keep fifty feet apart," O'Connor said. "In bumpy weather, close enough."

Compared with Harvards, Libs are ponderously slow to react. You've no brakes, so leave adjustments too late and there's panic to cut the throttles. One of the boys slid right under #1 yesterday, was leading the leader.

I think doing that to Sq/Ldr O'Connor would perturb him. A South African in the RAF with a DFC decoration, we haven't figured his position here. The way he bounces on landings, he's not an experienced B24 pilot.

"Most senior Squadron Leader in the RAF," he likes to tell you. Which sounds impressive, though as Steve Brodie pointed out, "It could also mean he's been passed over for promotion more often than anybody else."

We've done more gunnery practice; sometimes we'll be flying low enough to shoot up things on the ground. The gunners needed the work; even from 1,200 feet, the targets are nearly a quarter mile away.

The heat is always a problem. When aircraft are left sitting in the sun, the turrets must be covered by tarps. If not, gunners have to be careful not to touch any metal parts. On take-offs, the far end of the runway is just a shimmer of heat waves. We wear very little; for local flying, just shirt and shorts. Nevertheless, by the time you get off the ground, they'll be sopping wet; reach cooler levels and they're cold and clammy. My solution is to strip to under-shorts before getting in the aircraft; when we're above the worst heat, I unroll my clothes and get dressed.

Most guys are tormented by 'prickly heat,' which feels like a thousand needles sticking half an inch into your back. Something in the pores starts to fester and you want to scratch and scratch, but shouldn't. Doc says the only known cure is cooler weather, but a good tan might help. On bright days with the mercury trying to burst the thermometer, guys are out sun-bathing. It's been rumoured the natives think we're lunatics.

Hassim wasn't his usual cheerful self today. "Want go home, sahib," he blurted out. "Bengal... too much hot."

Cheez, even an Indian lad can't stand it. But I'll miss him.

I've had a good week, didn't even get whacked for running off the taxi strip. Flt/Lt Potter told me in the Mess he hadn't even reported the incident.

"Why would I? No damage done. No sense causing trouble if you don't have to. Yes, thanks, another Scotch would be lovely. A double? Two of them? Well, why not? Of course, if you'd cracked the wing, done any real damage..."

P-Peter did get dinged later. On a landing approach, I heard a "clunk" sound. A large bird was stuck in the leading edge of the wing, its long neck hanging down, still swinging. Mac pried it loose; he also gave the eulogy.

"Poor bird... never knew what hit him. They've had the sky to themselves for centuries... must hate this strange new breed, hulking monstrosities now cluttering up the skies, making flying dangerous."

Sgt Frey just said, "Another hawk? I guess we can't blame you for *that*, Mr Frazer." He knows my name now. "But we can repair it."

Dropping practice bombs — hitting a target from even 5,000 feet — is an interesting game. Even with one of those new Sikorsky things which can hover directly over a target, you'd still have to make allowance for any wind trying to blow your bomb off line.

But dropping your missile from a moving plane is as if the helicopter could only fire the bomb out of the machine in a horizontal plane — at about 160 mph, the speed of a moving aircraft. So a bomb-aimer has to release before the target is underneath, and allow for the speed and direction of the plane and the wind. If the pilot flies straight and level, and the bombardier hits the button at the precise split second, you get a bull's-eye.

Otherwise not. Which included us. "In eight trrrries, closest you got was two hundred yarrrds," was the complaint from the tail end.

Then we bombed in formation. With four aircraft each dropping a string of bombs, you should get a neat scattering of bursts over a small area. But four times we missed. That's what the crew said; pilots never see the bombs hit.

Today, we have interesting visitors to meet. Here's the crackle on the intercom now, Eddie's voice. "Fighters... three o'clock level. Mustangs... US markings."

American P51s? I thought they'd be Spitfires... didn't know we had Mustangs in India. But that's great; they have a longer range than Spits.

"Here they come!" For ten minutes they attack.

I've tried most games but nothing compares with this. And it's only a practice; the real thing comes soon. The next months could be interesting.

SEP. 9

Someone's sleeping in my charpoy. We get back to Jessore, it's mid-day, and strangers are in our beds.

"Don't wake them up," the Adj said. "The squadron's back from Kolar; the last group got in at dawn. Such big crews; don't know where to put you all. But Brodie's crew and yours... you'll take some leave."

Okay, we can stand that. In Cal, the NCOs have their billets; we're at Aircrew House, a hostel for junior officers. Run by some volunteer group, it's only five rupees a day — about $1.65 — and that includes three meals.

But for a special dinner you go to Firpos. Brodie knew the way. Up some steps, through double doors... and you're in another world. Table after table, the dining room stretches half an acre. Dozens of waiters move solemnly among the tables, colourful in white uniforms, red sashes, and turbans. Overhead, the whirring blades of fifty big fans kick up a marvellous breeze and a pleasant buzz. A spectacular, elegant sight.

"Try the prawn salad," Brodie said. "Just like shrimp." But I've never heard of prawns and my mother never served shrimp. Another wow! A heaping plate of the white meat with mayonnaise has to be the best meal I've ever had.

Another place where you can almost forget you're in India is the Calcutta Swimming Club, a swank spot strictly reserved for Europeans and their cousins. Right in the centre of the city, it's surrounded by a very high wall to insulate the members as much as brick-and-mortar possible from the sights and sounds and smells — and the people — of India. A white oasis in a Sahara of brown faces. And I enjoyed it, despite a vague feeling of unease. There has to be something wrong with a club in India that won't admit Indians.

Chowringee is a great street for meeting people. I spotted Ted Willing and, while we're talking, along comes big Robbie, my Stratheden room-mate.

Afterwards, back to the Grand with Ted. "Three orchestras play every night," he says. "Two of them just for drinking. But let's try the Casanova Lounge, watch the dancers. Yeah, I'm on leave, t'ike the tr'ine tomorrow for Naini Tal. It's one of the f'imous Hill Stations in the Himal'yas."

But what I want to talk about are his missions. He's done six now, six times into Burma and Siam, mostly mine-laying, skulking into Jap territory at night. Wouldn't experiences like that be traumatic? Even change a guy?

"Naahhh," Ted snorts. "That's cr'izy. You just fly to the t'irget, drop your load — bombs or mines — then point your nose back to b'ise. Their ack ack gunners can't shoot str'ight and you've got six gunners watching for fighters. What's the worry? Why would that ch'inge anyone?"

But I'm not convinced; maybe Ted's unusually brave. And yet... is that it? Is it courage? I heard in England that the guys in Bomber Command who have the worst time, who suffer the most fear, are the ones with imagination... those who can picture the terrible things that could happen. If so, could bravery sometimes come from a lack of imagination, some blindness to the laws of probabilities, some ability to ignore reality? If that's true, are such people not the lucky ones?

Another day I met Bill Jackson, at 355 now and expecting to do his first op very soon, likely as 2nd Pilot for starters.

"Phil Cloutier? He's with 358 Squadron now, joining 357 for clandestine work such as dropping agents behind enemy lines. Very secret, and dangerous."

There is now an RCAF Office in Cal, just opened. The reading room has magazines and home newspapers. This war has gotten terribly complicated, but the great maps in Life help you get the big picture — big arrows showing the Allied break-out into France, the Russian advance into Poland, the Yanks sweeping up through the Pacific, even the 14th Army advancing in Burma.

You can also laugh at the aircraft advertisements. I just wish the B24s flew nearly as high and fast as their ads say.

SEP. 15

We got called back from Calcutta. Until now, 99 and 215 shared the Jessore base, but Lib crews are twice as large. With 99 returning from Kolar, we'll have to move. Our new home? Digri, sharing the field with 159 Squadron. Just 15 miles north of Salboni, four Lib outfits will be close together.

"Should find enough guys for a softball game," Chota thinks.

"Our sixteenth Lib arrived today," the Adj said, "and we now have twenty-three crews, our full complement."

Yeah, we're getting ready for action. Sq/Ldrs Beadon and Webster are to head `A' and `B' Flights. I've met them both, but not the C.O. — Wing Commander Sindall.

Back from Cal, we didn't get our charpoys back; new crews like us sleep on our camp cots in a storage building. The humidity is terrible; you wake up lying in a pool of your own sweat — and that's sleeping `starkers.'

I bunk beside Steve Brodie, have decided he's one of my favourite people here. His real name is Charles, but most Brodies get nicknamed after the lad who jumped off the Brooklyn Bridge. Steve's from farm country just outside Toronto, maybe why he's part big-city slicker, part country boy.

He's quite average-looking, just a little black moustache to go with the twinkling eyes, but he's one hundred percent sane — which is certainly a lot better than average. In any discussion, he's the one most likely to come up with an answer that's so common-sense you wish you'd thought of it yourself.

And he has a great sense of humour. Lots of fellows can tell jokes, re-hash stories they've picked up from someone else, sometimes sounding

Royal Canadian Air Force

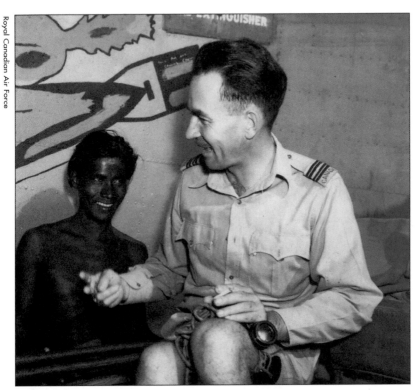

Steve Brodie

as if they've practised them in front of a mirror. Jokes are okay, and Brodie knows some too, but even better is his ability to spot the wry or ironic aspect of ordinary events, to make up his own jokes `on the fly.'

We leave here in two days. I should have foreseen it; a move always comes just after a shipment of cigarettes arrives. This time another eight cartons. I'm chain-smoking to get the pile down to a size I can carry.

CHAPTER 8

DELECTABLE DIGRI

SEPT. 16, 1944

Yeah, Digri is better — a rural area again, not quite a desert, but certainly not a jungle. And aircraft circling above, a real air base.

In another basha structure, I drew an end room. Ken Cox and Chota share the next one, just behind the paper-thin rattan, but neither are known snorers. Brodie and Potts have the third room, two RAF chaps the fourth. Other similar buildings are around us in a grove of palms.

Don't know where the Brodie guys are, but I'm ready for lunch anyway.

Laughter coming from the Officers' Mess — another thatched-roof affair — indicates a bit of whooping-it-up, perhaps to celebrate moving out of Jessore.

The truth is, I'm feeling just a bit ill at ease, very much a rookie, a new kid joining guys who have known each other for months, flown missions over Burma together. In this life, you get used to mixing with strangers, but these aren't just ordinary people, these are battle-scarred aviators.

From the door, I see that the lounge is crowded — guys sitting in chairs, sipping at drinks, chatting, waiting for the lunch bell. I wish I'd see someone I know. Or an empty chair. Ahh, one stool at the bar. Can't just stand at the door all day; I better take it. But what to do next? The fellows on either side are deep in conversation, ignore me, don't even see me.

Here comes the bar steward. Remembering all the war movies I've seen, I say, in a very firm voice, "Yes, corporal, a beer."

"Yessir, just got a shipment in. The ration's six bottles a month now; six pints, that is. But I only have the large bottles today, which count as two pints. That okay, sir?"

Cheez, I don't really want a large bottle. But would it sound right to refuse it? Still in a firm tone, I say, "Of course," very nonchalant.

So I get a whole quart of ale plunked in front of me, plus a glass, plus a chit to sign. The corporal is marking something in a book; I've just shot two-sixths of my beer quota for a whole month.

The label says "Indian beer" — potent stuff. A full quart in this heat might topple me off the stool. The bottle feels as if it's been sitting out in the sun all day but I pour a glass, drink it down in one long gulp. It's ridiculously warm, but I refill the glass and swing around to survey the scene. I'm managing to look pretty darn operational, I think.

I must have missed him before, but now I see Howard Johns sitting with three others at the table right in front of me. Two I've met, but not the one with the three blue stripes on his shoulder tabs. Of course! That's the C.O. — Wing Commander Sindall. I only saw him from a distance at Jessore.

But while I'm trying to give him the once-over, the WingCo gives a flick with his finger; oh, oh... I'm being summoned.

I slide off the stool and say, "Yessir," managing a quick nod to Howard at the same time. At least I don't have to salute; you don't unless you're wearing your hat. Which is lucky; I don't know how I'd have managed it holding a glass of beer in one hand and a quart bottle in the other.

"You're Frazer, I believe," the C.O. says, not sounding that excited at the thought. "You've met our Adj. This is Sq/Ldr Beadon and Flt/Lt Williams."

Their nods are almost imperceptible. What's this all about?

"Welcome to the Squadron," from the WingCo.

Still sitting, he extends his hand. To shake it, I have to get rid of the damn bottle, and the only empty space is under Sindall's out-stretched arm. When I put the quart there he pulls his hand right back; he extends it again, but cautiously, reaching around the bottle... likely concerned about knocking over my beer, which is thoughtful... maybe why his hand-shake is so limp.

Standing before him, I'm being given a thorough examination by cool eyes in a solemn face. It gives me a chance to look him over too. He's an older type of young guy, into his thirties but not far into. Dark hair, small moustache, good features with a firm chin — a sort of military look. He might even be a handsome fellow if he ever tried smiling.

"In this climate, Frazer, this temperature, do you really think alcohol makes sense at the lunch hour when you don't know what chores you may yet be asked to perform today?"

I glance at the table. All their glasses are filled with lemon-limes.

"Well, sir, I... uh... didn't expect... uh... large bottle... and... well..."

But it isn't coming out very polished at all, so I just finish with "Guess not, sir."

"Then I think you'd be right," he says. "But welcome to the Squadron."

But still no smile on his face. Any fool could see my operational career hasn't started off too great.

The C.O. resumes his conversation with the others; I've been dismissed. The only question: What do I do with the damn bottle still on the table? Just abandon it there? Offer it to Sindall? No, that wouldn't be a good idea. So I reach in front of him, pick it up, carry it back to the bar.

What a waste! Only one glass out of my ration for ten long, hot days.

But the corporal comes to my end of the bar, wiping at the counter, not actually looking at me. But I hear him say very quietly, "I think I could cap it... save it till tonight, sir."

And he did.

SEP. 23

Hey! Five divides into five exactly.

For three months, my crew and four others have been waiting for that many bombardiers to arrive. The quintet of bedraggled young Pilot Officers who just came into the Mess, a bomb-aimer's wing pinned on each sweaty shirt... hey, they have to be ours. And I've seen them first. I'll get first pick!

I'm alone in the Mess, more mail to censor. With big fans whirring, it's a good place to work. And then these five arrive out of nowhere.

"Come on in... take a chair; I'll find the bar steward, order drinks. Bomb-aimers, eh? Have you been assigned to crews yet?"

"Not that we know. All we've been told is to look for the five crews on this list. From Worli, we were shot off to Kolar. Four days on the train. We get there, the crews had left."

"Waited there six weeks," says another. "Then 'Go to Amarda Road, that's where they are.' Another four-day trip, miss them again. Very frustrating."

But I'm only half listening. What's important is to decide which one I like best, which one to invite into the crew. Besides a bomb dropper, the Frazer crew will have another officer in it; I'm going to have a room-mate.

How to decide which? It's another crewing-up problem. One chap has an accent that sounds as if he has a permanent, painful pimple on his posterior; his voice would drive me crazy.

"Then a posting to Jessore," says the one called Smitty. "Last moment, changed to Digri. Is this the right place? Do you know anybody on this list?"

Yeah, I like him best. Round face, brown hair, average height; not someone who'd stand out in a crowd, but a pleasant chap who'd likely go along with whatever the majority decided. I even like his accent. A bit shy, but that's not a fault. Arriving at a new place, anybody not at least a bit hesitant and uncertain is either overloaded with braggadocio or just plain dumb.

"That's me; I'm Frazer. The others are here somewhere."

What I'm hoping, of course, is that we don't bump into any of them right away. Walking them over to the Adjutant's office, detouring around the back way, I fall into step beside the Smitty fellow, chat him up, try to make up my mind. Wish I had more time to decide but, yes, I think he's the one.

"We have a very good crew, all first-class men," I tell him. "All we need is a bombardier. Would you like to join us?"

It's not a fair question. How could he know we aren't all maniacs? But I was right; he's an agreeable fellow, only had to ponder one full stride before saying he'd be happy to join us. So Alan Smith is our bomb-aimer; now we're eleven, a full crew. I'm glad it's settled.

Still haven't done anything here. The crews have been divided up; our crew and Brodie's are in `B' Flight. One surprise; Sq/Ldr Webster won't be our Flight Commander after all, has been transferred to 99 Squadron. In exchange — apparently an even trade — we get Sq/Ldr Percy O'Connor, the South African who some say is slightly... well, eccentric.

"Why the trade, you ask?" says Reg Grouse, one of the veteran Aussie captains. "You can bet there was a personality clash somewhere."

Each morning, a bit after sun-up, we're all at the little Flight Shack which serves as `B's' headquarters. P-Peter's dispersal is just a quarter mile away so we spend a lot of time there, are also getting to know Peter's ground crew. The boss is a Scot, Flt/Sgt Biggar, an `airframe fitter' by trade, which means his specialty is everything except the engines. The man under him is Corporal Baker, an `engine fitter' or mechanic;

Alan Smith

altogether, there are four fitters, one for each engine. Enrolled Followers help out. Specialists in aircraft instruments, radio equipment and such are available on call.

Are those men important to us, to our hopes to live a long life, be lucky enough to die with our boots *off*? You could bet your last rupee on it. It's comforting to feel they seem both capable and conscientious.

"She's in great shape, sir," Biggar says. "I understand your crew is to have first call on her. You can depend on us to do our best to keep her tickety-boo for you. We're very proud of our aircraft."

Hey! He said *our* aircraft. Does he think it belongs to *them*, the ground

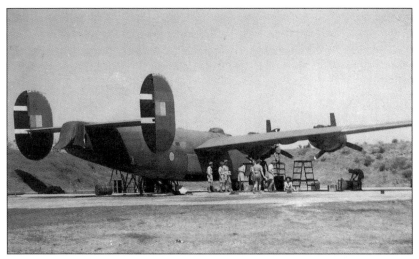

P-Peter — at dispersal

staff? That's crazy; it belongs to us, the guys who take her into the sky. But I've heard before that ground crews think the fly-boys only borrow the kite by the day, returning it to the real owners after each trip. Well, okay, I suppose it could make them even more conscientious. At any rate, it's not something to argue about.

"You heard that?" from Mac. "Our crew's to have first call on her. Isn't that enough? Let's pick a name... put our logo on her."

I suggested "Pachyderm"; Libs soar like birds in the air but on the ground they're more like over-fed elephants. But "Packy" got only four votes. Mac's suggestion — "P for Pirate" — got seven. I suppose we should be as democratic as possible, at least when it's not a life-and-death matter.

So Mac, somewhat of an artist, has painted a ferocious Captain Hook on the port side of the fuselage below the cockpit window. The plan is to add a small skull and crossbones for each mission. But "P for Pirate"...?

OCT. 1

Another month. Still we wait for the last crews to return from Amarda Road, for monsoons to abate. And 99 Squadron is treading water too; they've also left Jessore... are now at Dhubalia, north of Calcutta.

Though the weather's better here, the Met man says it's still duff over Burma. Across the field, 159 was briefed for ten missions in September; half had to be scrubbed. Both 355 and 356 aborted some ops, but did complete some. On a formation mission, there was a mid-air collision, one aircraft from each outfit. Poof... 22 men dead.

News like that is sobering. Truth is, I'm of two minds about this war.

Part of me wants to see some action. Hell, I've been preparing for nearly three years. But another part is thinking, "What's the hurry?"

Even without my help, our side seems to be winning the war now. I did volunteer; if I'm never used, is that my fault? And if I'm just left to sit on my fanny for another year or two, it might be all over. We're not living that badly — homesick and bored, but three meals a day, plenty of sack time, lots of friends. Doesn't that beat getting the chop?

But boredom is a terrible thing, maybe even worse than fear. Guys are so fed up with doing nothing they're asking to fly ops.

"Soon," O'Connor says, "action very soon now."

Sq/Ldr Beadon, rated a top pilot, is another whose promotion resulted from the shake-up following retirement of the Wimpys. I haven't figured him out yet; he's a big broad-shouldered fellow with a squeaky voice that doesn't fit with the physique. He also has one of those English accents which must have taken years, or generations, to cultivate.

"With sixty men in the Mess, you can expect a variety of types," Brodie says. We also have a big mixture of nationalities. Tommy Downs, an RAF guy, was figuring it out.

"I make it ten countries, counting English, Scots, Welsh and Irish as four. How many Canadians... eight? About fifteen Aussies, a half dozen each from New Zealand and South Africa. Then there's Tex Bonnar from the States, though he's in the process of transferring back to the US Air Force. And there's Pancho Pella from Brazil. How many's that?"

"That's ten. But you forgot Ray Singh, the Indian equipment officer."

"Can't count him. He's really with Wing HQ. But we have Enrolled Followers. And I forgot Flt/Lt Wallace who's from Fiji. That'd bring the total to twelve; I think we qualify as a real International Squadron."

Tommy was off in his count of RCAF; I make it nine. Four in Brodie's crew, Eddie Gilbert with Smokey Williams as his navigator, and three more pilots: Bill Waddington, myself, and Mac Gardner.

Old crews and newcomers are starting to mix, the process speeded up by parties like the one Saturday night. Tommy Downs seems our unofficial social director, can coax good tunes out of the old piano. The arrival of several cases of scotch helped get everybody in the mood for happy harmonizing. After a few choruses, Flying Officer Neville Bingham becomes "Bing."

I'm taking a little scotch now and then myself. The experts here tell me, "It won't leave you with a hangover, not as bad as the local gin, anyway." Well, maybe. It's just too bad it tastes the way it does.

When the weather clears up and cools down, I think we'll be fairly comfortable here. The Mess has just been enlarged and refurbished with lots of bright colours. And here the big fans run on electricity.

Smitty has now settled into our room. And we're in luck. We had wall outlets, a lamp, but no light bulb. But one of the boys found a dozen in Cal and I bought one from him, even though a carton of cigs is a steep price. Especially when he sniffed them first — which wasn't very damn neighbourly! —then refused to take the musty ones I'd planned to give him.

And we have a fan! A small one, but it blows its heart out, will reach both charpoys when they're shoved close together. It only cost three cartons. It's RAF issue, but the chap could have auctioned it off to someone else. He's posted back to Blighty, was out of smokes and liked the Exports I gave him as a sample. When I wouldn't give him any more, he decided to make the deal.

We're trying to hire a bearer but they're scarce here. Until we find one, Rog Tyrell, at the end of the billet, had his boy do a few chores for us; he seemed a good kid.

"Gone," Rog said. "Disappeared into the multitudes with the three hundred rupees I'd accumulated to go on leave. I suppose such a wad of money would be more than he could expect to see in a lifetime; the temptation was just too great."

I'm alone tonight, Smitty gone to the flicks. I'm writing letters, a never-ending chore. But to get letters, you have to write them.

A fine evening, the sky clear. The moon, big and round, has emerged from below the horizon, born again for another night. It's now about two palm trees high. Incredibly beautiful, if it only appeared every 75 years like that comet my Dad talks about, people would travel thousands of miles for a look and say it was the most marvellous sight the world has ever seen.

Through the trees, lights are flickering in the other bashas; the coloured ones are from the Mess. Until a few moments ago, you could hear guys singing, the muffled sound of voices and piano. Up close, it would be loud and raucous, but music and distance make a nice duet. But the drums have started again; there's a religious festival this week in the native village near the camp. It's hard to concentrate on this letter.

Here comes Smitty, back from the cinema. Last night we had a party for him to meet the crew. Also vice-versa, which was the part I was most concerned about; the crew is inclined to be critical. I overheard a few mutters early in the evening about "sprog P/O" and "just off the boat"; but Smitty comes across as a genuine kind of person and I think the doubters are warming to him.

And he was in Canada just six months ago!

"Yes, British Empire Air Training Plan. Worked in a bank, joined the RAF in `42. Twenty of us solo'd, but only three were picked to continue pilot training. The rest were given a choice... bomb-aiming in Canada, or navigation in Rhodesia. I chose America, went to Saskatchewan for bombing and gunnery, Manitoba for navigation school. Got my wings there January `44; back to England in March, some leave, then a month at Officers' School."

"Officers' School? What's that."

"Oh, lectures on Air Force law, RAF history, Rules and Regulations, tradition and deportment, making speeches, lots of things."

Hey, that makes sense. For months I was treated as just another aircrew trainee. Then one day was given my wings, started to wear an officer's uniform, got saluted. But there was no preparation for the sudden change. Maybe some instruction or training would have helped.

"You and the other new bomb-aimers saw the C.O. today. How'd it go?"

"Oh, fine. He asked where we came from, where we'd taken courses, where we'd done our OTU training. But we told him we'd never been to an OTU.

"He seemed shocked, but then asked how we liked the Mark 14 bomb-sight; we said we'd never seen one.

"'Omigawd,' he said, 'go drop some practice bombs right away.'"

"That's where we were this afternoon. Went up with Sgt Brooks' crew, dropped six bombs each on the practice range. Was that our OTU?"

Jeez! Two fighter pilots, a navigator straight from Nav School, a bomb-aimer who'd never seen the bomb-sight. We'll be the Squadron jokes.

OCT. 7

We wanted some flying? We're getting it tonight. If I had a second wish, I'd go for some moonlight. It's a black, black night. P-Peter... I mean Pirate... is five hundred miles out over the sea looking for a Lib down in the Bay.

The 159 boys went to Siam to hit a rail line north of Bangkok, attacking bridges from low level. Two planes were hit. Smoke coming out of one kite, it veered off and wasn't seen again. The other made it halfway home, their last message that they couldn't maintain height, would have to ditch.

A parade of planes has been out looking for it, 159 doing nothing else and other squadrons helping. From 215, both Shaw and Clark went last night, W/O Cameron's crew today. It's our turn tonight.

"You won't find the aircraft," the C.O. said. "The Lib is a very poor swimmer, would sink within minutes. How fast? Depends on how badly the soft underbelly crumbled on impact. Dip your hand in a pool of water and it feels soft; smack it and your palm will sting. Water is hard enough to smash thin aluminum. But there's always hope that at least some of the crew survived the crash, managed to clamber out, inflate the dinghy."

Cameron took off at noon, wasn't back when we left at 6:30.

A slow climb got us to the coast at sunset, then three hours to our area, the 1,600 square miles starting at 18° 27' North, 92° 52' East.

It's easy, of course, to plot those neat squares on a map in Calcutta, another matter to locate them out here. There are no street signs on the sea; in fact there's bugger-all out here. If our navigation, wind estimates or flying have been sloppy, we could miss our starting point by a hundred miles. The crew doing the adjoining area, no sight of land for seven hours, could miss its finishing point by more than that. The areas overlap a little, but there's still a big risk of missing something in the cracks.

We're at 2,000 feet, doing a 'creeping line ahead' towards the east. We're sweeping back and forth, a forty mile leg to the north, the same towards the south, then north again, each time moving a little closer to Burma.

The idea of edging towards a coast crawling with Japs doesn't thrill me even though Bob assures us we're still a hundred miles away.

Exciting work this is not.

What keeps everybody alert, though, is remembering that at any moment we could be passing over a little rubber boat bobbing on the waves, with several guys desperately hoping we don't miss them, knowing we're their last chance. Not that we'd see the dinghy in the dark, but we'd spot a light.

Now 2:15, we've been in the air nearly eight hours. With the runs a bit more than two miles apart, a couple more added to the 16 legs we've done will complete our forty mile square. I just awoke from a twenty minute nap; Jock had one earlier, so we're both wide awake. Never again will we let ourselves get so exhausted we both flake out.

You don't need all eyes searching full time so the crew shares look-out duties. Bob now has enough confidence in Smitty to let him take over as navigator for a spell — the timing of each leg, the interminable charting of each course change. Compared with that, Jock and I have it easy. Just sit, take turns keeping an eye on the gauges, smoke our cigarettes and think...when we can think of something to think about.

"Dinghy, a Hindi word for a small boat," the Intelligence bloke said. Strange I'd think of that... must have boats on my mind tonight.

Crackle. "Nose gun to pilot. Eddie here, skipper; Phil's taking a break. There's a light, a mile ahead, about eleven o'clock."

"Right, Eddie; tell me when we're abreast. I'll do a circuit around it, counter-clock. Everybody look sharp."

Hey, maybe this is it. But maybe it isn't; we've had false alarms before. The trouble is too many aircraft in the area, too many flares dropped for drift readings, flickering and flashing in the waves, looking a lot like Morse code. Then again, this could be the dinghy.

"Turn now, skipper. The light's at nine o'clock; you should see it."

Yeah, there it is. Fairly bright. Maybe too bright? It's certainly blinking; too bright for a flashlight, but could be an Aldis lamp. What are those letters? It's not S.O.S. It's not "di di dit daw daw daw di di dit."

I flick off George, tighten the turn to keep the light in view.

"What do you think?" I ask anybody. "Anyone read it?"

"I saw an 'H' and then an 'E', skipper," from Jonesy, keyed-up. "I think they were flashing 'help.'" There are other opinions. Everyone recognizes a letter or two, but not a whole word. But Mac says, "Just gibberish."

As a Morse Code man, he should know. But it's not the answer we want.

"Bob, what's wind speed down there? Approximate."

"Strong, twenty miles an hour."

"Then fairly heavy seas; there'd be a lot of pitching."

I think it's a flare, 95 percent sure. But that five percent is important too. I don't want to fly home wondering if we should have checked one more time. Guys in a rubber boat might be exhausted from hanging on, trying not to get bounced out each time a wave hits; they'd be hungry, thirsty... especially thirsty. You can live a long time without food, but not without fresh water.

"Pilot to crew. I'm going down closer, fifty feet above it. Everybody try to decide. Smitty, lead me over it. Are we ready?"

We're at a hundred feet. With solid black below, I'm afraid to go lower.

"Steady," Smitty is intoning. "Coming up to it... now."

Jonesy, unusually subdued, is the first to report. "I guess it wasn't a dinghy." Everyone agrees. But it's a big disappointment.

OCT. 15

The Lib that ditched wasn't found; the hunt's been called off. But the search did continue for a week. Our crew made a second trip in daylight but saw nothing. Everyone agrees the search was a good effort; even in petrol burned, the cost must have been tremendous. We all know we could be the next crew to go down; it's good to know the RAF won't skimp on rescue attempts.

I'm glad we did the two trips for other reasons.

"The more flying hours a crew puts in before starting ops, the better its chances will be." That was the word in England and I'm sure it's true; skill and confidence increase each time you fly. Also, it appears that the 24 hours we flew will count towards the total we have to complete.

In the UK, a tour in Bomber Command is thirty trips; a crew surviving that long is put out to pasture for awhile. Where ops flying is so dangerous, placing a limit on the number of missions is necessary. Crews have to be given some hope, a target to aim for. Maybe it's related to the saying that, "man can endure anything just so he knows how long it will last."

Surely flights into Burma won't be that dangerous. Nevertheless, we have a target number too. Because flights will vary greatly in length, it's to be calculated in terms of hours flown, the magic number being 300. But a dinghy search is more akin to patrols by Coastal Command where a tour is 500 hours. So the math is that sixty percent of our flying time on those two stooges will count towards our 300 number. Only 286 hours to go!

Big news around the Frazer-Smith household: we finally have a bearer. His name is Abdul. He's clearly not your typical servant-boy recently in from the jungle. Instead, he's a dignified fellow with enough pudginess around his midriff to prove that he has his own life organized well enough he hasn't missed many meals. It's hard to guess his age, maybe mid-thirties.

Abdul shows up at the door and informs us, in quite good English, that he is of the understanding we are in the need of a personal servant. He's wearing the usual pyjamas several sizes too large, but spotlessly clean, which isn't so usual. He has a round face, very much all-business at the moment, pleasant enough and not all that dark; another thing this laddie hasn't done is put in long hours working out in the fields.

He sports a small black moustache with eyes the same colour. They're good eyes, calm and confident. He can look properly deferential when he wants, but can also look you straight in the face.

Let's hire him quick. We're desperate, would take anybody, and this fellow looks good. I glance at Smitty, see he agrees. "Okay, you're hired."

"Sahibs," he protests, his palm pointing straight up like a traffic cop. Important business is not to be conducted in unseemly haste. Deliberately, he draws papers out of a purse, spreads them out, tries to smooth the wrinkles.

We glance at a few... letters of recommendation from former employers.

"Ver' important papers, sahibs. And here, most special important. Here is chitti from most last sahib, chief of policemen, City Deoghar. He speaks ver' high with me. Must read, sahibs."

The typewritten sheet has "Deoghar" printed at the top. Over the "Chief of Police" signature, the letter tells Whom It May Concern that the bearer, one Abdul Mukdar, was the writer's personal servant for one year, had proven himself conscientious, capable and honest, was leaving of his own volition.

"Then why did you leave?" Smitty asks.

"Pay ver' bad, sahib. Need rupees for feed family — one wife, two daughter — ver' much expensive, sahibs."

Ahh, he looks so much the perfect bearer, there had to be a catch. But if a Chief of Police couldn't afford him, how could we? When we ask how much pay he would require, he has his answer at the ready, no hemming or hawing.

"Ten rupees ever' month, sahibs. After two month when found perfect, twelve rupees ever' month."

Hey, is that all? Four dollars split between us? Trying not to sound too pleased, I check with Smitty and say, "That will be okay, Abdul. Of course, for that you'll have to do very good work. When will you start?"

"And rupees fifteen for uniform."

Yeah, I can guess what he wants. Some bearers in the dining room serve their masters in plain khaki; the more experienced ones are in uniform. Some question of status must be involved.

"To serve sahibs in dine room, ver' important for uniform, sahibs."

His tone is firm. "Okay, fifteen chips for uniform. When can you start?"

"Start now." For the first time, a smile appears. "Bring tea, sahibs?"

We're in luck; he's a marvel. A bearer's duties are not clearly defined anywhere; his job is just to be useful. Abdul is in at dawn to wake us up, shove a cup of tea into our hands, help us find errant socks or whatever while we pull some clothes on; he then scurries over to the Mess to serve our breakfast. During the morning, while we're away, he does household chores but watches for us to arrive back for lunch. He's entitled to his siesta time too, but shows up at four o'clock with our afternoon tea.

"How is it Abdul brings you cake while all our boy can get us is a dry biscuit?" Ken Cox from the next room complains.

I'd been shaving with water just warmed in the sun; it's a luxury to have it piping hot from the kitchen. If we decide to have a bath instead of a shower, he sets up the canvas tub and finds water for it.

"How come Abdul gets hot water when our bearer can't," asks Murray Potts.

He's always busy: running errands, fetching drinking water, making beds, hanging up clothes, polishing shoes. But with all the sandy soil here, a lot of it gets tracked into the room; we even bought a broom. But when I asked Abdul to brush the floor, he was quite indignant.

"Not sweeper, sahib! I personal servant, not sweeper. Never doing that!"

Ah, the caste system of India. The broom we have to push ourselves.

Mom's last letter asked what I did about washing my clothes; I think she was afraid we just didn't bother. But laundry — called 'dhobie' here — is well organized. Like other services around the camp, the concession is contracted out to a local entrepreneur. We pay this 'dhobie-wallah' a flat ten rupees a month and can send him all the sweaty clothes we want.

The service is fairly quick. But sometimes they over-do the starch; a little is a good idea as the stiffened fabric isn't as quick to stick to your sweat. But Chota Harris called us into his room.

"Look at these shirts. They're so hard I don't have to hang them up... just lean them against the wall."

But things do come back clean, surprisingly so because they don't use soap, just beat the dirt out. At the dhobie-works, I saw six men slapping wet articles against concrete slabs. Swinging hard. One effect is that buttons have to be replaced almost every week, a tedious chore I know Abdul dislikes.

I must have a mean streak in me. While he's at that job, I do get satisfaction in choosing that particular time to sweep the floor, saying, "Move your leg, Abdul," or "Raise your foot," while I sweep around and under him.

I've had one extra-curricular duty; an airmen died and I was detailed to accompany Sq/Ldr Reilly, the R.C. chaplain, to the RAF cemetery near here.

"A big mistake," I protested. "I'm not even the right damn religion."

"Just keep your mouth shut and try to look intelligent," Reilly said, "and no one will know you're a Protestant."

Everybody likes Reilly. Although you just know he'd be a good man to talk to if you had any problems that talking could solve, he can also sit in the Mess with a bunch of the guys, sip on his glass of beer, join in the laughter, tell jokes as well as anyone. He's fun to be with. Most R.C. priests I've met in the Air Force are like that.

Protestant padres, strangely, are usually a humourless lot who sit alone in the lounge, looking sad-faced and serious as if trying to stay in the right mood should someone suddenly pop a tragic problem on them. No one can explain why there'd be such a difference.

Late leaving the station, Reilly drove his Jeep at a very un-priestlike speed. Waiting at the cemetery was the lorry carrying the casket and a dozen of the airman's friends. I was glad the lad wasn't being interred so far from home without at least a few guys present who had known him.

It was a sad affair and I felt very uncomfortable. It wasn't just the boiling sun or having to wear a tie for the first time in seven months. It was also the thought of the airman spending eternity in what to me at least looked like a God-forsaken place.

Another part of it was having to listen to the mumbo-jumbo spouted by Father Reilly. It seems to me that one of the things this world sorely needs is a better funeral service.

I got conned! Formation practice, an 1,800 mile round-trip to Madras. With four boxes of four, we were slotted in #2 position in the third box.

"Look upon this as a final tune-up," the C.O. said. "A last rehearsal before we start the real thing."

Yeah, other hints too. The best: an assorted load of shiny bombs that arrived this week, surely sent for some purpose.

But Sam Dawson — a New Zealander, no dummy — asked, "Aren't you #2 in our box, Frazer? I'm #3, which is easier for the captain, but my second dickey needs practice at #2. Want to switch?"

"Well... I guess so." We've been flying #2 a lot, and #3 really is easier.

But I forgot one thing. Heading south, trailing the plane on your left, you're looking east, squinting into the damn sun six hours straight. When you turn to come home, there's the sun again, staring at you out of the west.

"Had that figured out beforehand, you say?" Dawson said. "No, no, never crossed my mind." But I don't believe him.

We get reports from the other squadrons. Like us, 99 is still waiting to get started but the others operated throughout the month. A mission 159 can be proud of was a mine-laying job all the way to Penang, a three thousand mile round trip within four hundred miles of Singapore. But two more aircraft were lost on that rail line north of Bangkok.

Momentous news is that 356, once with 355 along too, were on three joint missions with B24s of the USAAF. There really are Yank Libs in India!

Jap fighters jumped the bombers at Moulmein, their first attack on Libs in this theatre. The Americans took the brunt of it. Several 356 planes were also hit, but all got home. But they've had one aircraft crash on take-off, another crash-landed out of gas, and guns got a 355 plane in Siam.

Again I ask, "Hey, stupid, are you really that keen to start ops?"

Tomorrow, the end of another month. With today's trip, I now have 101 flying hours in Libs, about 75 of them solo. Is that enough hours, enough experience on B24s that we're ready to start flying into Jap territory? We'll be starting ops any day now. We all know that.

It must be enough; the RAF wouldn't send us into action unless we were ready, would they?

P-Peter, Air Crew

CHAPTER 9

MAIDEN MISSION

NOV. 3, 1944

Action at last! Not for me, the Squadron. Just four crews, but 215's first ever bombing trip in Liberators.

I didn't hear until this morning. Sitting in the shade behind the Flight Shack, we saw a Lib circling the field for landing. Strange... there'd been no take-offs. Within minutes, three more. Roy Williams, who runs `B' Flight when O'Connor's away, came out of the office with his field glasses.

"Liber'itors? Four of them? Wizzo, the crews on the mission last night."

"Mission? What mission?" we clamoured. "We didn't hear about any op."

"Aircraft 'V', that's O'Connor," Roy says, mostly to himself, glasses pointed at the runway a quarter mile away. "Good landing, Percy. Now 'B', that'll be Beadon. Here comes Jimmy Ross; very nice, Jim. Where's the fourth. Alright, there he is... that's the WingCo; wooooops... hold her str'ight, James. Okay, you're down."

Even without glasses, we can see that Wing Commander Sindall put another dent in our runway; a good pilot in other respects, he's famous here for terrible landings. Not that a few bumps are anything to be ashamed of; maybe we're even a bit proud of a C.O. who can make jokes about his bounces.

Everybody's excited, full of questions. Where did they go, what was the target? But Sid Clark, one of the older guys, says, "Not on the same trip? The C.O. and the two Flight Commanders wouldn't all go on the same mission?"

"Well, they did," Williams shrugs, "m'ybe because it was an unusual target... the shipyards at Vinh."

"Vinh! Where the hell is that? In Burma?"

"No, further east... French Indo-China."

We now know India, have seen Burma on maps, but what we know about countries east of there you could push through the eye of a needle.

"Topped up their tanks at Chittagong, then straight east. Like 355's op two nights ago to Hanoi. But the important thing is...they all got back."

"Roy, are those towns on your big map?" I have to see where places are.

Inside, we find Chittagong on the bit of India that runs a few miles down the Burmese coast. The Nips never captured the place, nor Cox's Bazaar another fifty miles further south; otherwise that's all enemy coast.

Hanoi is harder to spot but, yeah, there it is; and Vinh, a little further south. A long trip, but all the planes got home. It must be that the Japs didn't expect them; you'd never get that far in a Wimpy.

But long flights are what the B24 is all about. The Brits build bombers to carry big loads a short distance; American planes were designed for range... what's needed over big oceans. Maybe not too many bombs to drop when you get to your target, but better than not getting there at all.

We're filtering out. Williams, now back at his desk, waves me down.

"Wal, O'Connor left this to go on the bulletin board... tomorrow's Battle Orders. I'm just putting it up. You'll be interested."

Interested? Even my toe nails are tingling. I follow him outside, try to see over his shoulder as he clips it to a nail.

BATTLE ORDER... for November 4, that's tomorrow; BRIEFING... 1630 hours today; TARGET... to be announced at briefing; TAKE-OFF TIME... announced later; and other details, not important.

But there it is... AIRCRAFT AND CREWS. That's what I want to see. But everybody's crowding in. Who the hell's pushing?

A short list, six names. Who are they? "Aircraft B — Flt/Lt Grouse and crew; Aircraft C — F/O Clark; Aircraft F...

They must be listing the crews in the order of their planes. Yes, that's right... skip to the bottom.

There it is! Last name. It's us — "Aircraft 'P', F/O Frazer and crew."

Finally, finally, finally. Our first op. My heart is pounding hard. Gotta find the guys and tell 'em... tell them to get ready!

NOV. 4

What a beautiful morning... clear sky above, ocean below... blue on blue. Must be some chop on the water, though; where the sun reflects off the sea, it looks as if a billion diamonds were lying on the surface.

And how is the P-Peter gang spending this perfect day? A swim at the beach, a picnic in the park? No, we're taking a load of bombs into Burma!

Take-off at sunrise was scary; we're loaded. The aircraft manual lists the speeds required for take-off at various weights but the table doesn't even *go* past 60,000 pounds. But with two tons of bombs and 2,334 gallons of gas, our all-up weight was well over that. Runways here were recently increased to 2,500 yards; I breathed a little "thank you" for that as we passed the previous end-of-concrete mark, our 31 tons still stuck to the concrete.

But Peter did the job, a few feet to spare. Then the slow, agonizing struggle to wheedle some altitude, a few inches at a time, out of the groaning engines... fully aware that if any one power source so much as coughs, you and the crew, the aircraft, bombs and petrol are all going to make a most fiery mess on the ground below.

We've reached a thousand feet, still climbing, other aircraft scattered in the sky ahead of us. Jock takes over the controls and I swing around in my seat; Arthur is standing solemn-faced at my shoulder and I signal him that the guys jammed on the flight deck can go to their positions.

The next essential is a cigarette; Jock joins me. Arthur doesn't smoke, really doesn't like to see us puffing in the plane, but attached to the instrument panel is the ash-tray he made for us.

"I'll get dressed," I sign-language Jock as I climb out of my seat.

I'm dripping wet. The temperature can't be too high yet, and I'd stripped to undershorts, but I'm in a lather; half from the exertion and half from fright, I expect. Arthur hands me a towel, pretty dirty but all we have.

It's now 0755. At 4,000 feet, we're circling Sagar Island, our assembly point. Only five planes though; I guess W/O Cameron didn't get off. We were supposed to be the last kite airborne, following Cameron, but when we taxied past `M's dispersal, its engines were stopped, two airmen up a ladder looking at #4. Unless the trouble can be spotted fast, so they can take off and catch up, there'll be only five of us.

That won't win our maintenance boys any prizes; RAF ground crews are maybe still struggling over the switch from Brit Wellingtons to US B24s. Only five kites... a lousy grouping for defensive purposes too.

"Nose gun to pilot. Libs coming towards us, skippah. Twenty-two."

"Right, Phil, I see them... must be 355 and 356 from Salbani."

I can make out their tail markings as they cross above us, already in a formation of sorts. We swing in behind them. Briefing was for 215 to fly in two Vics. Norm Williams is the Squadron's leader in `O' and I can see him up ahead with his wing men. Stan Downie leads the second Vic in `D', and we're in the #2 position on his left. But such a gap on our right where Cameron should be. It doesn't look right to have that spot empty.

I wonder if I should be changing position.

As 356 have been flying missions for two months now, they're today's leaders; 355 is on their right. With us on the left, the three squadrons are thus in a Vic alignment too. It's a very loose formation, planes a hundred yards apart because we apparently needn't worry about Jap fighters out over the sea. A tight formation is dangerous when you're heavy-loaded and not very manoeuvrable. Besides being tiring for the pilots, juggling throttles to hold position is hard on gas.

"Next land we'll see," from Bob, "the coast of Burma. Three hours."

The rate-of-climb needle reads slightly above the horizontal, the numbers on the altimeter continually changing, but very slowly. It'll be a long haul to reach 12,000. But, even without instruments, you could tell you were climbing just by listening to the engines; they sound furious, like 4,800 wild mustangs snorting their disgust at being so hard-driven.

Jock has the wheel again and I can relax, try to sort out the thoughts bouncing through my head... buzzing like bees in a bottle today. Foremost at the moment is the talk with guys who were on the Vinh trip.

"Piece of cake," they said. "We dropped down over the mountains, bombed, got away before the Japs knew what hit them. A little flak, but not accurate. They weren't expecting us."

I wondered what the chances were of surprising them today.

"None at all," the I.O. said at briefing. "Expect heavy A/A fire over the target, the virtual certainty of enemy aircraft."

Jeez!

The WingCo started the meeting with a little speech. I guess it was intended as a pep-talk, but it didn't come over like that because Sindall is more a low-key type, wouldn't go in for razzmatazz stuff. Mostly he just wished us good luck.

"For those going on your first operational flight, just remember you are well-trained crews flying an excellent aircraft that is exceptionally well armed. If you remain alert... keep your wits about you... you should have no problems whatsoever."

I guess he was talking straight at us. We're the only rookies, the only crew of the six that hasn't done Wimpy ops. And yes, no doubt about it, I intend to do my damnedest to keep my wits about me.

The main interest at briefing was of course the curtain covering the map on the wall. But the Intelligence man droned on about Jap supply lines, how important Burma's railways are to them in supplying their troops on the Indian border. A long-winded S.O.B. Come on, pull the curtain. Eventually he did.

There it was, India and Burma with the Bay of Bengal in between. We squinted, strained to see. Where does the red ribbon go? South-east across water until it hits the Burmese coast near Cheduba Island. Then... then inland in about the same direction to... omigawd, it's Rangoon — the toughest target in all Burma! We're going right to Rangoon!

"No, not Rangoon proper," the Intelligence guy said. "Insein, a suburb just to the north... a railway centre with extensive marshalling yards. Your primary target will be the locomotive repair shops. A Photo

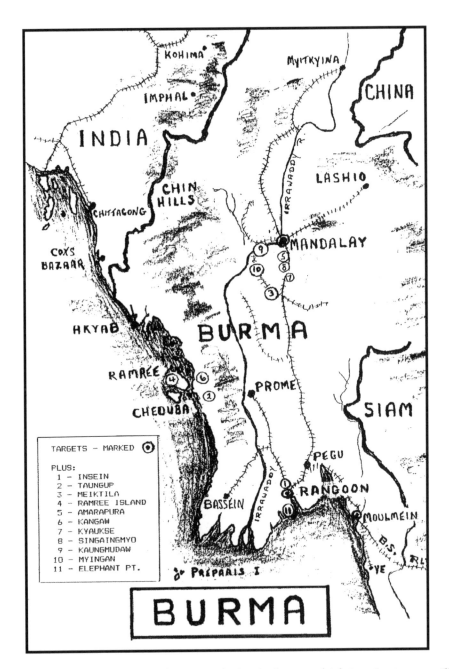

TARGETS — MARKED ⊙

PLUS:
1 — INSEIN
2 — TAUNGUP
3 — MEIKTILA
4 — RAMREE ISLAND
5 — AMARAPURA
6 — KANGAW
7 — KYAUKSE
8 — SINGAINGMYO
9 — KAUNGMUDAW
10 — MYINGAN
11 — ELEPHANT PT.

BURMA

Reconnaissance aircraft has brought back photos which bomb-aimers will study."

But I was more interested in other things — the type of formation, who's to lead it, what position we'll fly, the order of take-off. There are other details such as the time lorries leave for the airdrome, the time to start engines, similar stuff. You jot all this down; it's too important to trust to memory. But damn, I'd forgotten to bring pencil or paper. Cheez! I've been preparing for this for three years and don't remember to bring anything to write down whether we're to take off first or last. It held up the whole meeting — a helluva way to show you're keeping your wits about you. But Bob handed me a pencil stub, and an envelope I could write on the back of, and the briefing continued.

Sq/Ldr Beadon announced he had a surprise.

"For the first time," he said, masticating the words in his very English accent, "bombers of 231 Group are to receive fighter support. RAF pilots flying American P47 Thunderbolts — and another squadron of P38 Lightnings of the US Army Air Force — will meet you, escort you into Burma."

Hey, that's swell, that's great! It brought an immediate rumble of appreciation. But his next words brought them to a crashing halt.

"But we understand the fighters have insufficient range to go right to the target. You'll be on your own the last hundred miles."

What the hell! Surely where you need them most is over Rangoon. Right next to Insein is Mingaladon, a big Jap fighter base.

Then the I.O. talked about Contingency Plans, suggestions on what to do if we had to bail out. He showed the Escape Kit we'll carry which has lots of gimmicks, such as a silk handkerchief which becomes a map of Burma when wet, and a button which is a compass when floated on water. There's an English-Burmese dictionary and a letter in several dialects promising a reward to any native leading you back to India. And we each take some Burmese money, strictly on a loan basis.

Next he talked about Escape Routes; I wish he hadn't. Walking five hundred miles back to India, past Jap-held towns, over mountains, through jungles and leech-infested swamps... the idea's preposterous.

"Yes," the I.O. admitted. "It would be difficult to make it that far on your own. And little chance a Burmese would help you; most would take your money and also collect a reward from the Japs for turning you in.

"And stay away from the hill tribes in the mountains on the east side," he went on, banging at the map with his pointer. "Our information is they may be head-hunters, possibly cannibalistic. And we're not sure about the natives in these mountains either,"... jab, jab... "but if you can reach this area in the north, there's a good chance the Katchin people will help you."

That kind of talk puts rotten thoughts in your head.

At dinner, a parade of guys came by to wish us good luck. Afterwards, we sat in the lounge with Brodie's gang; they were all telling jokes, trying very hard to be amusing. Is it so obvious that Smitty and I need cheering up?

Nobody asked what the target was. It seems far-fetched to think that anyone on the base — the char-wallah or one of the bearers or coolies —

could be a Jap spy, could get word back to Rangoon to ambush us there tomorrow. Just in case, you're not supposed to discuss the raid, and nobody asked.

Except one. We gave Taffy, the bar corporal, instructions to wake us at O445 and left early. At the door we met Charlie Jensen, an RAF radio man. Jensen is sharp-eyed and sharp-tongued, not one of my favourites.

"I say," he asked, "isn't your crew going on the trip tomorrow?"

When we agreed, he lowered his voice to say, "Is it true? Rangoon?"

I wasn't sure what to say. But he took my mumbling for assent, shook his head, went off muttering, "You'd think they'd send a new crew some place easier for their first op."

I crawled into bed at 10:30, that comment still clattering around in my skull. In moments, I could hear Smitty snoring, but I was very wide awake. So many things to think about, to remember. In the morning, don't forget my sun glasses, pistol, the maps, my battle dress jacket. Leave my wallet and all personal papers behind. The lorry leaves the Mess at 5:30; that doesn't give much time to dress and eat.

How does it go again? Stay away from the head-hunters. But don't let the Japs get you either; they're not much better. If we had to bail out on the way to Rangoon, maybe I could make it back to the coast, find an uninhabited island, do a Robinson Crusoe bit until the war's over. Or try to walk north to Katchin country; nah, you couldn't get that far, not with a price on your head and the Burmese unfriendly. But if you were hit by flak, lost enough gas you couldn't get home, you might fly north as far as possible, jump, then hope you could find friendly Katchins before the Japs got you.

Maybe I should think that through again. Damn that Intelligence guy and his Escape Routes. Cheez, one a.m. I've got to be up in four hours.

Crackle... the staccato static of the intercom jolts me back to the present. It's Phil, sounding as if this was just another practice flip.

"Skippah, planes ahead are testing their guns. Can we do ours."

"Yeah, you first, the others in order."

I suppose the stink of the cordite, the deafening rattle of the point-fives, are as bad as usual, but they aren't bothering me today. I'm glad to hear them, glad to have them along.

It was tough getting out of the charpoy this morning, a terrible rush to dress, gulp some breakfast before the lorry left for the drome. I forgot only one thing — that damned envelope with all my briefing notes. What a panic when we got to the plane and it wasn't in any of my pockets! But Jock pulled a paper from his shirt. "Got all the same gen rrright heerre."

We're at 8,500 feet now, still climbing. But I have other thoughts. What I have to keep reminding myself is that today we are flying into Burma to drop bombs — big thousand-pounders which will make a mess of anything they hit. I have to keep telling myself this is actually happening.

The bombs will smash buildings and kill Japs, no doubt Burmese too if they're working for the Nips or just get in the way. And while we're doing this, their gunners will be firing up at us, shooting with real bullets, hurling live A/A shells into our path, trying to kill us any way they can.

I'll have to go over that again; it just isn't real. I know what reality is. "Real" is going to school, getting a job, going to movies and parties... things that make sense. That's what people do in real life.

But this is crazy. What lies ahead today is so remote from anything I've ever experienced that my head can't absorb it. Why, if it were true, in three hours I could be dead! The mind rejects such obscene thoughts.

It's not that I don't understand there's a big war on, a terrible lot of killing and dying all over the world these days. The part hard to accept is that the war — not just the training and sitting-around part, but the real thing — is now happening to me! I can now see that I've been moving slowly, inexorably, toward this day for many months. Now it's come.

Then how the hell did I get myself into this pickle?

I remember going to the recruiting office, taking oaths, signing my name. It was much more a crusade than a war; the Nazis had to be stopped from taking over the world. Obvious then, still is. We were sorry to be the guys who had to do it; a little older or a little younger and we'd have missed it. But an unfortunate fact; we just came along at the wrong time. Simply a matter of bad luck...and you can't do anything about that.

Two hours later. At 10,000 feet now, everyone hooking up to the oxygen supply. The aircraft's quiet today — no jokes, little conversation. Is everyone full of private thoughts just as I am? Or do most guys just go and do their damn jobs without all the useless introspection?

Jock's at the controls; we're a hundred yards behind `D-Dog', and the other planes are all ahead. A few clouds now but still a beautiful morning.

Hey, is that why I have so much trouble getting it into my head that today's flight is a deadly serious affair? Is the morning just too nice? That might be part of it. How can your mind contemplate killing, being killed, on such a perfect, peaceful day?

The sudden squawk of the intercom makes me jump. Yeah, I'm tense.

"Navigator to pilot. We're passing over Cheduba Island, skip. And here's a thought for you. There are Japs down there looking up at us."

"Mid-upper to pilot." Eddie's Lancashire accent; I can now understand him most of the time. "Fighters... ten o'clock high... hope they're ours."

Which starts about five guys all shouting at once, so loud I can't make out what anyone's saying. "Pilot to crew," I bellow, so hard I know I'm nervous. "Damn it, settle down. One at a time. Phil first. What do you see?"

"I think P47s, skippah. Radial engine, big blunt nose."

"Yeah... Thunderbolts," Eddie agrees. "RAF markings, about twenty-five."

Then Jim from the rear. "Tail gun to pilot. More fighterrrs above us. Double fuselage... have to be Lightnings. I count nineteen."

I take a quick peek. There they are, P38s, compliments of the US Army Air Force, glistening in the sun — a most marvellous sight. And now I spot the P47s higher up. Beautiful! But remembering they're just coming with us part way brings the sick feeling back to my stomach.

Across the coastline now, it's solid green down below. Rugged country, no sign of life. It's bumpy over the hills, our smooth air now full of pot holes. We disconnected George, are flying manually. At 11,600 feet, we've levelled off; the engines are happy about that, don't sound so angry now.

"Navigator to pilot. We're passing Taungup, down on the right. That's the secondary target in case Rangoon's socked in."

"OK, Bob." But who gives a damn about alternative targets right now?

Our ETA — Estimated Time of Arrival — is 1155 hours. Just 45 minutes.

Now that we're over Burma, the formation is a little tighter, but not much; too much turbulence. The other 26 aircraft are spread out before us. Flying #2 position in the #2 Vic, every other plane is ahead or to our right. Not only are we 'tail-end Charlie,' but away out in left field as well.

Which doesn't impress me even flying in a straight line. But we have to make two turns. At the I.P. — the Initial Point, where we start the run-in to the target — we swing south. After bombing, there'll be another turn to the west when we head for home. Both turns are to starboard... with us away out on the left flank! Won't that be an unhealthy position if there are enemy fighters?

Wouldn't it be better to tuck in behind `D', a sort of two plane box without wing men, all the squadron guns above us then? But can I do that... just change position? Well, we're told to use our heads and that's what my head is telling me to do. I warn the crew about the switch and swing Peter in behind D-for-Dog. Jock gives a thumbs-up. Bob comes on to say, "I think you're right, skip. I feel a lot safer in here."

Jock is flying; it's my chance to see Burma. Mainly it just looks peaceful. The land is flat now; we must have crossed the mountains, and are over the central plain. There are big rivers, towns, what look like irrigated fields. Maybe paddy fields; I think Burma grows a lot of rice.

Half an hour to go. We're still creeping across the landscape, all those little fields making a patchwork quilt of browns and greens. Very pretty.

Cheez, I sound like a bloody tourist!

What surprises me is... I'm reasonably relaxed. Oh, uptight and nervous enough; I don't know how deep you'd have to pry to hit the seam of funk. I'm sure it's there. But it seems under control. That's what you try for, hope for. Just keep the panic button covered... settle for that.

Crackle! It's Bob again, very formal now. "Navigator to pilot. I.P. in twelve minutes; a small stream into the Rangoon River... should be easy to spot. That's where we turn right... a straight run to Insein. Rangoon proper right behind it. At one-seventy-five mph... seven minutes to the target."

"Right, Bob." We got all that at briefing, but no harm reviewing it. We just follow the plane ahead but it helps to know what to expect.

I want to check with everybody one more time. Gotta remember to keep my voice as calm and confident as I can.

"Pilot to crew. You heard Bob. Everybody ready?"

One by one they check in. Four professional gunners in their turrets, Mac and Arthur at the beam windows. Joe Barlow reports he's on the intercom but with one ear on the wireless. Smitty says he's map-reading for Bob, will get on the bomb sight at the I.P. And they all sound so damn normal!

Okay, some voices show a bit of a short-of-breath kind of nervousness, but otherwise a hundred percent. I haven't checked with Jock Govan yet. He isn't on the intercom now; approaching the target, he listens out on the `formation frequency' in case there's a message from the leader. I wave to get his attention, point at my mouthpiece, and he switches over.

"Okay, Jock. Ten minutes to the I.P. Let me take over."

The formation is tighter now. D-for-Dog's big double tail is right in front — ten yards above, fifteen ahead. I can see the rear gunner revolving the turret from side to side, swinging his gun barrels. Say, isn't that Lawrie Lawrence, the Gunnery Leader? That's right, he flies with Downie. Hey, it's a break to have the Squadron's top gunner riding shot-gun above us.

It's Eddie. "Do you know our fighter cover is still with us, skipper? Weren't they supposed to leave before this?"

That's what we were told. A mistake? If so, I like this one. But no time to think about it; I'm having a helluva struggle to hold position in the formation. We've burned some petrol, but are still too damn heavy to be this close to other planes. Peter is sluggish and unresponsive, like driving a car with the brakes on. Add throttle and nothing much happens; reduce it and she wants to stop and die on the spot.

Flying tight on `D's tail, there's little margin for error; you're changing throttle settings continually. Of course, D-Dog is juggling its speed to stay with the plane it's following, that aircraft is making alterations to keep in step with the kite ahead of it. It goes right up to the formation leader. When you're Tail-end Charlie, you're at the end of the chain, have to adjust for everybody else's adjustments.

Crackle... squawk. Bloody hell, that did startle me! It's Bob again.

"Three minutes to the I.P. But I think the wind has changed. I'd like

Jim to take drifts now and after we turn. Can you hold her steady?"

Damn, we're sliding under `D' again. Throttles back... not too much... back on again. What did Bob say? Cheez, I'm trying not to knock Dog's tail off and all he cares about is the damn wind.

"Okay, okay... go ahead with the drift. I'll hold her steady."

Now we're into a swing to the right. It's quite gentle but, even so, Peter seems determined to slide off to the left, right out of the group. I have to fight the controls, force her to stay under `D's tail.

We've straightened up, are heading south. Seven minutes to go... this is it. In the next few minutes we'll find out if we live through this or not. Jeez, I hope we do. I do not want to die. I do not want that to happen.

"Jim, did you get that second drift for me?" For the first time ever, Bob sounds irritated, definitely tense.

"I'm trrrying. We'rrre bouncing too much."

"Okay, okay," I say. "Try again." And Bob gets his damn reading.

"Smitty, ready on the bomb-sight?" Again my voice is too loud, almost a shout. That's bad. Being loud when it isn't necessary means your nervousness is showing, and that can be contagious.

"Yes, ready. I'm changing... the wind setting. I'll use the... new one Bob just gave me. Can you hold... her steady on one-seventy-five. We're bouncing... all over."

"I know, I know... but it's bumpy."

Dammit, how do I hold the speed at 175 if the formation has slowed to 165? But I'll have to try; the bombs will miss if we're not close to the speed set on the bomb-sight.

"Flak ahead!" It's Phil's voice, not languid now. "Lots of it."

I have to take my eyes off Dog's tail for a quick look. There they are, the first I've ever seen. So that's what they're like, little wisps of smoke, grey puffs against a blue sky, five or ten feet across — an awful lot of them.

We're getting closer. The bursts look bigger, and more of them. Where there was empty sky — piff, piff, piff — three more ugly grey smoke balls appear from nowhere... just hang there. Right in front of us now, looking bigger and bigger. We're going to fly right through them!

"I see... the target, Wally." Smitty's excitement shows in his voice. "Straight ahead. Railway yards... just like the pictures. We're right... on line."

The planes up ahead are opening their bomb doors. I can look right up into Dog's belly, see the bombs hanging there.

Why the hell doesn't Smitty open *our* doors? Every other kite is ready to bomb. I'll give him ten seconds.

Still nothing. After three seconds, I can't wait any longer. "Smitty! The bomb doors." I shouldn't be shouting, but I am. "Open the damn doors."

Almost immediately, the metallic rumble of casters running in grooves, the noise muffling Smitty's voice, but I think he says, "I forgot."

"How long to the drop point?"

"Just seconds... thirty seconds." Smitty'll be stretched out full length on his stomach down in the nose, one eye on the eye-piece of the bomb-sight, one hand on the button, ready to squeeze it when the maintenance buildings appear in the cross-hairs. If this was a Yank plane, Smitty would actually be flying the aircraft right now, but we don't do that.

"Can't you hold her steady? We're bouncing all over."

"I'm trying, I'm trying." But the air's terribly rough. Maybe it's the mid-day heat, maybe the turbulence kicked up by all the planes ahead — packed pretty tight now — but I'd bet those puffs don't help either.

What was that? I felt something... as if a giant hand had given Peter a little slap. Was it flak... or my imagination?

"Steady," Smitty says, half an order, half a plea.

Jeez, we got slapped again. A hard, jolting whack — a lot harder. That was no imagination. The whole aircraft shivered and shook.

"Steady...another ten seconds... hold her steady."

I'm doing my damnedest to stay level, to hold the airspeed at 175. But I have to check D-Dog. Yes, there she is, right ahead. My eyes dart back to the instruments... speed about 170, close enough.

"Steady, steady... stea - dyyy... bombs away! Bomb doors closed."

A huge relief to be rid of that load of explosives. But I knew they were gone. Suddenly two tons lighter, Peter celebrates with a tremendous burst of energy, like a frisky colt let loose in the meadow. I have to pull back on the throttles... fast... before we run into D-Dog in front.

D-Dog? Bloody hell! I flip my eyes up from the instruments and there's nobody there. No `Dog'... no planes at all! Where the hell did they go?

But no time to look, no time to think. I hear Phil's voice, not breezy at all. "Bandit! Twelve o'clock level... attacking."

Omigawd! I see him. I hear Phil's guns blasting... other guns behind me. A terrible racket, stink. But there's the fighter — here he comes! A sight I'll never forget. Just a pip-squeak of a thing — single wing, radial engine — looks like a bloody Harvard. Coming straight at us, head on... strange lights flickering along its wing. Hell! Those aren't lights, those are... those are gun flashes! That little bugger is shooting at us!

I'm absolutely shocked. That's my reaction... shock, surprise, mad as hell. More anger than fear, more surprise and disgust than anything else. Of all the bloody nerve. That rotten little bugger actually firing at me... shooting real bullets, aiming them right at us!

It happens in a flash, over in seconds. I sense a shadow or something flashing by my window. Now it's gone.

But why is Jock pounding my arm and shouting? Can't he see I'm busy?

Eddie interrupts, his words tumbling out, "Bandits, bandits... above us, diving down, out of the sun. Look out!"

Omigawd, what do I do now? Where is everybody, where's the formation? Should I dive? Should I turn and twist, take evasive action? But I can't... I might dive into another plane. Where are they? Maybe right underneath.

What to do? Everything's happening too fast. I'd like to hide, but I don't know where. Do I just fly straight ahead... let the gunners shoot it out? I guess that's what we're doing. I don't know what else. It's pandemonium... chaos. All guns are blasting. The gunners have taken over the intercom, shouting to one another... yelling... barking out where the Japs are now. I'm right in the middle of it, but I feel useless... not doing a thing, just steering. The noise is deafening, the cordite stink everywhere.

All this happens in just seconds. The guns are still firing, Jock still banging on my arm... hard, insistent. Dammit, I'll have to find out what he wants. I drop the right wing to see out his window better, see what he's pointing at.

Good lord, there they are — the whole formation... over on the right, below us... already turned to starboard, already turned for home, leaving us behind. Bloody hell! We're several hundred yards — a quarter-mile — from the closest plane. And going in a different damn direction! Up with the port wing, down with the starboard. Point it at the ground. Jam the throttles forward, sharp turn to the right, a diving turn. Never did I make a steeper turn in a Finch or Harvard. Will the wings take it?

They do. The Manual says they'll stand three hundred in a dive; we're not much over that. Peter is still behind the others... but going in the same direction now... and gaining. Yes, we're gaining. The guns are still thundering, the cordite still stinking, but my only thought is to get back into that formation. Only a hundred yards... now fifty. I ease the throttles back and we slide right in behind the last aircraft.

I think it's D-Dog; not that I care. Yes, 215 tail markings, must be `D'. I'm tucked in so close I might scrape her paint. The rear gunner... he's waving at us, welcoming us back. Or is he telling us to get away, back off, that we're too damn close? But I'm staying right here. I don't want to get out of formation ever, ever again.

But something's different. Very different. What is it? Yes, the noise; there isn't any. Everything's quiet, suddenly quiet. No flak bursts around us. And our turrets aren't firing. Have the Jap fighters broken off?

As usual, Jonesy's the first to answer. "They're gone, skipper. Didn't follow us from the target... don't see any now."

The others agree. Then we're through it! We've made it! Already we're away from the city, over green fields again... with blue sky above, a sky not fouled with shells and smoke. We're going to be okay.

I feel wonderful! An hour from Rangoon and I'm still 'high.' Euphoric! Never have I felt so marvellous... bubbling over, head in the clouds. I want to laugh and sing, jump up and down, dance a jig.

The reason? It's very simple... I'm alive!

Leaving the target, I made the most wondrous discovery. I wasn't dead after all! Everyone in the crew was okay. I was sure we were gonners... then it came in a flash that we weren't. How could anything in the world compare with that? Our surprise, relief, joy — it shows up in our voices, our good humour, our bubbling high spirits. Is the word "ebullience"?

"Fairly... good bombing," Smitty says, still short-of-breath excited. "Our stick... undershot a bit but we... got hits... on the northern end. Others... got the southern part. The marshalling yards... got plastered."

"Someone got the building," Jonesy insists. "I think it was us."

"Maybe," says Smitty. "We'll see what the... photos show. But another thing; did anyone else see the lead squadron? What happened? They bombed right after... the I.P. — under-shot the target by six miles."

You shouldn't laugh at somebody else's snafus when you have enough of your own, but maybe we're in the mood for a chortle.

Arthur and the gunners are checking Peter for damage. We certainly took some hits; there are holes in the tail assembly that weren't there this morning. Only one looks serious — a big gash in the port aileron — but I do some gentle roller-coaster manoeuvres to test the controls. They seem okay.

Then Eddie, from the top turret, spots something wrong with the cowling on #2 just outside my window; a piece of jagged metal is sticking up. Can't tell if it came from flak or a fighter; what we can tell is it came damn close... inches from knocking out the engine, six feet from the cockpit. Peter has been hurt, but seems able to fly through her pain.

Now the gunners are talking about the fighter attack. Not Zeros, they say; a Zero is a Navy plane. Likely Oscars, perhaps Hamps or Tojos. At least six, maybe twelve. But they didn't all get to attack us. Our fighters were busy; there were dog-fights all over the sky.

"We got one of them, anyway," Jim is saying. "He rrrolled overrr on his way d'oon, smoking bad. A piece of wing flew off."

"We shot one down?" from me. "We did! I didn't know. Who got him?"

"Yes, skipper, yes. We got him." Jonesy sounds as if he's going to explode. "Pieces of the wing were falling off. I saw him hit... right beside the river. Got some shots at him... then my guns jammed."

"I firrred at him," Jim says. "And I hit him. I'm surrre of it... going to put in a claim forrr him."

"I fired too," from Eddie. "Several bursts. Maybe hit him. But other planes were shooting too... couldn't tell whose shells got him."

"I saw him," I contribute. "Coming at us from head on."

"That's right, skippah," Phil agrees. "A curve of attack, two o'clock to twelve o'clock. I got off a few rounds; you only get seconds. Then he dipped past on the left, going like hell. Didn't see him again."

"No, no," Eddie objects. "That's not right. He came in from the starboard side... the one I saw, anyway. Did a roll-off-the-top above us, then dived... right through the formation. A P38 was on his tail."

"I dinna ken wherrre he came frrrom," insists Jim, who often has the last word on things, "but he went past us frrront to back, into a wee dive, passed thrrrough a small cloud. When he came out, everrryone was firrring at him. But I'm putting in a claim for him, even if they all do, 'cause I hit him."

So a lot of disagreement, confusion. Each saw only part of the action and from a different angle. I suppose that's why you need de-briefing officers to sort out the different versions.

The best laugh comes from Mac at the port beam gun. "I had a good angle on the Tojo when he went by. But he was hard to see. It's not easy when your ring sights aren't lit. I forgot to switch them on, didn't get a shot."

Arthur at the other beam window didn't see any attackers. "Saw dog fights. And lots of flak, getting accurate; two blasts came very close."

"Coastline coming up, Wally," from Bob.

Yeah, a sharp transition from green to blue. We're used to having the ocean under us now. I prefer it, find it less threatening than the tangled jungle covering all those mountains with god-knows-what underneath. The sea is just simple straight-forward water — smooth, neat and uncomplicated.

And there's little risk now. This isn't Europe where bombers have to fight their way to the target and then all the way home. Here there's little danger after you leave the target area.

The formation's very loose; we're even using George again. Everyone's relaxed; we're going to make it home. I suppose the return trip is always an anti-climax. You pass the time with routine chores — eating your bully beef sandwiches, checking the petrol gauges and charting the consumption. In the cockpit, we're busy adjusting the trim tabs to keep the aircraft in level equilibrium, the centre of gravity changing as fellows move about the plane to trade jobs, stretch their legs, or visit the pail.

Yes, a bucket is what we're now using as primitive privy. There's also a rubber tube provided for pee purposes, but we've discovered a serious design flaw in the B24. When you use the tube, you spray the rear turret.

Jim gave us an ultimatum, "Eitherr ye' stop using the tube or I quit the crr-rew."

The formation has disintegrated. Planes are all over the sky, some out of sight. With Jock flying, I've nothing to do except twiddle my thumbs. This would be a good time to find out what happened over the target when I got out of formation. I'm embarrassed as hell about it... nearly got everybody killed. I don't even understand what happened. I suppose Jock could tell me, but shouldn't the whole crew be involved? I flick my switch.

"Pilot to crew. Let's talk about the bomb run. One moment we were right in position. I look down to check the airspeed. When I look back up there's no other plane in sight. What happened?"

Bob answers right away. "They made a steep turn to starboard, skip. I'd nothing to do on the bomb run so was watching. Smitty's right... the lead squadron unloaded their bombs miles too soon. They still had to lead the formation to the aiming point, but had nothing to drop. The flak was bad, but would be even worse straight ahead. They turned too early, too sharply."

"It was supposed to be a gentle turn," is my recollection. "They said, 'Bomb, then begin a shallow turn to starboard.'"

"Nothing shallow about it," Jock contributes. "Almost a rrright-angle turrrn. I think they knew of all the flak ahead and trrried to avoid it. I should hae warrrned you, but you were concentrrrating on the bomb run."

Three more hours. Okay, here's the Bengal coast, just emerged from the thick ground mist. Half an hour to go. A long flight — close to ten hours — but a satisfying one. What in olden days would have been called our "baptism of fire." For our first op, don't we get a pass mark? The crew were great. And maybe I didn't need to worry about them following my lead.

And the guy in the crew I was most worried about, the biggest unknown quantity of all? Well, not too great. I was terrified, and didn't hide it very well. Gotta stop making so many dumb mistakes. But it could have been worse.

Jock has gone back to the pail and Arthur's taking the opportunity to stretch out in the right-hand pilot's seat for a moment. Hey, I have an idea.

"Arthur, you could stay there for the landing... act as second pilot. Good experience; you might have to do it sometime if Jock or I get knocked out. You know all the procedures. Yes, we'll do that."

Neither Arthur nor Jock sound enthusiastic, but they don't object. Arthur straps himself into Jock's seat harness.

Almost home. Goodo, there's the airdrome. The crew are all packed on the flight deck ready for landing. With no other kites in sight, we can go right in. I call for undercarriage down and partial flaps; Arthur's doing just fine.

We turn crosswind, swing around onto the approach. Hey, I've timed the turn just right; we're in line with the runway. Is this my lucky day?

Add flaps, reduce speed, check fuel mix, prop pitch, everything else. Arthur and Jock are making sure I don't miss anything. Arthur's also calling off height and airspeed like a pro. One hundred feet, and we're just over the runway... just right. Fifty feet. Start easing off the throttles.

Kiss! We're down. We touched so gently I wasn't sure for a moment. Big surprise, I've made a good landing for a change.

What the hell! What's happened? We're swerving to the left — hard left, off the runway... right off the bloody runway!

The ground's hard, hard enough to take our weight. We're careening across the field, bouncing over ditches and bumps at ninety miles an hour.

"Arthur," I scream. "Get off the goddam pedals!"

"I'm not touching the pedals!"

But he must be, must have his left foot jammed on the rudder, maybe the brake... doesn't realize it. We're both shouting. I've never heard him sound frightened before. "You must be on the pedals!"

"I'm not!"

But we're still veering left. I can't steer at all. I've got the right brake pushed to the floor, but it does no good. We're completely out of control, bouncing crazily over rough ground, knocking down bushes, crashing through scrub saplings.

Omigosh, there's a bunch of palms ahead — a thicket of big ones. We're heading right for them. What can I do?

No, it's alright. We're still turning left, we'll miss them. And we're slowing down; I think we are. A really big bounce... must've hit a ditch. What a mess. What the hell did I do wrong? But we're definitely slowing. Another ditch, a final jerk... we're at a dead stop.

"Open bomb doors! Everybody out!"

It's a jam on the flight deck, everyone scrambling to his feet; a big crush to get to the exit, Arthur and I at the end. In the close quarters, like a rugger scrum. But now we're out... everybody's out... and we all run from the plane in case... well, I'm not sure what.

Poor Peter! The left wheel must be in a hole. That puts the starboard wing up in the air, the port wing tip scraping the ground. There are big dents where we knocked down trees. One of the oleo legs looks crooked. We can see the jagged piece of metal sticking out of the engine cowling, a big gash in the aileron. And holes we didn't see from inside. Poor Peter.

I still don't know what happened. If Arthur didn't freeze on the pedals, maybe the left brake locked on. What else?

Maybe I shouldn't have let Arthur help me land. I'll get hell for that, but I still think it was an okay idea. And Peter — our beautiful new aircraft, shiny and unmarked — only it's first op, and now it's a wreck.

And I did it. I was stupid, wanted to be captain, and now I'm in deep, deep trouble.

Here comes the lynching party. First the fire engine, siren wailing. Then the C.O.'s Jeep, Beadon riding with him. O'Connor's next. Then more lorries and Jeeps, all come to see what I've done.

What a mess!

A swirl of dust as the fire truck slams on its brakes, airmen jumping off, fire extinguishers at the ready. But then they stop... almost in mid-stride. They have nothing to do; there are no flames at all.

Peter just sits there, motionless and silent. Maybe looking tired out.

The C.O.'s Jeep jolts to a stop in front of us, brakes squealing.

"Anybody hurt, Frazer?" Sindall shouts.

"No sir... all okay."

"What happened... on the landing? You touched down quite nicely, then took off like a boomerang? What did you do?"

Cheez, that's the big question. That's what they'll be asking at the court martial. I have to come up with a good answer, but I'm stumped. Except maybe that Arthur might have... No, I better not mention that.

"The left wheel... um... it seemed to... uh... lock." I guess I'm stammering. "Like the brake had... uh... seized or something."

Sindall and the others are crowded around me like it was the Spanish Inquisition, faces showing they're not impressed with my answers.

A Jeep that was circling Peter drives up; Shaw, Squadron Engineering Officer — curmudgeon in his spare time — who hates pilots even when they don't smash his airplanes, gets out.

"The left tyre, James, it's flat. That would swing them off the runway."

"Yes, certainly would. Could you see what happened to the tyre?"

"Just had a quick look, but there's a hole in front of the #2 wheel nacelle... another behind it... as if a cannon shell went through, pierced the tyre on the way. They were peppered in other places too."

And instead of being dragged off in handcuffs, here's the WingCo pumping my hand! Congratulating me on getting the plane down more or less in one piece. Plus more of the same from everyone else!

But now I notice that Sindall and Shaw have gone over to examine Peter. I hurry to join them... to listen in, really.

Shaw is saying, "... bring a fitter and give it a thorough check, but there's considerable damage. We can patch the flak holes, bullet holes, dents in the wing, but the undercart looks twisted. And it seems the port wing hit the ground on one of the bounces; if so, that's serious. Offhand, I'd say we might have to scrap her... use her for spare parts."

Scrap her! I'm shocked. Peter is wounded, but surely not a terminal case... not so stricken she couldn't be nursed back to health. Did Shaw mean she might be put out of her misery, like shooting a lame horse. They wouldn't do that to Peter? But the C.O. just shrugged. No, they couldn't do that!

The lorry arrives to take us to de-briefing and then back to the billets. News travels fast. Smitty and I have just stripped for our showers when Eddie and Smokey come over from the next basha to tell us they heard we'd made a very good landing. That was a good landing?

It becomes a parade of fellows in bath towels coming into the room. The handshakes continue in the Mess, guys handing me drinks. Who would not find it all extremely pleasurable, maybe start to allow, after more gins, that... well, if you all think so, maybe it was a pretty fair landing at that?

After dinner, two strangers barge into the lounge yelling, "Where's this man Frazer who lands with a flat tyre... walks away from it?" It's Ted Willing and Johnny Johnson over from 159 Squadron across the field.

"C'mon," John shouts, "you're coming with us. We heard you just did your first op... some trouble but got back okay. That calls for a little `do.'"

"That's right, m'ite," from Ted. "We have a half-ton outside. Let's go."

By this time, I'm already both weary and woozy, but you can't refuse an invitation like that. And I find they treat visitors very well over at 159, especially if you know some of their guys, have just done your first op.

They plied me with liquids, except they wouldn't give me the one drink I really wanted — a bottle of Coca Cola. They have one, the first I've seen since Canada, and unopened... but it's just for looking at, displayed all by itself on a high shelf behind the bar.

A long sleep this morning, but then a big `all-crews' meeting to discuss the Insein trip. With the C.O. in Cal, Sq/Ldr O'Connor is in charge, and tells us that 231 Group is not too enthused about some aspects of the mission.

"Bombing results, actually quite good," he says, waving photos of the target, "even though the lead squadron had problems. When their leader opened his bomb doors, all bombs dropped prematurely because of an electrical malfunction. That can happen. But other bomb-aimers can't just push their buttons because they see the leader's bombs fall. Only when they see the target in their sights.

"Gunners are to be commended for beating off the Jap fighter attacks. Special congratulations to Flt/Lt Lawrence; confirmation has already been received from Group that he is to get credit for one Oscar shot down. And aircraft `O' gets credit for an Oscar damaged.

"But the formation flying? Not very damn good." Handlebar moustache twitching magnificently, O'Connor brandishes a sheaf of intelligence reports.

"Approaching and leaving the target, the formation was too loose. Over the target, bunched too close together... risk of collision much too great.

"But the big problem came after bombs were dropped. The leader of the formation can't just peel off into a steep diving turn. Possibly as a result of this, one of our aircraft — a new crew — got badly out of position."

Oh, oh... here it comes.

"It is most commendable to concentrate on flying straight and level on the bomb run. But, lordamighty, you have to stay in the formation too!"

Then O'Connor finishes by saying he thought 215 had done well for its first B24 formation trip. Of course, that's just standard pep-talk stuff; meetings always have to end on an optimistic note. So I'm not listening very carefully. But I perk up my ears when he says something about a crew getting shot up over the target, having to land with a tire punctured.

"And if Flying Officer Frazer hadn't made a damn good landing, a very soft touch-down, he'd have been in a lot worse trouble."

Hey! I always said Percy O'Connor was one of my favourite people here.

CHAPTER 10

THE ROAD TO MANDALAY

NOV. 11, 1944

Armistice Day. The date doesn't mean much here but I expect there are still big parades back home — bands playing, veterans of the Great War or the Boer War marching, commemorating comrades killed.

At school we were taught to honour those heroes, to stand silent at 11:00 a.m. and think on their sacrifices. But did we really feel great sympathy for the unknown dead, or the survivors who marched in the parades? To be honest, I don't believe I did. Sure, we were sorry there had to be wars, that soldiers had to die, that uncles had been killed. But it was all so long ago. And the marchers were such a pitiful bunch, missing an arm or a leg, or with a vacant look as if the poison gas had done something to their heads.

How could kids relate to old-timers like that? Even if you could imagine that such old gaffers had at one time been young men, must they not have been a dull-witted bunch to allow themselves to end up in such a miserable state? Any sympathy we felt, wasn't it mixed with even a trace of distaste?

Then 1939 arrived. Another war, and my generation's job to fight it. Hey, can that change your thinking in a hurry! Next year, the marchers came by, and those old men — they were us!

They were my friends and me — thirty, forty years from now. The dangers and fears that face us, they had faced the same worries decades ago... when they were our age. Guys just like us: ball players, hockey players, fellows from school. But now they're old guys, many gassed or crippled, just another bunch of men born at the wrong time.

If we live through this, will we look like that some day? Will young people years from now consider us just another bunch of silly old codgers, think we probably even began life as foolish old men?

That's when I wanted to go out on the street and shake the marchers' hands, thank them for doing what they at least thought was their duty, tell them I was sorry it hadn't worked out too well for many of them.

Around camp, since the Insein trip, a quiet week. We've even played softball... the equipment courtesy of the RCAF office in Calcutta, RAF and Aussies pressed into service to make up teams. Even in late afternoon it's hot work, the bat handle slippery from sweat. But you get a kick out of running around and shouting — acting just like you were care-free kids again.

Eddie Gilbert organized a poker game in the Mess. Nothing unusual about that except the C.O. joined us, saying he'd like to learn the game.

Cheez, would it be smart to bluff the boss out of a pot? Besides, every-one knows about beginner's luck. And that's what happened. The WingCo doesn't play a very good game, stays in every pot to the end, even with nothing — usually very expensive tactics. But not if you can draw wild cards like that. He certainly let his hair down, acted like one of the boys, had a marvellous time.

"Must have a game every week," he says.

My Dad plays a lot of poker, but he wouldn't play here. With versions of the game imported from so many countries, "dealer's choice" leads to some weird variations where you don't know the wild cards without a program.

"Bah, ladies' poker," Dad would say. "It's supposed to be a game of skill. But when you just stick to the end to see if you get undercut, or end up with three more wild cards, it's no more than a game of lay-down."

True enough, but still fun if you're winning.

A serious disappointment: P-Peter will fly no more! Never again will she point her nose skyward, raise a long, graceful wing in a steep turn. She has had it... she's going to be scrapped! When I heard that the death sentence had been pronounced, I broke into a conversation Flt/Lt Shaw was having with the M.O. Maybe he saw I was upset; he answered me.

"Might have patched it up, but needed a lot of work. And we can make good use of it for spare parts."

So Peter has been towed to the Maintenance Section. We all went to see her. To say goodbye, I suppose.

That's ridiculous, of course. It's dumb to feel an emotional attachment to a hunk of metal. And yet... those bits of aluminum have taken us across mountains and empty ocean, through lightning and flak, and never let us down. The four engines have willed the propellers to revolve a million times without a stutter, brought us home every time. Wouldn't you be bloody callous not to appreciate that?

But Peter, sitting silent and alone, is no longer a pretty sight. She is being nibbled at, has already been eaten half away. Bits of aileron, rudder, flaps — already gone. Props have been removed and there are gaping holes in the engine nacelles where #3 and #4 used to hang out. Wheels removed, she sits hobbled and immobilized on what look like bony legs with the feet amputated.

It's as if giant vultures had been clawing at her carcass, scared off by our arrival but waiting to return to their feeding. Peter can only crouch there, unable to defend herself, and wait for the end. And there's not a damn thing we can do to save her.

We headed back to the Domestic Site, sorely depressed.

NOV. 13

Rotten, rotten news. Johnny Johnson's dead. His crew, nine men, "got the chop" two nights ago... mine-laying at Moulmein. Other crews saw A/A guns firing, then a big explosion in the air.

The news hurts. Johnny, face full of freckles, was a brash, exuberant kind of person, very much alive. And now he isn't. Yes, wars are famous for turning live guys into dead ones but John was someone I knew, had partied with just days ago. My main reaction — anger! I get furious each time I hear of another life snuffed out because some dictator wants to rule the world.

An RCAF Liaison Officer dropped in today. His message: we should be using our abundance of spare time to prepare for post-war careers. The matter has come up several times in gab sessions, but the usual reaction is, "How can you plan your future when you don't even know if you'll have one?"

But he caught me at the right time. Dad has said my grandfather may be selling the family business. It's nearly bankrupt anyway, but at least it was a job. Assuming I make it home, I may have to find something else. So I signed up — an accounting course — study material to arrive in the mail.

Here come's Smitty back from the flicks. His father died recently and he's sometimes morose with worry about his mother alone in England. But I'm glad to have a room-mate to lessen the silence with occasional conversation. Not that he's a big talker or that we're inseparable; he has his own friends among the bomb-aimers he arrived with and I spend time with other groups too.

"The picture?" he says. "Terrible. The reel broke thirty times."

He sees I'm re-reading my mail. "Did I tell you I had a letter from my Mum today. She was worried to hear I'd be flying with one of those reckless Canadians, said I was to tell you to take good care of me."

"Hah! Tell her I promise."

NOV. 26

Eleven planes headed off to Burma this morning; I don't know where. I saw Brodie's crew leaving the basha early, but didn't ask. Going on their

Shower time.
Ken Cox, "Chota" Harris, Steve Brodie

first mission, they all looked tight-lipped and serious.

Another do-nothing morning. Smitty and I are back in our room, have lunched, siesta'd, tea'd and shaved. I keep checking my watch. It's six o'clock; our aircraft should soon be back.

There, I've finished my reply to Dad. His last letter said there was no decision yet about selling the family business. He had other news. Although I played with the Ottawa Senators, it was just their junior team. But, hey, my brother is trying out with the big club. Ron should make the team; even hockey players are in short supply these days. Because of a bout with pleurisy, the Army didn't want him so he's playing for Clarkson College in upstate New York, could only play week-end games with Ottawa. But I guess unusual arrangements aren't that unusual in war-time.

Peter's replacement arrived, another spanking new B24 —Serial EW 284. A black `P' has been painted on each side and Mac did another Pirate on its nose. Assuming she's at least more ours than anybody else's seemed to work the last time. Invariably, if we were flying and Peter was available, she was assigned to us. We'll try it again.

A plane is overhead now. Soon there are several, making a huge racket as they straggle in. We're all outside now, looking up, counting.

"Eight... nine... just two more to come. Yes, okay, there they are."

I'm anxious to see Brodie's guys, hear about the trip, but they'll be a while at de-briefing. There's time for a shower. Even from this distance I hear the yelps. The water comes from Artesian wells, ice-cold on hot skin, but they work well enough we've about given up the little canvas tubs.

Which will be a disappointment to the local population. Every afternoon a row of them would be sitting on their haunches a hundred feet away, grinning to see the white-skinned sahib officers trying to bathe in the ridiculous canvas pots. Not only do they think bath tubs a big joke, they also consider them unsanitary. A more fastidious person would either bathe in a stream or sponge himself down at a tap. Why would anyone wash in a tub and then continue to sit in the dirty water?

The Indians we come in contact with — admittedly not the Maharajahs and Princes of the realm — do seem an inquisitive people, maybe child-like in some ways, very curious about anything strange or new. Or is there just a shortage of entertainment in their lives?

I've never played softball in front of such a crowd. First we have to shoo them off the outfield grass; then there are rows of brown-faced fans lining the infield, sitting back on their heels, trying to understand the strange game.

Ed Gilbert flew an errand to a new base where flying machines are still a novelty. "For our take-off, villagers lined the runway for half a mile."

A letter came today from a fellow I didn't expect to hear from again. Tom Robertson was the navigator in my crew when we were finishing OTU in England, the one who was posted off to Italy when we were picked for India.

Did I have trouble finding a navigator there! The first fellow was in a terrible fog. Finally, on a night cross-country trip, he got us fifty miles off track, smack into the London balloon barrage. For the longest ten minutes, our radio picked up the whining bleeps warning us we'd blundered right into the balloons and their dangling cables. Then we were coned by search-lights, so unbelievably bright they blinded you.

Next day, nervous, I went to see the Chief Flying Instructor, a tough-talking old WingCo wearing wings he must have earned flying Sopwith Camels.

"I... uh... want a new navigator."

I felt rotten about trying to ditch the lad but it was clearly a matter of life-or-death. And we're entitled; we've been told it's important to have confidence in your crew mates. If the chemistry isn't right, ask for a change. Then why had the old CFI never heard of that?

"Ridiculous, a pilot changing his crew! What do you think's so special about yourself that a fully-trained man isn't good enough for you?"

Plus other questions I couldn't answer. But I kept insisting. He banged the table, repeated that he couldn't change crews on somebody's whim, there was no one else available anyway. Nevertheless, next day the DRO's spelled out that a Sgt Shugar was now the navigator in the Frazer crew.

Max Shugar had a lot of smarts, but after a couple of weeks he was sent to another station. I don't know why; maybe he demanded another pilot.

Tom Robertson, an Aussi, was his replacement and we became great friends. But when I drew the India posting, Tom was shot off to Italy. His letter mentions Capri and Sorrento; I expect both are prettier than Calcutta.

Here come the Brodie guys, looking hot and tired, but with grins from ear to ear. We're all out to greet them, ask where they went.

"Pyinmana," Ken Cox says. "North of Rangoon, half way to Mandalay."

"Good hits on the railway tracks," Steve answers me. "No opposition at all. But I want out of these duds, have a shower. Tell you more at dinner."

NOV. 28

"On the road to Man-da-lay-ay."

An old song, one a visiting baritone might sing at a concert in the church basement, the tune peppier than most at such affairs. And the lyrics do get you thinking about "paddles chunking from Rangoon to Mandalay," and the dawn coming up "like thunder over China 'cross the bay."

But I never expected to see the place, even from a mile up.

It was a combined operation, 99 and 215, Percy O'Connor leading. Past Chittagong, it's straight east over the Chin Hills. Pretty big hills. Mount Victoria is the grand-daddy at ten thousand feet, but not a worry in clear weather,

What would the opposition be? Flak? Of course, and heavy. But fighters? The Intelligence bloke wasn't sure. "Maybe yes, maybe no; about fifty-fifty."

Hah, that's clever; forecast something is a 50/50 proposition... or 60/40 or whatever... and nobody can say you were wrong.

Once over the hills and reducing height — coasting downhill, as it were — the engines were having an easy time, uncharacteristically quiet. Looking at the planes around us, I got a mental picture of birds drifting soundlessly across the landscape. To villagers down below, wouldn't we look like that, 21 hungry hawks — huge, ugly and terrifying — swooping over the mountain range, gliding silently into the valley in search of prey.

But our prey had already been selected — railway cars and locomotives in the marshalling yards in Mandalay, the third attack in a row against the enemy rail system in Burma.

"The Jap northern outpost at Myitkyina has been re-taken," the I.O. man told us at briefing. "The Japs are in full retreat. The next major objective is Mandalay. Our forces are now attacking Bhamo, just one hundred and seventy-five miles to the north. As almost all enemy supplies go through Mandalay, the rail facilities there must be smashed."

No fighters appeared; otherwise it was much like at Insein. Lots of flak — cotton balls floating in the air that start small, then grow. But with a short life span, they soon start to disintegrate, lose their roundness, get ragged at the edges. On their last legs, they drift past your window, a wispy shapelessness such as you'd see driving a car through occasional fog. But they mark where a shell exploded. Flak must be a lot like rockets in a fireworks show, a little explosion in the air and then all the pretty lights cascading across the sky. Except here they're pieces of metal, sharp and hard. If the explosion is close enough, it's a quick goodbye.

I tried to scrunch down, pull my neck into my shoulders, make myself as small as possible. That's crazy, but I couldn't stop myself.

There was the usual rumble as the bomb doors opened, the swoosh of air flooding through the whole plane as Peter's under-belly was uncovered.

Smitty put his bombs on the target, no flak hit us, and we flew home. Piece of cake!

NOV. 29

Just a seven hour trip, P-Peter was back from Mandalay at 3:00 p.m.

At de-briefing, the Intelligence Officer said all crews were reporting a good concentration of bursts on the target, about 75 percent of the sidings smashed. And three-quarters is apparently considered a hundred percent in this business. However, the I.O. listens to you with a frown, his manner saying he'll accept your report only when it's confirmed by the target photos.

Abdul arrived with our tea and biscuit even before we had all our gear stored away. An hour to relax, then a shave, shower, into slacks and bush jacket fresh from the dhobie, and over to the Mess. A stop at the bar to pick up a gin-lime, then into the dining room, all spiffed up, sanitized, hair combed down.

Sitting at a table, cutlery laid out before me on the white table-cloth, waiting for Abdul to serve the curried chicken, my thought is that today's flak over Mandalay seems very, very distant. Waging war by bomber raid is a strange business, our living conditions so different from infantry soldiers slogging it out in the field.

"Much like medieval times," an English guy agrees. "Like the Crusades. Knights would go off to fight the Infidel all day, but the battle was called off at sundown; then they'd all return to their tents where most of the comforts of home awaited them, sometimes even wives or girl friends."

That's admittedly more than we have here but, yes, some similarities. We went off to the battlefield this morning, were involved in the violence for a time, and are now home for the night. We think our comforts are modest enough but they'd look like luxury to Army guys fighting in the jungles north of Mandalay right now.

Most of the boys are still at the bar, just a few ready to start dinner. Mostly, we're the ones who missed our regular lunch today. Looking down the table, another thought materializes. I never noticed it before but each of us is looking as starched and laundered as he ever has in his life.

Hey, haven't I seen this scene in the movies? The very proper

Englishman, living in dark- est Africa or wherever, each night getting `dressed for dinner'? Though tigers might be pacing in the shadows around the camp, he would come to table dressed-to-the-nines as if dining in London with elegant friends. The scene was always presented as comedy, but... aren't we doing the same thing?

It's not a firm Mess rule. Come down late from flying and you can just eat- as-you-are; otherwise, it's into your finest khaki. Does it make sense? Howard Johns was at our table, and the Adj likes that sort of question.

"Hmmmm. Well, I suppose it does serve a pur- pose. We've all heard of people living in isolated places who become — is the

Dressed for dinner

American term `bushed'? — their self-discipline deteriorating over time to the point where they become less and less caring of cleanliness and appearance. Especially in this environment, this climate, there's danger we can become depressed, apathetic. It's something we all have to fight.

"I think it's especially important for you flying types to resist any tendency towards slovenliness. Your lives depend on staying razor-sharp. Might be difficult to prove any direct connection between neatness and staying clear-headed, but I'm not sure it doesn't exist. At any rate, a daily scrub-up can't hurt."

I'm enjoying the old Adj. "I was a teacher," he told me. "Small school in Devon. Taught English, Philosophy, other courses. Now I'm an Adjutant but I hope to get back to teaching some day."

I like to sit beside Howard; he has interesting opinions and comments to amuse or make you think. For example, the Signals Officer was telling us he was 39, had a birthday coming up, was bemoaning the impending mile- stone.

"If you're approaching forty," the Adj said, "and want sympathy, I think you'll have a better chance of getting it from someone not nearing sixty."

"An outdoor man?" he said another time. "Fisherman, hunter, devotee of the Great Outdoors... isn't that what every red-blooded chap is supposed to be. But I've decided I'm not like that. To me, the most exciting thing in the world is a new idea, a shiny, sparkling new thought I've never come across before. Call me an `indoor man' and I wouldn't be ashamed at all."

Another night, "Have you noticed that most people have specialties... certain fields in which they have considerable expertise, others in which they have none. A prime requisite of a smart fellow, it seems to me, is that he be able to distinguish one from the other."

"Middle-class morality? Oh, I think it's unfairly maligned. The upper classes often feel that ordinary rules of conduct are appropriate for ordinary people, don't apply to them. What some call the lower classes sometimes think, 'Why should we care about standards of behaviour? What have we got to lose?' Whether a society maintains any standards at all will usually depend on the middle class."

I want to get back to the room to re-read my mail — four letters from Jean and one from Dad — plus seven cartons of cigs. Two main items in Dad's letter: the family business has been sold and Dad is now looking for a job. Which is also what I'll have to do when this is over. And my brother didn't stick with Senators; they decided they couldn't rely on weekend players.

Dad's letters always include a joke, usually pretty bad. At his Lions Club, the man making the introductions was a friend of the guest speaker.

"We have had men address us here," the friend said, "where giving them a good drink and a good meal would almost certainly fetch up a good speech. Today's guest is different. Give him a good drink and he'll give you a speech that'll bring up a good meal."

CHAPTER 11

LAND OF THE FREE

DEC. 2, 1944

"Lea' me alone. What time's it? Four thirty? Bloody hell!"

But the voice keeps badgering, persisting. "Dammit, what d'you want? Who are you? Go away." But it won't stop. "A'right, what is it?"

"It's Taffy, sir... from the bar. You're flying this morning, have to get up. Sign here please... yes, right there. Very good, sir. You'll stay awake now? Mr Smith too? You won't go back to sleep?"

Cheez, my head wants to fall back on the pillow, but I can't let it. Guys have done that, were late for take-off or missed it altogether, then claimed Taffy didn't wake them. Now he makes you sign your name.

Yeah, I remember. It's another search mission, this time a US plane ditched in the sea, one of those new B29 monsters they call the Superfortress.

I'm sitting on the edge of the charpoy, lamp flicked on, rubbing my eyes, lighting my first cigarette of the day — if you'd call this day. Taffy must have roused Smitty too because I see him emerging from his mosquito net. It's a weird sight; pulling the folds of netting over his head, he looks like a larva coming out of its cocoon. Can you be asleep if you're amused?

I say "G'mornin," and he mutters something. His eyes aren't fully open yet but he remembers to knock his shoes together in case a snake spent the night there. Also, his head is cocked to one side, listening for mosquitoes; but I just checked, don't think there are any in the room.

Water sloshed in your face, you're a notch closer to full consciousness. You hang the towel on a nail and stop to listen to the silence, the stillness of the hour before dawn. Even the birds aren't up yet.

It's a noisy society we have here, not only people but raucous engine noises. Flying, it's hour after hour of those throbbing Pratt and Whitneys. Even on the ground you hear aircraft passing overhead day and night. At the drome, the ear-splitting racket of engines being run up at full blast — for testing or warm-up or take-off — is never-ending. We live in a deluge of decibels.

But not right now. The only crew going today, Smitty and I must be the only ones awake... could fantasize we're the only ones left in camp, that the others all folded their tents in the night and slipped away. To hear someone cough in the next room is vaguely reassuring.

Last night's briefing was a rush job; maybe you can't expect too much for a one-aircraft mission. But the I.O. said two kites from 99 were going and there'd be American planes out searching. But the plane's distress call was garbled. It's a big ocean to search if you can't zero in on one sector.

"Ready, Smitty? We're late. Got a torch?"

It's a nippy December morning as we make our way to the Mess. Dammit, no one was alerted to feed us; we have to settle for bread and jam. There's a suggestion of pink in the eastern sky as the lorry arrives, even lights in some bashas as we stop to pick up the others. Yawning, rubbing their eyes, they look the sleepiest ragtag of a crew you could imagine.

"Mac, is that all you have?" I've put McIlwaine in charge of rations, today from the Sergeants' Mess; the carton under his arm isn't very big.

"Did you tell them we'd be away all day... two meals for eleven of us?"

"I told them. They said this is all we get."

I do a quick count. Okay, ten plus me, so let's go; we're late. It's darn cool even wearing slacks and battle dress jacket. Maybe I should sit up beside the driver. Most captains do but, no, we're not that kind of crew.

P-Peter was due for maintenance so we're flying Q-Queenie. It's chief, Sgt Beddoe, told me yesterday they were still patching flak holes from `Q's` Mandalay trip but promised they'd be finished by take-off time. He and his men are waiting at the `Q` Dispersal, assure me the plane is ready.

"You're loaded up, sir," he said. "Petrol... three thousand gallons."

In the plane's belly, instead of bombs, four big auxiliary tanks, two on each side of the catwalk. Taxi-ing, Queenie is going to gurgle.

It's 6:30 already, but I won't rush pre-flight checks. At ten to seven, we're ready to roll. If we get lucky and find that B29 crew, they won't complain because we're twenty minutes late.

Q-Queenie gets us into the air, and the trip to our assigned search field is uneventful. The weather's okay — strato-cumulus at 3,000 feet — but we'll be staying below that.

At 1010 hours, we start to patrol. For ten hours, we patrol.

It's a `square search' this time, where you start in the centre of your zone and fly a square route around that point. You then begin another four-sided path just outside the first, then repeat and repeat with slightly larger patterns each time — what might be called `concentric squares' if there is such a term. The navigator must do a lot of record-keeping, the timing by stop-watch of each leg unending. The job is extremely dull. It's true, war can be unbelievably boring.

Such a vast ocean. I liked Brodie's story about the two country lads crossing the Atlantic on a troopship. With nothing but sea in every direction, Zeb says, "By heck, Zeke, that's a lot of water." And Zeke replies, "Yep, and that's only the top of it."

With visibility two miles, we're flying at 800 feet on paths three miles apart. Using binoculars to sweep the horizon, the boys on watch duty are satisfied the seas are empty on either side. Jock and I are being as accurate as we can with course headings. I'd rather miss a target with our bombs than miss a dinghy on the water.

Mac serves the lunch, a slab of bully beef between two pieces of bread, each more than an inch thick. The sandwich is too thick to go directly into your mouth; you have to nibble at the edges to get it down to size.

At four o'clock, the Brits must have afternoon tea even when it's only tepid water. But there's a biscuit each. And Mac has a nice surprise: a juicy mango is about as good as a drink.

We've seen the last of the sun for this day. When it's taken it's plunge over the horizon, the ocean becomes an even more lonesome place. And all this time we haven't seen a damn thing, not even a false alarm. If that B29 ditched in this area, it's beneath the waves by now.

It's 2030 hours now. We've had dinner — more bread, more bully beef — and both Jock and I had a half-hour nap.

Here's Bob: "We've now covered our search area. Of course, it's twelve hours since we saw land. If the wind has changed much and I've missed it, we could be out miles. What now?"

I'm feeling wide awake. We want to be sure we haven't missed any cracks. Also... and maybe this shouldn't be a consideration, but it is... we're putting in `op time.' Just the sixty percent variety — six hours for each ten — but we're doing it without getting shot at.

I check the gauges; we've lots of petrol. The auxiliary tanks have been drained and we're now drawing from the regular supply in the wings... not so much kept in the wing tanks as in self-sealing bags stored inside the tanks. The bags are two layers of rubbery stuff with a sticky substance in between. If a bullet goes through the bag, the gooey material congeals, seals the hole. A great invention, well worth a minor flaw: the gauges are then not completely accurate. But Arthur keeps a petrol consumption log as a double check.

"Petrol for four hours," he says.

That's plenty. It's only three hours to base. I get Jock's attention, draw a square in the air with my finger, and he shrugs. We'll do another half hour. Sixty percent of thirty is another 18 minutes towards our 300 hour total. Every bit helps.

Q-Queenie — after 17 hours

It's nine o'clock. But when I suggest we might still do another 15 minutes, Jock demurs. "Time to returrrn to base. It'll be midnight then... petrrol getting shorrt, and we could be away off course, have trrouble finding wherrre we are when we rrreach the coast."

Jock is often overly cautious, but this time he could be right.

"Okay, crew, we'll head for home."

The trip back is always impossibly long. Bob keeps busy taking star shots, gives us several course corrections. About 11:3O, we see the first lights down below, too many and too close together to be fishing boats. We're over land, but where? It's a long coastline and no road signs.

But we have the best navigator on the Squadron. There's just enough light from the quarter moon for Smitty to make out this darker blob on the water. The odd-shaped island — like a piece of jigsaw puzzle — is a perfect match with an island on his map. And we're only twenty miles off track!

One small course change and in thirty minutes the bright lights of the Digri field appear in front of us. I bump the ground hard on the landing, but who cares? We're home. My watch tells me it's 1155 hours; we've been in the air 17 hours and 5 minutes. Jock was right; that's enough.

Out on the tarmac, my legs need some practice walking before they can do it right. Sgt Beddoe, with one of his men, had been waiting with his torch to guide us into the Dispersal. He comes over to greet us.

"Welcome back, sir. How was Queenie? Any problems? We were starting to wonder how your petrol was holding out."

"The plane was great... in beautiful shape. Petrol? No problem... a hundred gallons left. Where's the lorry? We're ready for the sack."

"Be here any minute. They were waiting till they heard you overhead."

Waiting for the Transport lorry, I can do some knee bends. But here's Beddoe coming back — at a trot. He interrupts me in mid-bend.

"Mr Frazer! Airmen Thompson just checked your tanks. They're empty... almost bone dry. Not five minutes left!"

"What! That's crazy... got to be wrong. We had a hundred gallons."

"No, sir," the young fellow with him insists. He's holding a long stick, his voice breathless. "The wing tanks. Nearly dry... I checked... with the dip-stick... almost empty."

"Ridiculous. The logs showed lots of gas left. Gauges showed over a hundred gallons. Not exact readings, but they couldn't be out that much."

"But they could, sir," Beddoe says.

"Arthur!" I shout. He comes hurrying, almost running. There must have been something in my voice. He doesn't believe the airman's story either.

But one dip-stick is worth a thousand calculations. Arthur's gone up on the wing with the airman to re-check. The lorry is here now, but we've got to find out. Now he's back; even in the dark, his face is white.

"It's true. Almost dry. Not five minutes... even less."

Jeez! Not enough gas to make it home if Bob's navigation-by-the-stars had left us fifty miles off track at the coast instead of twenty. Or if we'd needed a few minutes to figure out just where we were. Not even enough to go around the circuit again if I'd misjudged the first landing approach.

And, omigawd, what if I'd insisted we fly that extra 15 minute leg?

Can you feel mortified, disgusted, ashamed, sick to your stomach — and lucky — all at the same time? You can, and angry too. All those feelings are jumbled together, but maybe the strongest is anger — but who at? At myself? I'll sure as hell get into that tomorrow.

We climb on the truck... once again everyone very solemn, very quiet.

DEC 4

Today's my birthday; I'm 24... already hoping for 25.

There was a 'do' tonight to mark it. Even the WingCo drifted back to the lounge after dinner for his buckshee drink; anyone notching another year on his belt buys a round all around. We get lots of parties started that way; with sixty officers, there's a birthday bash most weeks.

Another shindig was to celebrate Steve Brodie's promotion to Flight Lieutenant. Guys serving overseas are normally awarded the rank two years after being commissioned. But every squadron has an 'Establishment' quota; if short one Flight-Loot, the senior pilot of Flying Officer rank fills the spot. Steve's been an F/O the longest, is the logical choice anyway, and accepted the congratulations with the usual bemused twinkle in his eye.

Almost anything is an excuse for a party here. A national birthday is always a major affair. Even good war news can provide a reason. Liquor is not too expensive; you can get a birthday bash started for little more than a day's pay. A pleasant result is you have guys coming by to offer greetings.

"Happy birthday!" they say. "Hope you make it to your next one."

His chin bobbing up and down to add an "amen" each time, Smitty will have a sore neck tomorrow.

I'm enjoying the fellows in the Mess. Even from our first arrival, they were friendly enough, but the way you'd be friendly to a stranger. I wasn't yet one of them; they knew it and I knew it. But the Insein trip helped us become one of the group, largely because we got shot up a bit. Strangely, I think the veterans are quicker to accept someone who has been in a spot of trouble; don't know why that is, though.

And if any of them didn't know my name before, they know it now. After that episode when we stayed up too long, and landed with the tanks dry, my name may now be famous all through the Royal Air Force.

"Hey, m'ite, better t'ike an extra five-gallon can next time."

"I say, old chap, the Lib requires one hundred octane. Were you testing whether she'd run on zero octane?"

No worse than I deserved, the remarks were mostly made in good humour, especially by other captains who seem careful not to bad-mouth others in the same line of work. Maybe like doctors. I've never been offered a membership card, but I suspect that somewhere a society exists — perhaps called "The Brotherhood of Aircraft Captains."

Yesterday, I marched into O'Connor's office to talk about gas gauges.

"You admit, Frazer, that classroom instructors at Kolar did mention that petrol gauges weren't perfectly accurate, even if they failed to warn you they could be wrong by a hundred gallons. And no flying instructor mentioned it? Bad show, right? Perhaps we should put a notice up. Or is everybody here quite knowledgeable about the problem now? Thanks to you, right? "

He didn't believe me! I was starting to doubt my own memory. But guys who had been with me at Kolar agree little was said there about the gauges.

Bob and Jock and I then had a session with Arthur to look over his calculations based on tables giving the gallons per mile used at various engine settings. His figures checked out.

But Flt/Lt Shaw made an unprecedented stop at my table during lunch.

"Heard you were checking your petrol figures, Frazer. We convinced your Engineer there was zero chance your tanks had not been properly topped up before take-off. Also, that the consumption tables we supply are accurate under normal conditions. But was there anything unusual about your trip... apart from its length? Seventeen hours is rather pushing things a bit. But I was wondering, for example, if you had your ball turret extended for long."

"Well, yes... maybe ten hours. Our ball gunner likes it there."

"Then that's your answer. With turret down, there's extra drag, would increase petrol consumption. The tables we prepared wouldn't fully allow for that. I'll get a bulletin out right away."

So that was it. How many other things about the B24 do we not know?

I'll try to finish these letters. But what can I say? Officers' mail isn't censored but it's not smart to blab about ops. And I certainly can't tell them I almost flew our plane out of gas.

I'll tell them about our meals. Breakfast was different: a huge duck egg to go with the beans. Lunch was rice and stringy mutton. For dinner, a big treat: tomato catsup all the way from Canada to spice up the spam. I could add that, with a big crowd at the tables, the fans whirring at full speed, and a lot of joking and laughter, the Mess can be a very happy place.

Maybe I'll add that the M.O. has ruled, "No more wedge caps or officers' flat hats. To protect against the sun, either an Australian bush hat or a pith helmet." But who'd want to be seen in a pith helmet?

Down at the Flight Office today, some good news — word that two gunners of a 355 crew shot down in October are prisoners; the Nips don't usually report POWs. But two kites from 99, on a formation trip to Siam, collided at 10,000 feet —crashed in the sea, no survivors.

Before the gunners headed off to clean and oil their guns — a daily chore because of blowing sand getting into everything —I talked to Jim Slight. He's still peeved he didn't get credit for the fighter shot down at Insein, that the Gunnery Leader did instead.

O'Connor has decided to re-assign all aircraft to different dispersal pads. The ground crew aren't allowed to taxi planes, so Jock and I got the chore this afternoon. Still managed a few minutes with my feet up before dinner. The news that I was having a birthday spread quickly and a big crowd was waiting for me at the bar. All in all, a pretty good day.

DEC. 10

Today — Siam.

That's the old name. Since 1939, they prefer Thailand — "the land of the free." Though maybe not as free as they'd like now they're allies of the Japs, the flag of the Rising Sun flying high in their country.

At the briefing, a geography lesson. It seems the Nips have a major problem keeping their army in Burma supplied with war stuff all the way from Japan. The sea route — the South China Sea to Singapore, then up

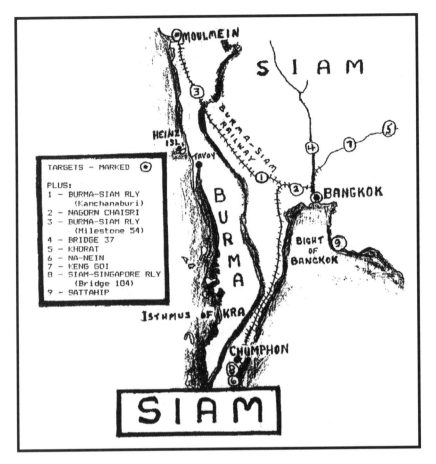

TARGETS - MARKED ⊙

PLUS:
1 - BURMA-SIAM RLY
    (Kanchanaburi)
2 - NAGORN CHAISRI
3 - BURMA-SIAM RLY
    (Milestone 54)
4 - BRIDGE 37
5 - KHORAT
6 - NA-NEIN
7 - KENG GOI
8 - SIAM-SINGAPORE RLY
    (Bridge 104)
9 - SATTAHIP

the Indian Ocean to Rangoon — is almost four thousand miles. And since Uncle Sam whomped the Jap fleet at the Battle of Midway, Tojo no longer controls the seas.

To forge a new route that's less vulnerable to warships and submarines, also a thousand miles shorter, they've built this Burma-Siam Railroad which cuts across the land bridge separating the Indian Ocean from the Pacific. A bit of line at either end was already there. The new addition — 250 miles —means trains can now run from Bangkok on the Gulf of Siam to Moulmein on the Bay of Bengal, then right into central Burma.

"Our people surveyed the route for a rail link years ago," the I.O. said, "but abandoned the idea — impossible terrain, jungle, monsoons and malaria. But starting in September of `42, the Japs completed the line in just over a year. How did they manage the feat? With slave labour!

"Thousands of our men, taken prisoner at Singapore and elsewhere, as well as civilians over-run in the Jap advance, were forced to labour on the construction, were worked unmercifully hard under appalling conditions.

A great many died of overwork, disease, malnutrition and beatings. Native Siamese, Burmese and Malays — two to three hundred thousand — were also conscripted for the job, and treated no better.

"Since completed about a year ago, train loads of war supplies have been flooding into Burma. Your job is to reduce that flow to a trickle."

But I'll also do my damnedest not to end up in one of those prison camps. When the railway was completed, most prisoners were returned to Singapore, some were sent to Japan, but many are still there to maintain the line.

The railway has already been bombed once by Libs. This time we have nine planes. Also, 99 Squadron is coming with us, but not in formation. Each aircraft will get there on its own, choose targets within the area assigned.

I know fighter planes are sent to seek out "targets of opportunity" — but four-engine bombers?

Our area is at the far end. Kanchanaburi, one of the main towns, is seventy miles from Bangkok; we have the stretch west of there.

"Navigator to pilot. Should be seeing those Preparis Islands by now, Wal; that's where we turn east. Everybody watch for them."

It's 1300 hours. We left Digri at 0830, came down the Bay of Bengal over water all the way. Instead of short-cutting across the main part of Burma, we're skirting around it. But that makes it a long mission — 14 hours, 2,200 miles round-trip — so we don't have a big bomb load. With 2,500 gallons of gas and the usual 972 pounds of oil, that leaves room for nine assorted bombs totalling 2,900 pounds.

It feels strange there are no other planes around us. Not that flying alone over the sea is so frightening to us now but, going all the way to Siam, I'd prefer a little company. There have to be other kites... twenty of them... but we haven't seen any for three hours. Not one.

Yet 215 all took off in sequence and started on the same heading. We're proceeding independently, of course, each navigator choosing the course for his crew. You have to expect some difference of opinion as to wind shifts. Maybe small differences, over time, mean you end up miles apart.

Yeah, maybe that's it.

Ten minutes later, still no islands. Bob did sound puzzled; if we keep pointing south, we'll hit Antarctica before anything else. We better talk.

"That's right, skip, ten minutes overdue. Maybe we missed them."

"Yeah, wondering about that. What now?"

"I suppose we should turn east, make a landfall somewhere, then figure out where we are. The coast runs north and south so we'll hit it some place. But right now... sorry 'bout that... I don't know where we are."

Cheez, six hundred miles since we saw land, and we're lost. Not that

I blame Bob; it's easy to do on a long sea leg. But it's not a good feeling. High, high on the list of things needed to give you a secure feeling in the air is knowing where the hell you are.

I swing Peter to port and Jim drops a smoke-pot to take another drift reading. Bob is back on the line. "Wind has picked up. Instead of ten mph, it's over twenty. We're a lot closer to Burma than I thought. Change course to oh nine five. We should hit the Tenasserim Coast within two hours."

Tenasserim? Yeah, that's the land that runs down towards Singapore, Burma on one side and Siam on the other. Further south where it gets even narrower — only thirty miles at one point — it's called the Isthmus of Kra. Then it becomes Malaya, but we'll never get that far south.

This trip is a repeat of the op two days ago. Bombing from low level isn't something we've ever done so I talked to guys who'd been on that one.

Number one, they said, no Jap fighters. Second, A/A fire was minimal. But flying as low as 300 feet, they were peppered by machine guns, even rifles. The gunners strafed trains, but several crews admitted the majority of their bombs missed.

Which doesn't surprise me. At 170 mph, you're approaching the aiming point at 250 feet per second. To place a single bomb on a target, the bomb-aimer needs split-second timing; push the button one-fifth of a second too soon or too late and you've missed by fifty feet.

Dammit, still no other kites. Could Bob have miscalculated? Are other planes all flying in a bunch, only P-Peter out of step? Or were all planes recalled to base but we missed the signal?

"Nose gunner, skippah. Land ahead. But they're just islands. Several... one, two, three... one after another. Lots of water behind them."

Bob answers: "In that pattern, they could be the Heinz Islands. Is there another one... a bigger one on the left? That'd confirm it."

It checks out; we know where we are again. The wind has blown us fifty miles off track. Bob gives us a course correction. We come to the coast, and then big hills. Across them now, the terrain is less rugged, solid green again with a few villages. Smitty, map-reading, confirms we're now over Siam.

"Top gunner to pilot... a Lib! Ten o'clock level!"

Hot damn, there it is, a friendly B24. We're not here alone after all. Our paths are converging and we're close enough now to see its tail markings. Yeah, one of our 215 planes, either `O' or `Q'. Someone at the beam hatch just waved. How about that; come to Siam and meet your friends.

"Ball gunner to pilot!" Jonesy's in his turret. "Another Lib, below us. It's a 99 kite... a white circle on the rudder."

Double good, more company. But below us? Yeah, we're still at

Royal Air Force

Bombs over Burma-Siam Railway

5,000; maybe I should start letting down. The plan is to patrol and bomb at about 2,000, depending on visibility, surrounding hills, amount of gunfire. Bob checks his maps, confirms we'll be safe enough at 3,000 feet for now.

"Watch for the railroad," he says.

"And other planes," I add. The two aircraft from 99 colliding last week — that shocked me! Now there's another Lib ahead. With 21 aircraft in the area, cruising the same rail line at low level, it could be a traffic jam. Maybe too much company isn't a great idea after all.

"Skip," — it's Bob — "Smitty's not well. Maybe you should talk to him."

"Smitty, what's wrong? Should Bob take over on the bomb-sight?"

"No, I'm okay... just a touch of flu. I'll be fine."

Crackle. It's Phil. "Bob, there's your railroad... down in a gully."

It's following a small stream; we stay to starboard to keep the tracks in sight out my window. Our altimeter says 2,000 feet; the hills on either side are almost that. Concentrating on not running into one, I can only afford the occasional peek. But it's easy to see it was a tough construction job. In several places the rails are laid on rickety-looking trestles hanging onto cliffs right over the river gorge.

Then Smitty, map-reading: "A hamlet, two small streams coming into the river from north and south." It's a good pin-point. Bob says we've reached the stretch of railway we're to cover.

What a weird mission for bombers: "Locate and attack." And I don't really care for being this low, only a few feet above some of those hills.

What if the Japs have gun batteries on them?

"Phil here, skippah... another Lib ahead... about a mile. He's turning, coming back towards us. Maybe swinging around to make an attack on something. Yes, yes... a train, stopped on the tracks. Can we fire?"

"Uh... yes, I guess so."

Our guns start blasting. I chance a quick look. It's a train, medium-sized — a locomotive, ten wagons, steam rising from the smoke stack, dust kicking up where our shells hit. Now we've passed it. I also spot the Lib on our beam, a quarter mile away, going in the opposite direction.

The gunners are excited, shouting they got some hits on the railway cars. Not the locomotive itself; armour-piercing shells would puncture its boiler but then you'd see steam escaping.

What now? Circle around, make a bomb run? Or does that target belong to the other crew? What's fair? We weren't told that. But we're already past it. Should we go on... find our own target? We were told there'd be plenty for all. But the hills are suddenly higher than we are. Push the throttles forward and pull the nose up. We've climbed to 3,000. The locomotive's behind us now; okay, we'll leave it, go on ahead.

"Nose gun here. A Lib... away below us... just skimming the river."

Cheez, we weren't briefed to go that low. Now I see it, away below the hill-tops. It makes me ashamed to be up at 3,000, especially as the hills don't seem as high again. I'll let down to 2,000... low enough.

It's Smitty again: "We're crossing a bridge, another trestle affair. We could go after that... though I'd rather try for a train."

"Sure... okay... keep looking."

Now Phil reports another B24 ahead... but it's coming towards us, over on the left. Whishhh! I just saw a flash of something go by, much too close! Damn, it's too crowded here.

Smitty, sounding sweaty: "A train, two locos... parked on a siding, under camouflage netting; almost missed them. They'd be worthwhile."

"Okay, let's get 'em. I'll circle back. Anything behind?"

I get an "all clear," make a big swing. "What you want to drop?"

"Just one bomb, a `sighter'... get the range."

The gunners are pestering me, asking if they can fire. Why not? They're likely more accurate than the bombs. So don't waste ammo but strafe anything interesting. All except Eddie; the top gunner can't see the ground anyway and we need somebody watching for other aircraft, both Japs and ours.

"I see them," Smitty tells me. "Turn ten degrees to port. Doors open... left, left!" Our guns are blasting but I hear him say, "Bomb away."

Phil shouts, "Machine gun... underneath... firing. Get it, Jonesy!"

Then there's bedlam, Jonesy never so animated. "I got them... machine gun nest... on the hill, straight below. I got some hits... right in the middle.

I'm sure I did... they stopped firing!"

"Missed the train," Smitty says. "An overshoot. Let's try again... two bombs. I'll release earlier."

We've circled to attack again from the same direction. But I'm more concerned about the Jap guns. "Gunners, those machine guns. Ignore the train till you're certain they aren't firing."

We're approaching the target again. Both Phil and Jonesy are shouting, "Nothing from the machine gun... go for the locos!"

And now Smitty's yelling, "We got it. Maybe not the locos, but at least some of the trucks; there's stuff flying everywhere. Now it's just a cloud of dust... can't see a thing."

The gunners are shouting too — what they hit, what somebody else hit, agreeing the bombs landed right alongside the train. All jabbering like a flock of crows. I bellow to get them to shut up.

Just back from Siam

"Settle down! We're not through yet. Smitty, what next? Another run, try for the engines, give the gunners another crack at it?"

We're swinging around for another attack but the downwind leg has to be extended. Two more Libs are coming down the river, one behind the other, a mile apart, passing on our left. Now the way is clear again. Here we go. Smitty's set his switches to release three bombs. The smoke from the first attack should be clear by now.

But it isn't. "It's all smoke and dust. But I'll estimate... I can still see the track. Hold her steady... bombs gone!"

As usual, there's a wait for the bombs to hit, to hear the results, but not a long wait when you're this low. Meanwhile, our guns are making a racket, the stink terrible. Then the shouts start again. Mixed reports.

From Smitty: "Couldn't see where they hit... too much smoke... but one landed right in the middle, maybe right on the locos."

"Got some wagons," from the gunners. "Hit several. Some on fire."

All's quiet again. What now? We still have three bombs left. What should we do? Cheez, what a crazy kind of mission — haphazard, disorganized; you're not sure what to do next. What we are doing is just following the rail line. A glance at my watch tells me we can still afford a little time. I guess if we see another target we'll go after it; otherwise there's Kanchanaburi.

Jock has the controls and I can study the railroad and the thick jungle on both sides. Now we're passing a spot where the tracks squeeze through a deep cut in solid rock. And occasionally there's a compound with poor-looking bamboo huts that look unoccupied. Is that where the POWs were kept?

We pass another train, freight cars burning well enough they don't need more attention. The gunners want to fire anyway, are unhappy. I say, "Dammit, save some ammo. Jap fighters could show up."

Next is the dummy; we were told about it. Out in the open, under a net that doesn't camouflage it very well, sits a single solitary locomotive. It looks real, but it's a fake, just cardboard and lumber.

"Navigator here. Kanchanaburi in five minutes, skip."

Cheez, already? That's our secondary target. I guess we'll take it. But I forget what we're to attack there.

"Railway station," Smitty says. "Storage sheds south of that. A POW camp alongside... close. And a gun position beside it. I'll be careful... aim for the station, but make sure any error is to the south. Can we do a dummy run?"

"No. Just one run, then we get the hell out of here."

It really is time to think about our petrol. Another reason... 2,000 feet is damned low when the town has guns. Okay, here's the city — buildings and streets ahead. Here we go. Just wish my stomach would stop churning.

Smitty feeds me the course changes, then says the bombs have dropped. But my mind is mostly on the damn flak. It's not thick, not like Rangoon or even Mandalay, but accurate. We're only at 2,000, and every gun is pointed at us! I'm holding my breath — how long can you hold your breath?

I think the puffs are getting scarcer already. Yes, they're done.

Now Smitty's shouting. "A good hit! We got the stores buildings... right in the middle..."

Jonesy, and Mac at the beam gun, are hollering to confirm this. When they slow to catch their breath, the voice from the rear turret is agreeing.

"Rearrr gunnerr heerre. One building exploded... big firre going."

I've swung Peter to starboard, away from the town, out over thick jungle again. Now Jock and I have to go to work, get this aircraft home. Already, Bob is giving us the course to follow, and our ETA at Digri.

"What's that? Eleven o'clock?"

Cheez. Seven hours to base!

DEC. 13

Photos developed, the assessment is that the Squadron did worthwhile damage to the Railroad: eight locos shot up; fires started on four trains, one carrying ammo because the recce plane saw it still exploding an hour later; in Kanchanaburi, several buildings left burning.

But a prize to the kite collecting the most punctures would go to the WingCo. Other crews keep tabs on the C.O. and Flight Commanders as to the trips they go on. Any indication they were skipping the tougher ones would be noticed. But that's not happening; it's more the opposite.

In fact, does a C.O. have to set an example, attack from lower than anybody else? Sindall's run at a train was made from 800 feet, and he went into Kanchanaburi just after us, but at 500 feet. On the way home, he spotted a Jap ship in Heinz Bay and strafed it from mast level.

Am I ashamed I never ventured below 2,000 feet all day? I'm not. The rear gunner in the WingCo's plane was killed when shrapnel got him. I might rate as a 'chicken' captain on the day's effort, but we're all live chickens.

All our planes got home okay though Len Cameron in Queenie was a day late, stopping at Chittagong for gas. We can do that; in an emergency, landing either at Chitters or Cox's Bazaar on the Burma side of the Bay of Bengal will get your wheels on the ground at least an hour sooner.

The M.O. slapped Smitty into sick bay, but didn't seem perturbed. "One of the Anopheles ladies got him. But I've become quite expert at treating malaria... guarantee to pull him through."

CHAPTER 12

MERRY CHRISTMAS!

DEC. 17, 1944

So much cash! Bundles of the tiny rupee notes, rolls of coins. A quick peek at the last page and I see "Total — Rs 39,960."

Along with the one-day job as Payroll Officer came a corporal from the Pay Office, a long list of names and amounts, and the satchel of money.

"Want to count it, sir? You're responsible for any shortage, of course."

Did I? I counted it twice.

In alphabetical order, each man approaches the table, salutes, gives his name. The corporal reads off the pay amount and I count it out into a pile. The airman picks it up, signs the sheet, flicks another perfunctory salute, and is gone... and the next man is waiting. Great fun — for half an hour. Then tedious. You have to keep the line moving or you'll never finish.

"Too much, sir. You gave me ten chips too much," one lad says.

They're all watching, counting too. So I re-calculate his little pile, retrieve a ten-rupee note and wave my thanks. But how many mistakes did I make which weren't corrected?

You feel sorry for the AC2 erks who draw just a pittance. I had to fight the impulse to reach into the bag and say, "Got lots here, take a few more."

At all levels, the Brit pay scale is very low. An RCAF Flt/Lt calculated that his salary was more than the C.O.'s. Smitty and I are the same rank, but I think my pay is double his. No, I'm not sure of that; it's something we don't discuss — a taboo topic.

In addition to flying duties, most officers get other chores. Don Mathieson, a New Zealander, drew a tough assignment —Mess Officer.

"Didn't know how to boil potatoes; now I have to provide two hundred meals a day. I have a corporal who knows what he's doing, but still lots of headaches."

But he's doing a good job, somehow keeping mess fees to fifty cents a day. And he just arranged a real coup with a Yank B24 squadron. Our beer ration is still a miserly six pints a month, but we get an adequate supply of Scotch; the Yanks' situation is just the reverse. A trade was arranged — a bottle of beer per ounce of whisky.

The accounting course came but it's stashed under my bed. Didn't look very exciting. Or is there another reason? I guess I'm queasy about doing anything that presumes I'm going to live through this, anything that smacks of counting my chickens before the barn door is closed. Wouldn't training for a post-war job be doing that?

"Don't tempt fate!" is the rule. Yeah, flak makes you superstitious.

More formation practice this week: four squadrons across India in tight formation to Bombay, home after dark. But two kites from 99 didn't make it.

"Abandoned aircraft through lack of fuel," was the report. Both crews baled out. But two planes lost on a training flight! B24s are expensive, over $200,000 per plane, the wages of a hundred men for a year.

We've been back to Siam, a formation attack on a bridge at Nagorn Chaisri, twenty miles from Bangkok. Taking Smitty's place was Ken Silcocks. We dropped our load and got away completely unscathed. Trouble was, the bridge didn't get scathed either. Silcocks said our line was good but the last bomb in the stick undershot by twenty yards... every aircraft the same. Between us we'd dumped ten tons of explosives in the water.

The fish must have thought it was Judgment Day.

I turned to get a glimpse of the bridge as we pulled away. It was still standing erect — intact, unmarked. Can a bridge laugh at you? And all that grey water suddenly turned white — like an ancient miracle! How many fish floating belly up does that trick take?

Returning, we stayed in formation all across Burma, only one excitement.

"Tail gunnerrr to pilot. One airrrcrrrraft behind us, six o'clock... a fighterrr... a mile back, below us."

"What's he doing? Coming this way?" A message like that wakes you up fast. "You said fighter? Is he coming after us?"

"Single engine, rrradial, too farrr to tell what type."

"What's he doing? Coming after us?"

"Naw, flying acrrrross our trrrack. Doesn't even see us. Climbing up, then diving. I think he's prrractising."

Hah, that's a good one! A Jap pilot putting in a little training time. Wouldn't he get a surprise if he looked up!

But what a waste today was! Bombs, oil, petrol — all squandered. And yet, a heretical thought! It is not crucially important to me whether our bombs straddled that bridge or fell short. Yes, that's mostly because

Abdul

we bombed in formation. When you're flying alone, and miss, it's your own fault, your own incompetence. But today it was just follow-the-leader.

As I see it, my job was to take us to the target, then — top priority — make sure we all got back to base. Safely home, I feel I did my job, won't commit hari-kari because the formation missed the target. My over-riding philosophy about this war? By enlisting, I agreed to face some danger, can't renege on that. You have to do your job, never let crew mates down. But I've no ambition to be a hero. My military goal is very simple — survive this thing! I'm not proud of that ambition, but that's how it is.

The formation broke up over the Bay. Normal cruising with the plane empty is 160 mph, but we were at a sluggish 140, the most economical if worried about gas. Arthur assured me we had adequate petrol but I still get nightmares about four engines suddenly coming to a stop.

Back at camp, it's tea time and I see Abdul coming up the path from the Mess. He really makes me smile. With short little steps, he glides along smoothly, sedately, his tray balanced on upturned palm at shoulder height. In uniform and turban, he always reminds me of the genii who popped out of the bottle. Unhurried, unflustered, but with a purposeful manner proclaiming that he, at least, knows what he's doing, he pitter-pats along the path in bare feet, straight-backed and head high, the Jeeves of the Boondocks.

"Hi, Abdul," I greet him. You have to like the little guy. "What do you have today? Biscuits? Four of them? Great!"

"Sahib." He acknowledges my greeting in formal fashion, but then just a flash of conspiratorial grin as he hands me a plate with double the usual ration. "Mess corp'l forget Mister Smith at sick hospital."

His English is surprisingly good; also the writing and spelling. On the table is the chitti he's preparing for the next load of laundry; it lists "5 shirt,

2 pannt, 4 sokk" — more or less correctly.

He's a big help. In this Air Force life, I've done all the housekeeping chores — darning socks, sewing buttons, polishing shoes, making beds — but now Abdul does all that for us. And on mornings when he sees us strapping on our gun belts, he stands at the door to say, "Good lucks, sahibs."

He's likely the best bearer in the camp. There's only one problem with that: he thinks so too, is quite sure of it. The result is that every month he wants more pay; we now know his spiel by heart.

"One wife, sahibs, two daughters. Daughters go schooling now. Ver' big expensive, sahibs. Must needs ten rupees addition."

British families in India are horrified at how much we pay servants.

"Ridiculous, pushes up wage levels everywhere, ruins it for all of us," is a common complaint in Letters to the Editor. I suppose we're guilty of that. Smitty and I now pay Abdul sixty rupees, about twenty dollars a month split between us, maybe double what any other bearer here is getting. But we're hooked; he's made himself indispensable.

To make matters worse, fellows come up to us in the Mess with their eyes flashing. "This Abdul fellow... your bearer, isn't he? Right? Well, do you know what he's doing? He should be thrown off the camp.

"When my bearer comes into the room today, he's got your chap at his side. This damned Abdul tells me, cool as you please, that I have to give my boy a rise in pay. The lad will quit if I don't give him another six chips a month! Your Abdul's doing all the talking; my boy just stands there, staring at the floor. Bloody hell — six rupees. It's highway robbery! But he's a good kid, don't want to lose him. I'll have to pay it. Damn! A bloody trouble-maker, that's what your man is!"

Hah, I have to cover my mouth; it wouldn't be a good time to laugh. So Abdul has a second vocation. When he isn't being the perfect bearer, the rascal's a labour negotiator, marching in to meet the bosses on behalf of his clients, cool and businesslike. The picture amuses me.

He'd be good at that job. Smitty and I should know. This month he even brought his two daughters into the bargaining session. Just their pictures... little black-eyed girls about six and seven, very pretty dark-haired things though shabbily dressed.

"For going school now, need uniforms, sahibs. Ver' important. For daughters, for schooling uniforms, need ten rupees addition, sahibs."

What could we do?

I'd like to know what he charges the other bearers to represent them. It wouldn't be gratis, not Abdul. And with the nights getting nippy, he asked if he could use Smitty's two blankets until he gets out of hospital.

Use them? I'd bet anything he's renting them out.

Jeesh, I was never can-veyed... convoyed... home b'fore. Wup, nearly shlipped. But I din't fall. Somebody's got holt of my arms.

"Jock and Arshur, right? Hi, fellahs, good party, eh? Okay, okay... I'm alrate... don' need ten guys to take me home... speshly a buncha drunks like you fellahs. Good Chrishmus bash, eh? An' how'd yuh like our Mess? First time there? Is that right? Gotta have more pur... parties there.

"Leggo my arm. I'm a'right. Jus' drinkin' soda, y'know. Yeah, you were tryin' t'dump gin in m' glass. But too shmart for yuh... kept my glass full'a soda, filled up, no room for gin. So I'm okay, I'm sober... just tired. Say, were we up at four ayem? Was that t'day? Hey, tha's a long time.

"There's my basher. O'course it is... oughta know my own charp, eh? It's okay, Mac, I c'n take off my own damn shirt. Alright, Joe, maybe the shoes. Yeah, okay, pull down the net... keep the old mossies out, right? Okay, fellahs... g'night. Find your way home now? Yeah, see ya tomorrow. Merr' Chrishmus."

They're gone. But I feel terr'ble. The room's underla... undulating, up-and-down, down-and-up. Then it slides to the side... slithers like a snake, and my stomach slides with it. Quick! Out the back door, out on the grass.

It's later, much later. I'm just sitting here. My dinner's gone. Those drinks... potent! But I feel better. I think I do. A cup of water and a gargle... that helps too.

Cheez, I'm bushed... too tired to sleep. We really were up early, middle of the bloody night. Take-off was 5:30... still needed runway lights.

Maybe I'll have more water. It's cool... from our `chatti'... earthenware urn, colour and texture of a flower pot. Condensation through the purrous... porous walls... keeps the water almost cold.

The op today was short and easy... to Taungup, the big supply dump near that Cheduba Island. Hoped for a milk run, that's what we got. Some days war is easy. The four regular RAF bombing outfits — 41 aircraft — were joined by two USAAF squadrons for the biggest raid yet into Burma.

So a long day. Except for the half-hour before dinner, I've been awake nearly 24 hours. But I don't think I can sleep yet; my stomach's still jumpy. Maybe another glass of water.

Hope we can finish our softball tournament. The four-squadron meet at Salboni was a great day. And big surprise! So many RCAF there — the first crews being specially trained for Libs at a place called Boundary Bay near Vancouver. One fellow told me his crew was in Canada a month ago. A staggering thought... just thirty days ago!

Our hosts, 356, have a C.O. — WingCo Beale — a Canuck, though in the RAF with a mostly Brit crew. Many Canadians, Yanks too, just went to Britain and enlisted. But some people don't understand how someone who joined the RCAF could end up on an RAF squadron. But the RAF had squadrons in place, they needed replacements, and Canada had the air crews. I've never felt there was anything unnatural about it. We're all in the same war, aren't we?

Hey, I wonder if it's true about tracks — panthers or tigers — seen just outside the camp.

"Yes, sahib," Abdul assures me. "Tigers. All bearers ver' scare."

No wonder. Bearers and other workers live in the native quarters at the edge of camp, sleeping on the open ground, nothing between them and the bush. A story in the Calcutta paper said tigers take fifty lives a year in India. The danger's worse in the Sunderbans near the coast, but the natives here are sleeping close beside one another — even Hindus and Moslems together — and bonfires are kept burning all night.

I'm ready to sleep now. Tiger tracks? I'll lock my door just in case.

DEC. 25

My khaki Christmas! Clothing, thatched roofs, the whole landscape — everything brown.

Will I remember the Christmases of these war years by their predominant colours? Last year it was grey. Uniforms added touches of blue... often well-faded blue. But leaden clouds, dingy unpainted hangars and Quonset huts, even the general scene in all the dank and misty weather... mostly grey. At least that's how I'll remember winter in wartime England.

The year before that? White! A bitter cold, mountainous snow drifts glistening under the sun. Taxi-ing a Harvard when snow banks piled on either side were higher than the plane, flying a solo cross-country over empty Ontario backwoods after an overnight blizzard had obliterated all traces of roads, railways, rivers — any topographical feature at all — and you were lost over an expanse of unbroken white, white, white.

Last night was our Christmas Eve party. But it never peaked. Maybe everyone is more subdued than usual, thinking of home, family and friends.

But this was a good day. It was a complete `stand-down,' no flying or other chores, but I woke at nine. It may have been the "swish-swish" of Abdul polishing shoes, or maybe my subconscious remembering the packages with the "Do not open till Dec. 25" labels.

Mom's was a food parcel — fruit cake, chocolates, other goodies. And Jean... hey! A camera, a little Brownie with two rolls of film that look in good shape. And a 1945 calendar with scenes of Ottawa in seasonal poses. The final item: the photo of herself I've been asking for. Great!

Some cake sufficed for breakfast, then I checked out the laughter in the next room. It was the Brodie foursome getting in the right mood for the big day. I got there in time to hear Steve's story about the woodchopper felling trees, another of his yarns that leaves you pondering a little even after the punch line's been given.

"He was the hardest worker in the bush. Chop, chop, chop. Never slowed down. But his axe was always dull. His buddies told him, 'Take a few minutes, sharpen it, you'll cut more trees in less time.' The woodsman stopped, wiped his brow, thought for a moment, but went right back to swinging his axe. 'Can't... no time... too busy.'"

At the Mess, all the NCOs came in for a drink before we walked en masse over to the Airmen's Mess to serve their Christmas dinner. There the men all sat at long tables, every AC2 to corporal, knives and forks at the ready, shined up and waiting for the role reversal to begin. It was good fun.

"Sir, over here... on the double... more potatoes."

"Sergeant, where's the tea? We want another pot of tea."

"Wing Commander Sindall, this cup's dirty; a clean one right away!"

With as many servers as diners, it was a chaotic scene, waiters vying to see who could deliver an order fastest. Great platters and pots were carried in — soup, roast fowl and vegetables, pudding and sauce, jellies, nuts and fruits — with a bottle of beer for each man as a gift from the Sergeants' Mess. Spiced with joking and laughter, a very merry affair.

After that there were games, the main event a soccer match between airmen and officers with the latter decked out in crazy costumes. Then I watched some cricket where Jock Govan was one of the best players.

Our own big meal at night, presided over by a Group Captain from 185 Wing, was a formal Mess Dinner with tables in long rows, and place cards to tell you where not to sit. It was a swell feast — turkey, chicken and duck with all the trimmings. From the pudding, you could get a hangover.

"Whisky, rum and brandy mixed with a dollop of flour," was the M.O.'s professional analysis.

Then the port was escorted in and ceremoniously passed down the table... and I made my big gaffe. Chota on my right got the end of a carafe, only half a glass. It seemed fair to offer him my new bottle to top it off.

"No, no, you can't do that," I was instructed. "Port is always passed to the left... never, never to the right."

After that came speeches and toasts, followed by more speeches, more toasts. Steve Brodie, speaking as the senior RCAF-er, keeping his remarks very short, got the most applause of all.

"Canadians are not noted as particularly good talkers. On the other hand, I believe we have a world-wide reputation as proficient drinkers. I propose we now dispense with the former and concentrate on the latter."

At the Drome
Bill Waddington, Smokey Williams, Murray Potts, Ken Cox,
(Workers in background)

Which likely speeded up getting to the C.O's closing remarks. But his words didn't get any applause whatsoever.

"You have all heard the rumours. I now confirm that we will be moving to Dhubalia, rejoining our friends at 99 Squadron as part of 175 Wing. You will receive more details later. Suffice for now to say that the transfer is to be made as expeditiously as possible, to be completed within the week."

Damn. Then it's true. More changes, more musical chairs. After three months, we're fairly well organized here, are reasonably comfortable. Now we have to move and start all over.

We've all settled into the lounge to discuss the news. Only Brodie, slumped in a chair with a glass in his hand, doesn't seem that concerned.

"Ahh, don't get so excited. It's an inconvenience, but not life-or-death. Nobody likes changes, but you have to learn to live with them.

"Have I told you about the two old farmers? Over eighty, retired, both sitting in their rockers on the front porch. Just sittin' and rockin'. After a long pause, Silas says to Zeke, 'Y'know, Zeke, there's bin a heap o' changes aroun' here in the past sixty years.' Zeke thinks a full minute, then says, 'Yep... that's right... and I'll tell yuh somethin'. I been agin every dang one of 'em.'"

Nobody laughs harder than Chota Harris. Some guys have faces that invariably look as if they've just received bad news; others always appear angry. I'm in the group, I've been told, that usually looks worried. But Chota is one of the lucky ones. Even asleep, I expect, his expression would make you think he'd just heard a good joke.

"Hi, fellas." Bill Waddington pulls up a chair. "What d`you hear from the Coast, Murray?" They're both from the Pacific Ocean end of the country.

Bill's another very good guy. He's flying as 2nd pilot with the C.O. and I don't think I'd like that. Of course, Bill maybe didn't choose the job; maybe the WingCo chose him.

And here come Eddie Gilbert, Smokey Williams and Mac Gardner. Hey, all the Canadians in one group. Gilbert isn't a rookie. According to Smokey, Ed flew in the Aleutians, did Wimpy ops in the Middle East and was with 215 in India before the switch to Libs.

What do we talk about? In hockey, will the Toronto Leafs win this year? Which part of the country has the coldest weather? Is zero Fahrenheit with a raw wind colder than thirty below on a still night? Should guys be allowed to defer enlisting while at University?

Through the evening, we've been having a few drinks. I have no use for drunks, guys who down more than they can handle, even brag about how stinko they got. Hell, what's clever about that? Now if someone could down a whole bottle of whiskey and still stay sober, that would be something to boast about. But just get knee-walking blotto? Any clot can do that.

As an older RAF gent once lectured me, "Only a dolt drinks to `get drunk.' However, imbibed with sophistication, alcohol has its uses. The demon rum with all its cousins, adulterated with fizzes and mixes... sipped with continence in the company of convivial comrades... does indeed furnish the lubrication often needed to grease the gears of gregarious gab, provide a passport to pleasant palaver, a palliative potion potent enough to paint a place in pretty pink."

Pretty pink. I guess that's how I'm seeing things tonight. It's been a nice evening. It was a pretty good Christmas.

CHAPTER 13

DUSTY DHUBALIA

DEC. 29, 1944

Buildings here at Dhubalia are the same as at Kolar, Salboni, Digri. The landscape's also similar — flat, parched and dusty. We're told the nearby town has six thousand inhabitants, another twenty villages in the area. That's surprising; looking to the horizon, you see nothing, could believe you were on the moon.

Smitty and I have adjacent rooms; the Brodie four share the other two. One difference is the furniture; there isn't any. Half the officers are on their camp cots. To provide all our airmen with a bed, charpoys had to be commandeered from Enrolled Followers over at Wing HQ. If Abdul lived there, he'd be leading the sepoys in another Indian Mutiny.

But I have a charpoy, the deluxe model; instead of rough hemp rope to serve as springs, they're canvas strips — smoother, firmer, and you don't lose any skin if your legs come in contact. Got to find a fan, though, before the heat returns. I thought of smuggling my Digri blower with me, but precious items like that are closely counted.

"Transferring all squadron equipment and personnel from Digri in just three days... quite a feat. Counting Enrolled Followers, nine hundred men were transported by road, rail and air," the Adj said. "We're invited to a welcoming party over at 99 Squadron, but we have to get set up here first."

Wing HQ, also across the field, supervises the two Squadrons, provides such services as church and padres, cinema, payroll people, Intelligence boffos, Control Tower staff and medics.

Smitty's in Cal for a final check-up. If he's okay, he'll get recuperation leave. But I brought Abdul here. He didn't want to come and it took all my persuasive powers to change his mind. Plus another ten rupee raise.

We were at the Flight Office today to study the diagram of the runways and taxi strips, and visit Peter. Jock Biggar and his men were working on

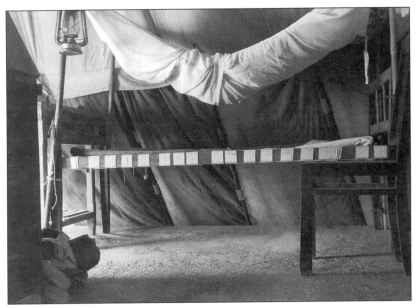

Charpoy — Deluxe Style

her. After our party last night — just ground crew and air crew — I've now got all their names straight. I was anxious to have the get-together to make amends for being so dumb at Christmas. I'd wanted to give the ground guys some small gift, but what? One commodity I always have is smokes.

"Much apprrrreciated," Jock told me. "But the C.O.'s crrrew got whiskey! D'ye ken they don't have harrd liquor in the Airrmen's Mess. Biggarrr said that's what would've made them all feel just grrrrand."

And all they got were crummy cigs. I went to see the Mess Secretary, said I'd squeal about the C.O. getting a bottle if I didn't get one.

The party was a great success, the Haig and Haig label making their eyes sparkle a lot brighter than the cigarettes did. Before it broke up, we were shouting toasts to "the bes' damn groun' crew on the stayshun," and they were downing drinks to "the bes' bloody damn aircrew in the whol' bloody damn RAF." Which, as everyone knows, is proof of a good party.

Our only chore has been to give Peter a 'compass swing.' A big problem with navigation in the air is that a compass needle will be deflected by any nearby hunk of metal, which an aircraft mostly is. So we take Peter to a quiet area of the field, run up the engines to flying power, and Bob reads the aircraft compass. Arthur, the outside man for the day, notes the true reading on a separate compass distant enough not to be affected by the plane's metallic content. The difference is the 'deviation' on that heading. Repeat the drill on eleven more headings and Bob has useful information about compass compensations needed to get us where we want to go.

P-Peter, Ground Crew

Another problem is 'magnetic declination.' Navigation would be simpler if compasses pointed to the true north, if only the Creator had thought to put Magnetic North smack on the Pole. However, the declination in Bengal is only one degree, can be ignored.

Jock Biggar says everyone's pushing to get aircraft in tip-top shape in a hurry. The word from the C.O. is that we'll be into a heavy schedule of ops beginning the first of the new year.

JAN. 3, 1945

"Hey, Wal. You awake? Time to go."

With Smitty in Darjeeling on leave, that's Chota checking on me. Brodie's crew is flying today too. I join them on the dark trek over to the Mess, and we pick up Eddie and Smokey on the way. We're going back to the Burma-Siam Railway, the target so often lately the I.O. just calls it the "B.S.R."

Alf Reed, renowned for having the widest handlebar moustache on the squadron, is subbing for Smitty. He's already at breakfast, and I join him. With just eight kites on the trip, there are only about twenty at the tables. Nobody's talking much, not at this hour.

Or maybe we're thinking of Sq/Ldr Beadon's troubles two days ago when his H-for-Harry took a hit from an A/A shell. The tail gunner was killed, the rear section set ablaze. W/O Combes, second pilot, went back to empty the fire extinguisher on the flames, beat them with his jacket, dumped drinking water on the embers, and got the fire out. Despite damage to the elevators, Beadon got them back to base. Nobody complained about being a bit thirsty.

The crew decided to walk over to have a look at `H' yesterday, and we met Steve Brodie and Murray Potts on their way back.

"No, you don't want to see it," Steve told us, the twinkle missing from his eye. "The gunner is still in the turret. They haven't removed his body, cleaned it up yet. Believe me. You... don't... want... to... see... it!"

We said "Oh," and turned back.

So, 215's first casualty since switching to Libs — a landmark of sorts. But our good luck couldn't last; other squadrons have been taking their lumps. Fighters attacked a 159 formation on the B.S.R., but were beaten off. But W/O Stewart's plane crashed in flames while mining the Rangoon River estuary. We don't get much news of American losses but know that several 99 crews were out searching for another B29 down in the drink.

Of course, that's nothing at all like flying into Germany. Terrible losses. We lose one man here and the whole Squadron goes into mourning.

"A record cold snap," the Met man said at breakfast. "Last night... thirty-nine degrees." Okay, so at home that'd be a January thaw, but we had furnaces and insulation there, didn't go riding in open lorries before sunrise.

It must be tough on the natives. We're just passing coolie labourers now, men, women and youngsters trudging to the drome where they're building the new taxi-strip, their grey-white clothing picked up by our headlights. What an unhappy lot. Most have a cloth or sheet pulled over their shoulders or their heads, but they're all shoeless. Their feet must feel like blocks of ice! It's almost enough to make you feel guilty about your own little complaints.

Here's our Dispersal; Alf and I jump off. The rest of the guys are already there, shivering. Here comes a Jeep, driving fast. It's the C.O.

"No problems, Frazer? Ready to go? Good luck then," and he leaves. He's not on today and we're impressed he came to see us off.

Jock checks his watch, says, "It's time."

Derek Slack, one of our erks, points his flashlight and we duck under the fuselage to go in by the bomb-bay; with five hundred-pounders hanging from the racks, it's a tight squeeze. Jock and I stash our chutes on the hooks behind each seat, buckle ourselves in. He points at his wristwatch again; time for start-up.

There's now enough light I can make out Biggar standing behind a torch. With the cockpit light on, he can see me give the `thumbs-up' to crank up the engines. Start-up procedures are routine now, #3 and #4 purring already.

Now #2. A flick of the `mesh' switch and it sputters and catches. Move the mixture control to `auto lean,' check the oil pressure comes up to normal.

What the... ! It doesn't! The little arrow stays on zero.

What's the matter? You can't run a big Pratt & Whitney for long without its full ration of lubricant. But maybe it's just the gauge, the needle stuck. That can happen. I tap the glass hard; it still reads zero.

I'll try running up the engine. With mixture control back in auto-rich, ease the throttle forward. The R.P.M. indicator goes to 1800... 2000... 2200, a terrible racket. But the oil pressure still shows zero.

What now? Wash out the trip? I better re-check everything!

I heard of a pilot in England who aborted an op because of some engine malfunction where it was later decided he'd simply left a switch 'off' when it should have been 'on.' When that happens, especially just before leaving on a mission, it raises a serious question: Was it carelessness, or intentional... stupidity or a case of 'L.M.F.' — Lack of Moral Fibre?

We've been told that the captain of an aircraft is in the same position as the captain of a ship. Responsibility for the safety of passengers and crew is entirely his. No one can order him to go against his instincts, take his vessel into unnecessary danger. It's entirely his judgment, his decision.

Which is balderdash! In wartime, if one plane doesn't take off with the others, the captain better have a bloody good reason. So Arthur and Jock are both helping me check. But if I've missed anything, we don't find it.

"Get Biggar in here."

The sergeant's been watching, curious. He comes into the cockpit.

"Try different engine settings," he suggests. But the same result.

"You'll have to scrub the flight, sir," he says. "It's the oil pump."

I check with Arthur, who nods. We cut the switches, and the engines sputter to a stop. The sudden quiet is startling.

"Trip's scrubbed," I shout. "Everybody out; take all your junk."

We're on the tarmac. Peter stands very still, motionless, head sort of hanging down. I think she looks ashamed.

The other Libs are coming by now, moving slowly along the taxi strip. In this half-light, their delicate wings fluttering like an insect's antennae, they look like giant beetles, crawling through the dark, noses dipping up and down, foraging for food.

Or maybe like a string of elephants in a late-night circus parade, one behind the other, almost close enough to be holding the tail of the one in front. Yes, that's it. With noses and tails slowly bobbing, bodies yawing from side to side, Liberators do resemble ponderous pachyderms. I still think Peter should have been called `Packy.'

There's Wallace in `O', followed by Brooks in `U', then `R' which is Ed Gilbert, and four more, the last one Brodie in `D-for-Dog.' Brakes squeaking, they slow in front of our Dispersal, maybe wondering what's wrong with us, but are moving forward again.

"Here comes the C.O," Jock warns me. With a squeal of brakes, the Jeep slides to a stop. "What's the matter, Frazer?" His voice is decidedly unhappy.

"Number two, sir; no oil pressure."

"Damn... another oil pump. Leaves us with seven." Mostly he's muttering to himself. "Your engineer checked it? Your crew chief? Alright, once they're all off, I'll arrange transport to pick you up."

It'll be a long wait, low on his priority list.

But there goes the first plane now. You could hear the terrible racket of the engines being run up behind those bushes... then the noise moves from left to right, still out of sight... and finally the big bird appears just above the tree-tops, struggling to maintain height, starting a slow climb.

That's the first one away, the crucial one. Now you know it can be done, the take-off weight not impossible.

Do I wish we were going? Hell, no! A 14-hour grind to Siam isn't what any sane person would want. And any day you don't get shot at is okay with me. Preparing for an op, not knowing what to expect, gets me very, very tense. To feel that tenseness now dissipating makes me wonderfully relaxed.

There's the second plane climbing away... now the third.

On the other hand, we were primed for it — briefed, loaded up, ready to go. Dragging ourselves out of warm beds, was that wasted too? And, yes — hardest of all — we'd prepared our minds for the trip, reconciled ourselves once again to the necessity of doing the lousy job. We'd girded our loins, whatever that means.

There's the seventh kite leaving; that'll be Brodie. Yeah, I am sorry we're not going with them, but just to get the 14 hours in the log-book. We'll have to do our 300 sooner or later. Maybe we should be going, get it over with one way or the other.

With the aircraft gone, it's a quiet world again — just low conversation and a few "clink" sounds as the airmen start removing the engine cowlings. The decibel level certainly goes up and down around here.

Here's Mac: "What about the rations, skipper? Take them back? Why don't we eat them? I didn't have time for breakfast this morning."

Unless maybe you're Druids or something, sunrise is an unusual time for a picnic, Peter's kraal a strange location. It's crowded in behind the oil drums but Biggar says it's better in case the Engineering Officer happens by.

The conversation? Mostly it's about how long we'll have to stay in this country, a common topic. But it reminds me of the Canadian troops who've been in Britain since 1939. Jean's last letter had a note about one of those guys, Doug Honeywell, who played on our hockey team when we were kids.

Doug was one of the first to enlist. He married Evelyn and was sent to England almost immediately. But before the war heated up, while steamship lines were still in business, Evelyn booked passage, followed him to Blighty where they set up housekeeping. Jean said she had met Ev's father, who reported he was now a proud grandfather.

He also showed her Doug's cable home, an absolute marvel of brevity: "Mother well. Daughter well. Honeywell."

It's after dinner now. We had the day off and I got some letters written, even read several pages of the accounting course. But compared with real life, it's dull stuff, and is back under my bed.

Tonight, a bridge game. My partner is `T.J.' which are Lt Hawkins' initials. The five South Africans here are all pleasant guys, good-humoured except on one topic: they don't like people with off-white faces.

You might call this an International Match because our opponents are from England and Australia. What we're really doing, of course, is putting in time, waiting for our planes to get back. It's after eight; they should be home soon. Ah, there's one now. Roy Williams goes out to check the sky, comes back in to report, "Two kites in the circuit." Within minutes, three more. Only two to come but we're all starting to look at our watches.

"You were at the briefing, Wal," Roy asks. "What was their ETA at base?"

Roy's concerned; a lot of Aussies were flying today.

"Wasn't a formation trip... they all went on their own, looking for trains and stuff, the usual... then home on their own. So it'd vary. But... eight-twenty now... I think they should all be back, Roy."

We've called off the bridge game. The Mess is uncommonly quiet, everybody listening. All aircraft took the same fuel load, wouldn't have much gas left by this time. Of course they might have stopped at Chittagong or Cox's; I guess that's what we're hoping for now.

Sq/Ldr Beadon comes striding across the room, a taking-command gait. With the C.O. at the Briefing Room, he's the senior man here. Taffy hands him the bar telephone; he's finished in a moment.

"The Tower confirms five aircraft landed, and a signal from Chittagong that Flt/Lt Wallace stopped there. No news about the seventh. I'll call the C.O. at de-briefing; the crews returning might know something."

Another short conversation. He puts the receiver back on the hook, turns to face us. We're all trying to read his face.

"Rawtha' bad news," he says, his high voice much lower than usual. "Very bad news, I fear. The report is that one of our aircraft was seen to crash. There were no parachutes... no survivors... no chance at all."

A stunned silence, then a tumult of shouts, of questions.

"Which aircraft? Are they sure? Who was it? Which crew?"

We all have particular friends in one crew or another. But I'm not shouting. I can't. My heart's in my mouth, blocking off the air.

"My information is... it was Flt/Lt Brodie's crew."

Oh, no! Not Brodie. Omigawd!

Steve and Murray and Chota and Ken — my best friends here! Two others from the Mess — Nisbett on the bombsight and Flt-Lt Sao substituting as top gunner. And six NCO's, Washbrook and Irvine the RCAF guys I knew a little. Eleven men... the whole crew... and no survivors!

It can't be. They were so alive at breakfast. There has to be a mistake... the wrong crew, maybe. Some kind of mistake. God, that's terrible! I feel sick, punched out, like a punctured tire tube with its air gone. But it's no mistake; I know that. My best friends!

Someone just handed me a scotch, shoved it into my fist. Wah! It's gotta be a double... a triple. It scorches my throat, my innards, brings tears to my eyes. Or were they there already?

Guys come by, tell me how sorry they are, bring me more drinks. Do I look as if I need the fortification, was about to conk out? Their thoughts should be for the crew, for the guys who are dead now. Everybody liked Steve and his bunch — one of the best-liked crews here. And now they're all dead.

I have more drinks. Is even Taffy at the bar being generous with his measurements. I'm getting unsteady, woozy, but maybe... maybe that's the way I wanta be. But I think I'll go t' bed now.

It's not that late. There are still lights in billets... sounds of guys talkin', laughin'. Except in our basha, my basha... everything's very quiet. Not a light, not a sound. O' course, Shmitty's away. His room's empty. And... the other rooms... the other two rooms...!

I've never felt so rotten, so sick of heart, in all my life.

JAN. 6

Another sortie to the B.S.R. today, but we didn't get far, only to the scrambled eggs, before we heard, "Bad weather over Burma, mission's scrubbed."

The loss of Brodie's gang is much on my mind. I think of them several times a day, remember some wry comment Steve made, or notice there's no sound from the next room, realize I'm not going to hear Chota's laugh ever again.

Eddie Gilbert came in yesterday. I like Ed — a straight-forward kind of guy, just a bit sardonic at times when he's trying to sound cynical and tough. But not then. He admitted he was badly shaken.

"I saw Brodie crash, you know. Three of us went after the same bridge, and a locomotive stopped halfway across. It was in a valley, steep hills on both sides. We were at five hundred feet, lower than the hills.

Wallace, the Fiji guy, went in first. Steve followed him, and I was right behind.

"There were gun positions on the hills, both sides of the bridge. They hit Wallace, then they got Steve, hit his #4. I could see the flames. Steve and Murray did a good job... everything they could... jettisoned the bombs, got the prop feathered... as fast as anybody could. They tried to climb, but there wasn't room. Hit near the top of a hill, just one big explosion.

"It happened so fast, just seconds. Some, like Chota and Ken, wouldn't have known what was happening. The others... well, they didn't have time to think about it. And Steve... he didn't panic... did everything he could. You can't expect more of a captain than that."

So that's how it happened. Wallace's kite was staggered too, but they got their bombs jettisoned, scraped over mountain tops, put out a fire and nursed the aircraft to Cox's Bazaar... throwing out equipment, radioing Mayday.

"The locomotive was a decoy," the crew said. "They were waiting for us; we were just lucky to get away."

But Brodie's guys... not lucky at all. Eleven men killed.

I heard one comment that really shook me. It came from Geoff Burton, an RAF navigator type, a bloke with a high opinion of himself, not one of my favourites here even before he collared me to offer his piece of wisdom.

"I'm sorry about Brodie; great bunch of guys and all that. But do you realize it was to our advantage?"

Our advantage? I should've hit him right then. But I was flabbergasted, had to find out what in hell he could mean by that.

"Well, we've been very lucky here with losses. So it was overdue, had to happen. Now that it has, the rest of us can breathe easier for a while."

What was he saying? That there's some Aztec-type god up there who must be mollified by the sacrifice of an occasional crew? When the offering has been made... the god appeased... the rest of us can feel safe for a time?

Or that there's some law of averages that predetermines the losses you have to suffer? A sort of quota for each squadron, a target number to be met? With that thinking, losing a crew means you can cross out one of the `crash' spots on the quota list, be happy there's one less to be filled?

There's a certain plausibility to the idea but... No! That's crazy!

You have to remember that, "Dice have no memory." As with flipping coins, even if `heads' comes up ten times in a row, the coin isn't smart enough to remember that. It's still a fifty-fifty proposition the next time too.

Flying ops isn't like flipping coins or rolling dice. There's no mathematical formula to tell you precisely what your odds are on the next trip. But I don't think that should matter; whether the odds are one in ten, or one in a thousand, the odds aren't changed because a crew was lost on the previous flight. You could also say that "airplanes have no memory."

I checked with Howard Johns who has some mathematics.

"Oh, yes, you're right," he said. "There's a lot of sloppy thinking about numbers, gambling odds and such... a great deal of superstition. Losing a plane might increase your knowledge of the operational risks involved, correct your assessment as to what the odds really are. But it doesn't change them."

Mac Gardner had another question. "Do you know the game of 'curling,' Howard? Something like lawn bowling but on ice. It's a Scottish game... played a lot in Canada. It's a big advantage to have 'last rock' — the final throw on each end —and you flip a coin to see who gets this advantage to start off. I was told you should always let the other team call the toss because they'll usually lose. The majority of the time they'll shout "heads"; however, as the chances of it being heads are only fifty percent, they'll be wrong more than half the time. What do you think?"

Howard laughed. "I say, a most interesting twist... one I've never heard before. Not correct, of course. It's still a fifty-fifty bet every time."

I'm glad to know I wasn't benefiting from Brodie's death. I'll make a point of getting Burton straightened out too — make damn sure he doesn't get any satisfaction from it.

Maybe I'm in a bad mood. The Adj gave Ed Gilbert the job of clearing out the Cox-Harris room. I got the Brodie-Potts stuff, have been sorting through their belongings. I didn't object to the chore; it's just that going through all their personal effects is a sad business. You pack up anything of value or importance to send home, give away or throw out the remainder. You have to make decisions: uniforms with wings and rank insignia go home but not underwear; log book and hard covers but not paperback mysteries; pictures and photographs, not magazine pin-ups.

Letters are a problem. Those from parents, wife, church minister and the like get packed. Anything from a female has to be looked at. Unless clearly from a sister, cousin, aunt or old school teacher, I threw them out.

Both had enough money in their wallets to pay off the bearer and their mess bills, the remainder going to the Adj for the Airmen's Welfare Fund.

The job took two days. My fee? Yes, I charged a fee. I charged them one fan. It's RAF issue, of course, and someone was going to get it. I like to think they'd have chosen that it come to me.

A lorry came by today to collect the boxes for shipping. Tonight the room is very, very empty.

CHAPTER 14

SOME OPS, SOME OOPS

JAN. 11, 1945

At dusk, even with shadows on the ground, it's still pale-blue above. Won't any object in the sky make a clear silhouette, be easily seen from below while those in the plane will see only black underneath?

The shortest way home from Siam is a direct line across Burma. Our track takes us between Rangoon and Mandalay but there are lots of lights flickering down there. And many of those cities have fighter bases.

Wouldn't Jap pilots be gleeful to find a big, dumb bomber come lumbering through their air space, all alone, etched against the sunset? Attacking from below, out of the darkness, their guns could fill our belly with slugs before we knew they were there. Grinning, one of them could be getting us centred in his gun-sights... now!

It didn't happen. But maybe he's going to start firing... now!

Again, nothing. But such lousy thoughts to have tumbling through your head for over an hour. We can only inch across the sky, damn the sun for being so slow to get out of sight, and curse whoever mis-planned the mission.

Not a great week for 215. The bollux in Neville's kite has to be the worst I've ever heard. Approaching the B.S.R., their engines sputtered and stopped. The problem? Switches accidentally flicked off, or petrol cocks switched to already-empty tanks? No one will say.

Our gunners saw the plane going down, propellers twisting idly. Starting from 8,000 feet, Neville jettisoned his bombs but they were still losing height fast. At 3,000, one of the crew jumped; his chute opened okay. But just after that, the plane levelled out, all props turning again. Problem corrected, the aircraft started climbing to catch up. But bloody hell! They were short one member of the crew!

The story next day? Engines starting to cough, Neville warned everyone, "Get ready to jump."

The escape hatch was opened, and the crew crouched around it, scared, awaiting orders... the wireless op staying in contact with the captain over the intercom. When the problem was located, engines again ticking over, Neville reported the good tidings. The radio man got the message, passed the news to the others with a happy 'thumbs-up.' It was the wrong signal, too easy to misinterpret. The ball gunner jumped out.

The poor kid! Swaying in his parachute harness, seeing his plane climb back up to re-join the formation, then to fly home, he must have been the loneliest man in the world!

He landed in a clearing. We've no idea what happened to him after that.

Here's Bob. "Still trying to get a pin-point, but the ground's too dark. Everybody watch for something we can recognize."

"Ball gunner on the job, Bob."

Jonesy's disgusted with me lately. Except over the target, I haven't let him lower his turret. I suppose it's crazy having a gunner just ride as a passenger, but it saves gas. Tonight, though, we need his guns.

Today's raid: a rail line running north from Bangkok. Six of us flew out together and then split up, our responsibility Bridge 37, a low-level attack. With ten five hundred-pounders in our belly and Alf Reed to push the button again, we located the target, a single-span stretching sixty yards across a river meandering through paddy fields. A pretty thing. No gun fire, no opposition at all, made it a sitting duck. I almost felt sorry for it.

At 165 miles an hour, from only 300 feet, the landscape rips by at a helluva rate, everything a blur. When the target shows up in the cross-hairs, the bomb-aimer has to be very quick with his trigger finger. Damn! Alf wasn't quick enough. An over-shoot, fifty yards.

We tried again... the other five bombs. Damn, damn! Missed again. Closer, but a clear miss. So far to come and nothing to show for it. This wasn't formation bombing; we can't blame anyone but ourselves.

"Wait, there were only four explosions," Jonesy shouted. "Not five."

Arthur hurried back to the bomb-bay. Yes, we'd had a 'hang-up'; one of our quarter-tonners was still there. We could have another try. If we couldn't connect with a stick, I had small hope we could do it with a single, but it was a chance. If this were another Hollywood war movie, our last bomb would leave the bridge upturned in the water, gasping for air.

A big circle, then "bomb away." After that, the suspense. From 300 feet, it takes no time for the bomb to reach the ground but then there's the 11 second delay on the fuse to let us get out of the way.

But this was definitely not a movie with a happy ending. As usual, the first report came from Jonesy. He must have lightning-quick reflexes, might have made a great bombardier.

"Missed," he shouted, his voice a mix of excitement and disappointment.

"But close." The consensus was, "Very close, another over-shoot, but only twenty yards, maybe near enough to at least weaken the abutments."

But why not a direct hit? I think I had Peter where it was supposed to be. Could the problem be the bomb-aimer? I don't think so. The bomb-sight? There have been questions whether the Mark 14 is adequate at low level. But I think it's a matter of practice — or lack of it. We've never dropped one practice bomb from this height. Why send us a thousand miles to practise in Siam?

Our route home took us past another of the day's targets: Bridge 26. "Look, it's down. Somebody got it. The main span's in the water."

It was a beautiful sight, one of the end sections badly twisted, a big gap in the middle. Why couldn't we have done that?

"Look, a water tower!" from Phil. "Somebody's filled it with holes."

It looked funny, a tank up on long legs, water gushing out in ten places. But all that was two hours ago. Right now it's Phil's voice.

"Nose gun to navigator... coast coming up."

Good, we're okay now, can relax, finish our rations, maybe even a nap.

But Bob spoils it. "We're south of where I expected, skip. We have a headwind, right in our face, at least twenty miles an hour. We're past the Jap base on Ramree Island but we'll have to detour around Akyab. About three hours to Digri. How's the petrol?"

Damn! 'Headwind' is the ugliest word in the English language.

"Engineer to pilot... harrumph." Arthur clears his throat when he has something to say he'd rather not. "Might be close. I estimate petrol for three and a half hours... but could be out thirty minutes either way."

Dammit, petrol problems again; I burn more fuel than anybody. Other captains tell me, "Learn to fly 'on the step.' Same as in a power boat. Don't mush along in a nose-up attitude. To cruise economically at, say, one-sixty, you add power and put your nose down until you're doing one-eighty. When you ease back on the throttles, the speed will drop back to one-sixty but your nose will stay down, you'll be 'on the step,' and save gas."

We've tried many times, still can't be doing it right. So we're always the last aircraft home, stooging along at 140. Sure, it's embarrassing to see birds passing you, but they don't need petrol.

"Bob here, skip. Wind's more like twenty-seven."

Cheez, it'll be close. But there is an alternative; we could stop at Cox's Bazaar. We have enough juice to get there if we swing back to the Burmese coast very soon. Someone there would give us the petrol to get home. But we'd likely have to stay over till morning.

Landing at a strange field at night doesn't thrill me. Set the plane down and you're amid a thousand coloured lights marking runways and taxi strips all around you, going in every direction. From above, a recognizable pattern. Sitting amongst them, they're a jumble, so confusing you have to beg the Tower to send someone to lead you out of the labyrinth.

Even when you find a parking spot, it's report to the Tower, get a signal back to 215, find beds for everybody. In the morning, more problems: wangle a ride back to the field, organize some gas, get a boost for start-up. Others who've landed there say they'll look after you, but you have to wait your turn. They have their own aircraft to service.

Maybe we should fly straight home. If we make it, we'll breeze through de-briefing, and then to bed — our own beds —and sleep till noon.

The ship is quiet. Everyone's weary, but they're also wondering what we're going to do. And it has to be my decision. I can't ask somebody else to make it for me. I think we could make it home, would put our chances at nine out of ten. But isn't there a risk that Bob some night will end up confused and lost, that Arthur's calculations might be wrong, that our engines could sputter and quit. Damn! I've got ten guys depending on me not to make more dumb mistakes.

"Pilot to crew. Likely enough petrol to get home, but there's some doubt. We'll stop at Cox's. Bob, work out a course."

"I think you're right, skip. Turn to zero four oh."

He answered so fast he must have had it already worked out.

JAN. 13

Big changes in squadron personnel. Sq/Ldr O'Connor has completed his tour and gone. Others too: RAF-er Norm Williams; Downie, the New Zealander; Coulin, Graham and Grouse, the Aussies.

You have mixed feelings, happy for them but sorry the Mess will be a lot less merry. For certain, each departure means big profits for the bar.

"We'll not be getting a lot of new crews as replacements," the C.O. said. "Second pilots will take over existing crews, a few newcomers added."

O'Connor's replacement to lead 'B' Flight? Someone transferred in from elsewhere? The WingCo made a big production out of it, ordering Roy Williams to stand at attention before the bar; accomplices put a blindfold on him and slipped new insignia tabs onto his shirt. Blinkers removed, Roy's shoulders had an additional thin blue band between the two wider ones.

Our new Squadron Leader's promotion got big approval. Fairly serious for an Aussie, Roy's very much a 'gentleman' type, likable and capable. Some guys you know you'll be happy to work under.

Our recent detour into Cox's worked out okay. Close enough to the Japs that it's blacked out, the runway is lit with about five-watt bulbs. I haven't had to land in a dim-out since Britain and we bounced hard. But the `Pilots' Best Friend' was waiting, a Jeep with a `Follow Me' sign on the back.

A USAAF petrol bowser pumped in enough gallons next morning to get us home, Yankee gas into an RAF bomber. Was I expected to pay for it, and if so, how? But not even a chit to sign. On a forward base, I guess nobody has time for petty details like that.

Home in two hours. Still had to be quizzed by the I.O... admit we'd wasted bombs and gas. Strangely, he didn't seem to care. Why? Other crews had knocked down two bridges and damaged a third. The op was already "successful."

I'm still missing Brodie and his guys. Both padres spoke to me; neither said anything useful. But Howard Johns had a quote: "Death and Sleep are brothers." He said it came from Homer, an old Greek poet. Sounded interesting, so he lent me a book on Greek Mythology. It'll be a change from whodunits.

The news out of Burma continues good. Last week we skirted around Akyab. It wasn't necessary; Brit forces have now re-taken it. Our troops are also closing in on Mandalay.

That's where the boys went today. I was Marshalling Officer so was at the briefing. For the first time, the target was people — Japanese staff in Fort Dufferin, the old British fort in Mandalay which is now Jap HQ there.

Dropping bombs is a very impersonal business. Attacking a bridge, say, you aren't really aware of anybody down there. There must be, but you don't think about it; your mind doesn't 'see' them. So far, anybody killed has been hit accidentally, an incidental result of war. Going after them deliberately is a bit different. But if they're enemy troops? Well... you can always say, "They started this."

As for civilians, the truth is that shells coming up at you leave little room for thinking about much else. You're too busy worrying about yourselves to have any thoughts for unknown, unseen strangers. That may not be right, but it's how it is.

Still rattling around in my skull is the discussion last night. If there was a topic, I suppose you'd say it was 'fear,' not something we normally talk about. Not seriously, anyway, though there's nothing wrong with making jokes about your fright.

At present, we're all doing the 'mouth-twitch' routine. Ask someone how things went on his last trip, he'll say "fine," but the corner of his mouth then goes into nervous spasms. Some people are very good at it; I've received compliments myself.

But you don't admit to fear, try not to show it. You don't suggest the opposite either, that you consider yourself a fearless fellow. Oh, we have a few who drop hints to that effect, but it's bad form. However, listening to a group at breakfast, before an op, you'd think they hadn't a worry in the world, their nervousness well papered over. But that discussion in the Mess last night likely revealed more than their voices or their eyes.

"Supposing..." one fellow said. Isn't that how a lot of your very best conversations get started?

"Supposing the Devil approached you... yes, Satan himself... and offered you a deal. Something like that Faust fellow. He would guarantee that you'd live through this war if you would agree to accept your death at some time in the future... the date to be settled now. In such a bargain, what age would you settle on?"

"You mean... if Satan offered me age fifty, say, and I agreed, I'd live until then, guaranteed, but no longer? Otherwise, just take my chances?"

That started it, everyone thinking, arguments going full blast. It's one thing to have vague concerns; being forced to zero in on them, to face just how serious they are, is something else. As one of the college guys said, "The question makes you quantify your fears." And it's not just a dollar amount. If you signed the papers for age forty, how would you feel when you reached 39?

And what did we decide? Opinions varied, of course. A few optimistic ones would accept nothing less than a full 65 years. Some of the gambler types — who usually like to make bets — said they'd accept no deal at all.

Or would that *be* their gamble?

At the other extreme were the ones — maybe thinking of Brodie's crew or so many others — who would settle for as little as fifteen or twenty years of guaranteed post-war life. Doesn't that indicate some guys are feeling very nervous, even worse than I thought?

The average? Somewhere in the forty to fifty range. That's what I'd say too. To have your life snuffed out — all life's pleasures, present and future, suddenly snatched away — that's a most awful risk, a terrifying possibility, something to be avoided at almost any cost. If you could take out a kind of insurance policy against that happening, wouldn't it be smart?

But what about the cost? It's a terrible lot... you wouldn't want to make a mistake. Age forty, eh? Of course, by that time you've already had most of the good things in life — marriage with a loving wife, kids, a job, a home, good times. You'll have experienced all that.

And if you didn't live past fifty, would it be such a tremendous loss? My own parents don't care that much any more for dances, big parties, for having a ball. I wouldn't say their life is over, but it has certainly slowed to a crawl. Wouldn't it be smart to trade those faltering years of old age to guarantee the next twenty?

Yeah, I think that makes sense. But forty? Or would I hold out for forty-five... or fifty? I'd have to think hard on that.

Royal Canadian Air Force

Official RCAF Photo
Author with Enrolled Follower

JAN. 21

Our third op in six days.

On the 16th — Rangoon. With 99 and 355, the big Zayatkwin airfield. At the same time, 356 combined with USAAF B24s to attack nearby Mingladon, the main Jap air base in Burma. What air support: P38s and P47s, 88 in all, a most beautiful sight! Clearly, our air strength here is increasing.

A man from Group confided we now have 2,600 aircraft in this theatre! That counts everything, of course. But 200 Libs! And 90 Mitchells! I'd never even heard of B25s here. Counting the five Hurricane squadrons of the Indian Air Force, we have a thousand fighters. Most are RAF kites though it's the longer-range US planes that do the escort jobs. Transport aircraft total nearly a thousand. I thought they'd be mostly RAF units but 800 of the planes are Yank C47s and similar.

"You'll need the escort tomorrow," Intelligence told us at briefing. "A pack of fighters recently jumped a US formation over Moulmein... shot down one. They'll surely come up to defend their primary bases."

The trip had me extra excited. For the very first time, the Frazer team was to lead a Vic. Roy Williams was maestro of 215's nine-kite contingent. We were Number One in the second threesome. How about that! Okay, you have to maintain position in the formation but there's still some flexibility to move closer in or farther out. Instead of gluing your plane to someone else's wing tip, two others are formating on you.

Hey, I liked that. Jock and I even took turns flying little zig-zags, to left and right, just to look back and see the other two following us!

To top it off, we had our very own target! Other aircraft went straight for the main airdrome. Our trio was assigned to veer off and attack the 'kutcha strip.' That's any secondary runway, often unpaved, but for us the most important target in all Burma.

Pulling away from the main formation, I worried some if a three-plane group could protect itself. But no Japs appeared. The only non-Libs were Lightnings and Thunderbolts... circling above, guarding us.

But if fighters weren't a problem, clouds were. Most bombardiers never saw Zayatkwin, had to 'gestimate.' But for us, a crack opened up over the kutcha strip at precisely the right time. Reed had us at the perfect release point and all three bomb loads found the target. I could have kissed him.

Next trip, we again led one of the four Vics. Bill Waddington, who's now taking over the C.O.'s crew, was in #3 position. W/O Combes flew as the other wing-man. The target was at Meiktila, another airdrome.

"The aim is to knock out runways," the I.O. said. "Complicate life for Jap aircraft harassing our troops, just seventy miles from Mandalay now."

Roy Williams led us again, a dozen aircraft from 99 tucked in behind. We were riding P-Peter again with Smitty back on the bomb-sight.

"Feeling fine. Darjeeling? A great place, but too cold in January."

It was a fine sunny day with beautiful big cream-puffs hanging in the sky. Hundreds of them. Not the gigantic ones, but house-sized to city blocks, well enough spaced it wasn't hard to find a path through them. Good sport, in fact. If Roy veered around one, I'd have to judge how much speed to add or subtract to keep my brood in position. When the whole formation changed direction, the planes moved in unison, like marchers in a parade.

When flying, the sky is your constant companion; for hours and hours you can study clouds. In a million snow flakes, it's said no two are exactly alike; the same with cumulus. Such weird shapes! You could imagine you were watching a circus parade of bizarre creatures captured on some alien planet. And against that backdrop, the bevy of aircraft... darting this way and that... looked darn nice. Even a stubby old Lib — off the ground with legs tucked up and wings spread wide — can do a good impression of a swallow.

But when clouds got thicker, gaps smaller — only wide enough for three planes at a time — we'd have to swing in behind Williams' Vic, drop below his slipstream, follow him through the opening, then re-form. And beware what the other Vics were doing. When I saw a particularly narrow passageway ahead, I got my smart idea. Rather than follow Roy through the gap, I'd go around the cloud, re-join him on the other side. Risk of collision would be reduced, less juggling of throttles would save gas.

So we did that. A gentle do-si-do to the right to pass the big cumulus, our wing-mates following, while the other nine squeezed through the hole. The cloud was bigger than I thought, a whole lot bigger, but no problem. We'd hook up again as soon as we got past. Except...

Where the hell were they? Where did they go?

Miraculously, not an aircraft in sight. Vanished... like a magic act. Clouds, lots of them, but surely not so thick we couldn't spot nine big B24s. Jeez, I had to find them. To left and then right, peering behind one cloud bank after another, my wingers stuck with me; we must have looked like three chicks hunting for the mother hen.

But nobody there! Just clouds and sky! We had to give up, carry on into Burma. No big problem; Bob could get us there. But what happened?

Tee-Em — the Training Manual the RAF puts out as a magazine, which we always read because it tells about all the dumb things aircrew types have done each month — I'll be in the next issue! "Bomber formation over Burma changes direction," the headline will say. "P/O Prune fails to notice, continues straight ahead."

We finally saw nine Libs in the distance. It took extra petrol but we caught them at the I.P. — five minutes from the target —and slid into position, trying to look as nonchalant as possible.

Bombing results were good, photos showing bursts across both runways. Fighters were seen on the ground, but none came up after us.

Roy Williams, in a puzzled tone, asked me at de-briefing where I'd disappeared to just as he made that course change to port.

"I thought it was too dicey squeezing through those narrow openings," I lied. "Safer to loosen up the formation, tighten up again at the I.P."

Roy nodded, slowly. Too slowly, I'm afraid... likely why I'm not leading anything today. Four Vics line astern and we're flying #3 to Bingham.

Today's mission is special — an invasion! The British Army is going into Ramree Island to re-take the main Jap base on the Burmese coast.

To open the attack, the Royal Navy will shell coastal batteries. Yank B24s will bomb Nip Headquarters. Four RAF squadrons will then go after fortifications, 215's target being Mount Peter, a wooded ridge thought to conceal ground defences. Shelling will resume until landing barges get to the beaches. As our troops scramble ashore, fighters will strafe anything that moves.

"Sandwip Island... three minutes," from Bob. "We join 99 Squadron there."

"Planes ahead, skippah," from Phil in the nose. "Circling, a thousand feet above. I say... their ground crews are on the ball. I count sixteen. Can't see their markings yet but... Omigawd, they've hit!"

"Collision!" Eddie adds. "Two planes. Terrible."

It's raining debris — scraps of metal, pieces of fuselage!

"They just disintegrated!" Phil is shouting. "One turned right into the other... I think looking into the sun. One moment, two planes... then none. Nothing but falling scraps."

I check Bingham's aircraft again — it's well known that auto crashes are worst when motorists slow to view an accident — but I take a final look. Two kites... 22 guys... not even a ripple left on the water.

We're heading south over open water now, everyone subdued. The remaining 14 planes from 99 are in place behind us.

Two hours later, we've reached Ramree Island. Fifty kites, but it's not really one big formation. We're to arrive together, bomb at the same time, but each squadron has its own target.

"Ships, skippah. Explosions. The Navy must be shelling the beaches."

"Top turret to pilot. More Libs ahead... away above. The Americans? Their bombs are dropping now. And more Libs to starboard... the other RAF squadrons?"

"Landing craft, skipper," Jonesy's voice, bubbling. "Two rows of them, heading for shore, a mile to go."

"Target ahead, Wally," from Smitty. "Just a hill-top... but I think it's the right one. The shelling's stopped. Bomb doors open!"

Our four Vics are in line astern. I just follow the leader, keep straight and level. It's mostly Smitty's responsibility, Smitty and his finger.

Bombs gone, we're doing a slow swing to starboard, heading back to sea. If there was flak, we didn't see it. Smitty's sure he bombed the right hill but there's no way to tell if there was anything under the trees.

We pull away; the Navy starts shelling again. Now they've stopped, the landing craft almost on the beaches, our fighters buzzing above them.

And that for us was the invasion. Do we take the island? Do the Tommies and Ghurkas meet tough opposition? We don't stay to find out.

It's like leaving a movie 15 minutes before the end.

CHAPTER 15

LAHORE LEAVE

FEB. 1, 1945

Sixteen days leave, and I'll be glad to get away. We've seen too much sky lately: three ops this week, eight in 23 days. Most trips have been to Central Burma, though — only six or seven hours — and no fighter attacks. Of course, that's what you find when you get there; you don't know beforehand. So I always expect the worst. And worry.

A trip to hit Amarapura, near Mandalay, was different in that Jock had the day off and the rest of us flew as 'screens.' That means an experienced crew going with a rookie captain. Yes, that's exactly what the C.O. called us — "an experienced crew."

Then an unusual job. The Army has cleared the Japs from Ramree Island, is pursuing them inland. Stopped at Kangaw, they requested 'close support,' a job usually done by small fighter bombers. The target — a patch of jungle. We would see a dirt track, then three wooded hills. Our troops held one, the middle was 'no man's land,' and the Japs were in fortifications on the right, behind the revetments we were to smash. But how to hit the correct hill?

Bombardiers got photos to study, but were warned over and over, "If you're not absolutely sure, bring your bombs home."

Roy has forgiven me enough that P-Peter lead a Vic. With no opposition, we apparently hit the right bit of greenery. A message came in from the Army saying they were very pleased with the results.

A 'piece of cake'? Not at all. Without even leaving Dhubalia, it's the closest we've come yet to splattering ourselves over the Indian landscape.

"Group thinks we take too long getting into formation," Sindall told us. "So no more than forty-five seconds between take-offs."

Alright, we'd show them. With no dawdling, barely thirty seconds behind the plane ahead, P-Peter charged down the runway. We'd staggered off with no more trouble than usual, had climbed fifty feet when... bloody hell!

Without warning, we flipped over on our side. The starboard wing popped up — nearly straight up — and the port wing went down, almost scraping the ground. I was straining, pulling on the control column... trying to rotate it, to raise the wing tip, get it up and away from the surface... screaming at Jock to help. If the wing so much as touched — the end!

It was inevitable. Fully loaded, a Lib on take-off will barely stay aloft with wings horizontal. Almost vertical, not a hope!

In a spot like that, time stands still. For two minutes — or maybe two seconds — we hung there, suspended in that narrow band that lies between being in the air or spewed over the ground... in the thin strip of whatever it is that separates being alive from being dead.

Strangely, I became fairly calm — for me, anyway — and stopped shouting at Jock. I guess I'd resigned myself. Hanging sideways in my straps, I stared straight down, studying the distance between wing tip and ground, but in a detached way — a spectator with a front row seat.

Could I jettison the bombs? No, we're too aslant. There was nothing to do, nothing except wait to see what would happen... as when the dice have been thrown, are tumbling and bouncing crazily. With no control over the outcome, you can only wait to see what numbers come up.

Guys watching felt sure we were gonners. But then... a miracle! The wing popped up, not gradually, but with a sudden lurch! Jock and I were pulling so hard we nearly did a complete roll. But not quite. We reacted in time, got the wings levelled, straightened out and re-commenced the climb.

The intercom buzzed when the crew got to their stations.

Lahore Street

It must be terrifying to be bunched on the flight deck, hear the engines screaming — and in a tone you don't recognize — feel the unaccustomed 'G' forces and know something is terribly wrong, wonder how much longer you have to live.

I could tell them what happened, but not why. Slipstream? Too close behind the plane ahead? I wished Peter could tell me but the engines were now pounding away as if nothing whatsoever had happened... nothing at all! No, you can't ask airplanes; they have no memory whatever.

Following that, another 'screen' job, this time with W/O Appleby who's moving up to captain. With his crew this time, a motley group of recent arrivals and guys left over when the rest of their gang went tour-ex.

Cheez, I hate that... flying with people when you don't even know their names. And gawdamighty, the navigator was on just his second trip!

"Re-check the oil on number four," I told Appleby. "Run up the engine again."

By then, I figured, the swirling prop-wash from the plane ahead must surely have dissipated. It had. And Appleby managed the take-off so well I relaxed some.

The target was a place south of Mandalay. It's "Kyaukse" on the map although the I.O. called it "Chalk-see." I'm not sure whether the difference is the result of our rotten pronunciation or their lousy spelling.

Whichever, it seemed a petty target to warrant a four-squadron effort. It's not my job to think on such matters but I had little else to do; new captains like to do their own flying. But it was my chance to see the bombs dropping from other planes, also the cascading snow-storm of propaganda

Tennis — Govan, Smitty, Howse

leaflets written in Burmese we toss out on most trips.

I also wondered why I had to risk my neck, even a minor amount, to such little purpose — especially with my bags packed to start on leave.

Arthur, Mac and Eddie made other plans, but eight of us are going to Lahore. It's in north-west India, only three hundred miles from the Afghanistan border, out of the Ganges plain. It's reputed to have a pleasant winter climate, a sizable European population, and not be over-run with uniforms.

Tonight's chore? Write up my log-book. Ops total... 143; almost half-way.

We go into Calcutta tomorrow morning, leave there at midnight.

FEB. 12

Lahore: a fine city, a Rudyard Kipling city. It figures in his book about Kim; there's even an old cannon in a park called "Kim's gun."

It might even be worth the trouble to get here.

For a pleasant journey — luxurious accommodation and excellent cuisine — wait till the war's over and try the Orient Express. For a steady diet of tea, bread, potato chips, and half-cooked eggs... and three nights sleeping on an upper shelf... the train to Lahore would suit you fine.

Everyone's heard of India's caste system; I think they got the idea from the British military. It's ridiculous that a crew can't all stay together even on leave. The guys were herded off to a hostel for NCOs.

Smitty and I got into Faletti's Hotel — swimming pool, fancy ballroom, an attractive dining room with swell food. We even had a suite — bedroom plus sitting room — but it held five beds. Of the four in the outer room, two were occupied by Aussies. Nothing wrong with that, but disconcerting was the gold-braided full Colonel who emerged from the bedroom.

"Good morning, men," he said, obviously trying to be jovial. "We are indeed being subjected to a degree of wartime crowding, but I do not wish it to interfere with your well-deserved leave. We will therefore not stand on rank. If you arise before I do, feel free to use the bath to wash or shave or whatever. I shall not insist on first use."

First use? Did he really have to give his permission? I guess I don't know much about dealing with senior officers.

"Aw, he's ok'y," from the Aussies. "Even said we could help ourselves to his bottle of rum."

So we didn't stand on too much of that rank stuff, just took care to clean up the bathroom after we'd 'first-used' it.

The white population did seem genuinely friendly, even ran a weekly dance to which they committed their daughters in sufficient numbers that there were occasional partners for everyone. The ladies also operated a

On Leave — Lahore
Barlow, Govan, Slight, Smith, Done, Howse

little coffee shop where we met each morning to plan the day.

A temporary membership in the fancy Gymkana Club let me take the others to use the pool, tennis courts and other facilities. To feel like a civilian again, I even trotted out my green jacket and slacks.

Saturday night, I had a date. The attractions at the coffee shop included volunteer waitresses, one especially blond and pretty. Her father, she mentioned, was head of an Army unit there. A colonel's daughter? I was surprised she accepted my invite to the Dinner Dance at Faletti's.

Jean will be interested to know that dating here is very different. I didn't go to the girl's home. She was delivered to the hotel by a chauffeured limousine which waited for her till the party was over.

Why are all British girls great dancers? I could have danced all night. But we were at a table with a group of Yanks. They were short a couple of partners, and with a war on you have to share.

Mixing Yanks with anyone in a Brit-type uniform — even one with 'Canada' badges on the shoulders — starts with suspicion. We smell each other out like dogs sniffing dogs. But the wariness only lasts till you get to know one another. It turned out they were another B24 crew — 7th Bomber Group of 10th Air Force — so we had a lot in common there. In addition, all of us were far from home on a Saturday night.

I'd never spoken with USAAF Lib flyers. We talked some shop, found we've even been on some of the same missions. The reason we didn't hear of them for several weeks was they'd been diverted to flying gas and supplies 'over the Hump' into China, something we've never done.

As a crew, we spent a day at the races, a course littered with fences and gates where a horse has to be more hurdler than runner. Mostly they had Indian professional jockeys, but some amateur riders too, who fell off a lot.

"Would you care for a mount yourself, sir?" I got asked.

Hey, the chance of a lifetime — a real horse race! That'd really be something! But just then a stretcher went by with an RAF guy on it... moaning! That's when I remembered I know nothing about horses, even get nervous on the merry-go-round if I draw a frisky one.

But today we're just lazing around the pool. I've got a knee that's too bruised for anything much, and maybe we need to rest up for the trip back. With card games, movies and such to fill in odd moments, we've had a busy time, a great time, and I could stand another six months. But some are saying it's time to start back, their cash about gone. I guess we've been living it up pretty well at that. There are several night clubs and we've visited them all, including the one last night where I banged my knee.

One act in the floor show was a Russian dancer, a slim woman with long black hair who did acrobatic twists and turns to strange music. She later sat with British Army types, sometimes fox-trotting with one or the other.

It was Phil who suggested, "Hey, skippah, you like to dance. Why don't you ask her? Go on, I dare you."

Everyone thought that a grand idea, except me. I thought it very dumb. Sure, I dance a bit, but not recently. I'm way out of practice. No thanks.

But they insisted. Maybe there are times when it's necessary to show a little courage, accept a dare if it's only half ridiculous. Also, I'd had a few gins. Whatever, I found myself standing at the girl's table, suggesting she might join me on the floor.

I even made a little horizontal circle in the air with my finger... in case she only spoke Russian. I guess that was dumb too.

The Majors and Colonels sitting with her were scowling something fierce. She stared at me, cold-eyed, gave a sour look as if her feet hurt already, but nodded and stood up. Maybe it was in her contract.

But what a dancer! She knew what I was going to do before I did. Not that I know fancy steps, but I used to be considered fairly fleet of foot. We went wheeling around the floor, twirling round and round, in tight circles, tighter circles, faster and faster, twisting, spinning like a top. But eventually a top starts to wobble. I was getting dizzy, thinking I definitely should have passed up that last gin, not sure how to get stopped. I don't think anybody else was on the floor by then. Other couples had stepped aside, maybe to watch, maybe to take cover.

Somebody tripped me!

I am definitely of the opinion that one of the dancer's Army pals stuck out his toe as we passed that table. What's certain is... we ended up in a heap on the floor, stretched out and hurting. The music came to a crashing halt as the Army rushed to her rescue, helped her to a chair. Remarks made to me were unfriendly, even uncomplimentary.

She had a few words for me too. Oh, yes, she speaks English. Definitely does. Unless, of course, cuss words are the same in both languages.

FEB. 22

We're back at Dhubalia, on the job again, not happy about it at all. If I said I hated this war with a passion, it would be no exaggeration.

It puts a pall over everything. Really does! Coming in the front gate, I was fully aware of a dark shroud hanging over the place. The blanket isn't always low-hanging and oppressive, but goes up and down. Before a mission you know will be dangerous, it's thick, black, heavy. When you've landed, don't expect another outing for several days, it'll be high and wispy.

It's still there though. We try to ignore it, disperse the overcast with laughter and jokes. Our parties are raucous affairs, the revelry at times maybe even noisier than the amusements warrant. We do enjoy ourselves — no question about that — but always lurking in the corners is this smell of fear, the occasional whiff of aromatic nervousness.

Which doesn't surprise me. Crews would have to be witless not to be frightened by this rotten business we're in, and these are not dumb guys.

My first stop at the Mess was of course the mail rack. Hot damn... 18 letters! Then into the lounge where everyone was waiting for the dinner bell. The boisterous welcome was nice to hear.

"Hey, Fraz, where's my drink?" someone yelled. The shout became a chorus. Then the C.O. was shaking my hand, saying, "Congratulations, Flight Lieutenant Frazer." Wizzo! Drinks for all. It was a great homecoming.

Abdul had the camp tailor-wallah whack up new shoulder tabs — two blue rings instead of one — and I check out every mirror I pass. It's not that I've suddenly become handsome, but the double rings are definite proof I'm no longer a rookie. Apart from extra pay, I'll get more respect now. The whole crew will. Smitty is now F/O Smith and all the others are Flight-Sergeants. I guess we truly have become an `experienced crew.'

The squadron had been busy. I liked the score: Missions - 9, Losses - O.

One was 15-hours-plus against the railroad running down to Singapore. And at Rangoon, Oscars and Tonys finally came up to attack, but were beaten off.

"Yes, 215 gets credit for one Tony shot down," the Adj said, "but so many gunners claimed it, credit is going to the Squadron as a whole."

The other seven trips were all to central Burma in support of our ground forces closing in on Mandalay. That was our target right after getting home, Peter leading a box. We're going again today, not as a leader, but flying Q-Queenie in the tail-end-Charlie spot.

That's disappointing, especially as I'm a Flight-Lute now. But Roy says, "We have more Chiefs than Indians; everyone will have to take his turn."

So Harry Shaw in `O' leads our box; we're directly behind. Two Flight-Sergeants are on the wings — the Aussie, Cameron, and Tom Brooks, the blond English lad. But why fly so tight? Ridiculous. But if the NCO captains want to fly this close, I'll bloody well show them I can do it too.

We're not expecting much trouble today, maybe nothing at all. Flak is likely, fighters unlikely. But you never know.

From Bob: "I.P. in ten minutes. Target should be easy to spot today."

Yeah, an unusual one. A small place, close to Mandalay. The town has two names — Kaungmudaw or Paganyat — something to do with it being a Buddhist religious centre. Smack in the middle is the Great Pagoda, supposed to be very old, large, world-famous. I hope I see it before we knock it down.

Because of the Pagoda, the town has been off-limits, never bombed before. It seems a shame to smash it but the I.O. blamed the Japs. Surrounding the big Pagoda and eight smaller shrines is a high wall, and the Nips have made a fortress of the place. With our troops just a mile away, the complex is giving them trouble. It has to be levelled.

We've made the turn, are on the bomb run. Damn, I forgot to look for the Pagoda. Too late, now it's underneath us. I was concentrating on the other planes in the box. We're still ridiculously close.

"Big temple," Smitty is shouting. "Right ahead. Doors open."

Other planes are also ready to drop; I can look almost straight up into `O's' belly. The big double tail is above us, close but not too close. It's the wing men who worry me, especially Brooks on our left. His starboard wing is inside our port wing. I can see almost straight up into his bomb-bay too. That's crazy! Why the hell's he crowding us?

"Bombs... away!" Queenie tries to bolt ahead. Eleven thousand-pounders are also coming out of `O' just ahead of us... falling right in front of our nose.

Damn, maybe I'd crowded up too far... but, no, it`s okay, they missed us. But at the same time I get a glimpse of `T' on our left — except now it's almost directly above, crabbing across the top. The bombs are dropping from his plane... falling right in front of us. Cheez, I hope they are... there's damn little room to spare.

Ahh... okay. They all slid past our nose.

"Jock! What's that?" Something black — small and black — is coming this way. It looks to be coming directly at us, but of course it isn't. Bombs from other aircraft always look as if they'll hit you, but never do... they always drop in front. So will this one, although...

"Duck!"

It hits us, the window in front. A "splatt" sound, then a blast of air. But the thing missed me. At the last moment, I ducked... jerked my head to the left. I think I'm okay. Is that blood I taste? I feel alright. Except...

Except I can't see a thing. I don't think it's the blood. It must be the wind, blowing in my face. A hole... there must be a hole in the windscreen!

The wind is coming in, blowing like a typhoon. Worse than that, it's blowing in at our airspeed — at 16O miles an hour —worse than a hurricane. You can't look into that, not straight into it.

I try turning my head. I think I see Jock there, and he looks okay... but you can't face the wind. Your eyes water, blur, you have to shut them. I guess I automatically jam the nose down, ease back on throttles. We're losing height... only a gentle dive, I hope. My eyes are shut tight but I don't hear any collision... not yet anyway.

Now I've stretched to the left; the wind isn't as bad right against the side window. I get my eyes open, can see a little. But scrunched to one side, can I fly the plane? Don't think I could land it. But the immediate problem — stop the dive, level out, get back in formation — maybe I can do that.

But I feel the control wheel move without my moving it. Jock's taken control. I shield my eyes to look; he gives a tiny wave. His body's tilted towards his side window too, but not as much. He'll be able to get us home. I try to shout to him, but he can't hear. The whistle of the wind is terrible.

Here's Joe Barlow battling the gale to wipe my face. He's our medic, appointed keeper of the first-aid box, responsible for minor repairs. There's blood on the cloth, but not much. He daubs some ointment on my nose, sticks a bandage on it. I can't hear his words, but his wide grin tells me I'm going to live. And Jock has us back in the formation.

So what happened? It's obvious there's a hole in the plexiglass. The cockpit window in front extends back over our heads, but there's also a small triangular panel in each corner. That's what I'm hiding behind because part of the main section is gone. Maybe a piece of it nicked my nose.

Arthur taps my shoulder. Now he's down on his knees between the seats, picking something up. It's a piece of steel, the size of a fist, machined and shiny with curved flanges.

Yeah, a 'propeller.' It's screwed into the pointed end of a bomb, keeps it from becoming 'live' until out of the plane. As the bomb drops, the air working on the flanges makes the safety device revolve. This unscrews the thing, it twists off, falls free, and then the bomb is ready. But it's not supposed to drop off so soon.

I call the crew. The noise is so loud I have to bend over, hold the mike at my knees. Now I can hear them; they're telling me about the Pagoda.

Damn, I forgot to look at the ruins as we turned away.

"No, it's still there," Smitty's saying. "Good bombing. Our bombs, other bombs... we blanketed the compound, all around the Pagoda. But didn't hit it... I don't know how, but it's still standing."

We're on our way home. Jock is flying, says he can do the landing. It's drafty as hell, though. At 6,000 feet over the Chin Hills, it's even chilly.

But I'm still fuming. That metal piece... I'm sure it came out of 'T'. Even mis-performing, it wouldn't have done any damage if T-Tommy had been flying parallel, not crossing above us. You can bet I'll have a chat with Brooks about that. And yet... was I at fault too? I shouldn't have been jammed up so close to the lead plane.

"Cats have nine lives." Isn't that the saying? What about pilots? I hope it's at least that many. I've used up half already.

CHAPTER 16

BOMBS TO BANGKOK

FEB. 25, 1945

Another midnight, and we're nearly home. But a problem. Crossing Burma, north of Rangoon, we became aware of it. We were completely out of cigarettes. Eight smokers in the crew and not one butt between us! And nowhere we could stop to pick up a pack.

I'm smoking too much — take-off to landing, non-stop. It's not that I can't do without them, I just prefer smoking to not smoking, could give them up anytime. But I've gone through every pocket fifty times. Must have left my extra packs in the room, could near kill myself for being so stupid.

Another long one — 13 hours to Siam — and I'm bushed. When you bomb at dusk, half the trip has to be in the dark. Buckled into the shoulder harness, you get stiff, tired, fed up with grinding out the unending miles hour after hour, staring out at all that interminable black nothingness.

Yeah, that's what I'll do. Next time I'll put the cigs, the extra packs, right in my flying boots the night before. That way I can't forget them.

I'm proud of the new boots, black leather almost to the knee. One of the boys had them made by the local shoemaker, found them too small, sold them to me for two bucks. If you had to bail out, walk home, they'd protect you from snakes and blood-suckers. I just wish they were a size larger.

We needed a successful op today; our last two have been embarrassing. At Taunggyi, the lead plane's bombsight went kaput just minutes from the target. Bombing "by the seat of your pants" doesn't work.

The day before that — Myingyan. Bombardiers got only glimpses of the target. Unfortunately, a gap opened up just as the bombs hit... unfortunate because we brought back pictures of all our loads landing in a river.

Today was better, not that the weather was so marvellous. Waiting for

Royal Air Force

Pattern Bombing — Khorat, Siam

us as we reached Siam was this brigade of loathsome dragons — what the old Greeks called Gorgons — monstrous creatures lined up like hostile border guards, feet planted on the mountain tops, heads breathing steam to 17,000 feet.

I hate those ugly cumulus, their fluffy exteriors masking the violence in their hearts. We had to go over the top, sucking oxygen and hoping the turbulence wouldn't loosen Peter's rivets. But central Siam is flat. We let down to 4,000 feet to bomb.

The target — Khorat, never attacked before — is north-east of Bangkok on a rail line used for bringing supplies in from Indo-China. We did enough damage to at least slow the operation. No lucky shot brought us down and Peter's engines didn't quit on us. I was glad; it would have been a long walk home. Especially when your boots are a bit tight.

When we land, that first drag will taste wonderfully pleasurable. Not that the Adj would agree. "No, no... you get no real pleasure from smoking," he natters us. "You chaps have developed a need for nicotine, a serious addiction. All smoking does is temporarily relieve the craving. It eliminates a displeasure... doesn't *give* enjoyment. You're no happier smoking than if you'd never started puffing in the first place."

But what does Howard know? He says he quit years ago.

We've landed. The wheels hit the runway with contented "plunks." I'm close enough to Peter by now to know she's glad to be home too.

You wheel into the Dispersal, cut the engines, then sort of collapse.

And Jock Biggar doesn't let me down. He has cigarettes and it takes only a few long drags to get rid of that ache in my innards.

Then to the De-briefing Room. How the tiredness peels off as you go through the door. Maybe it's the lights in the room —shockingly bright after the hours of darkness, but waking you up. Or could it be all the people, a hundred guys milling about, greeting each other, joking and laughing, helping themselves to biscuits and drinks?

Crews arrive in multiples of 11 and replace those who are leaving. It's a party atmosphere, everybody in a great mood, glad to be home, happy the war's over for another day. It gets you all charged up again.

Motor Transport drops the crew off at their billet, the "good nights" sounding sharp and loud in the late night air. From our Mess building, Smitty and I walk over to our own basha, and we're home.

Snap on the lamp, and my room looks as neat as my grandmother's front parlour. I left it a mess this morning but Abdul's been on the job. And there they are, three packs of cigs on the table, but under a newspaper clipping. Yes, next time, into the flying boots.

The clipping is a big joke. From the Calcutta Statesman, it's the report of our raid last week where we aimed at the Giant Pagoda and the bombs dropped all around it. "Magnificent precision bombing by the RAF," the news item read, "evidence of the great care taken by British forces to ensure that structures of cultural or religious importance to the people of Burma not be damaged in the struggle to rid the country of its Japanese oppressors."

But we only missed it by accident!

But after fighting to keep my eyes open for the last three hours, now I'm wide awake. What can I do at three in the morning? Not Greek Mythology, not bookkeeping lessons. But it's the end of the month; I could write up my log book. A record of all your flying, it's almost a diary of your time in the Air Force. You note aircraft flown, crew members, destination, any other comments you wish. There are columns to analyze flying time by categories. Add the totals to date, ink them in and get the C.O.'s signature, and you've got those hours locked up in your bank.

Of course the only column that matters right now is the one headed "Operational Hours." Not too much added in February. Those little six and seven hour jobs don't add up very fast. Today was better; you could say, "one Siam equals two Mandalays."

There, I've finished. Total to date: 177. Yeah, if we hadn't gone to Lahore, it'd be over 200 now, but you shouldn't think like that. I'm happy we're half-way to the magic 300. And I do enjoy looking at the totals all inked in — underlined in red —ready for the C.O. to sign.

But should I put the book away, try to sleep? Wasn't King Midas the fellow who was obsessed by his gold, spent his days looking at it, holding it, counting it. Could I be getting as bad... counting and fondling my op hours?

MAR. 2

Tonight it's Bangkok — the Makasan railway workshops where locomotives are serviced and repaired. Another long one. Only a nine man crew. And almost the entire trip will be flown in the dark, getting to the target after midnight. We've never bombed at night before.

For SEAC, it's a big operation with all five RAF squadrons. But you can't fly formation at night. We have to get there on our own, home the same way, just like Bomber Command into Germany. Another similarity: we're to try the `path-finder' technique. Each squadron is sending two planes out early to mark its target area with flares. Other bomb-aimers can then just dump their loads on those markers.

Sounds a good idea, if the indicators get placed in the right spot. The C.O. said he'd be picking two of our best crews for the job, and we certainly weren't the only guys hoping we'd be chosen. But Sindall picked Beadon, an obvious choice, and W/O McPhee, the New Zealander said to be a top pilot. I was disappointed, but not for long. I got over it fast when I heard the Pathfinders were to go into Bangkok, a big city — at 300 feet!

It's now 2300 hours, a beautiful night. Coming down the Bay of Bengal to skirt around Burma, the full moon has been in front of us all the way. Big and round, it gives enough light to provide a horizon, faint but helpful. Our only source of entertainment, she arrived as a flaming redhead, became a platinum blond; now, more mature, she's getting silvery. Like people, I suppose.

We've turned east. It's bright enough we should spot another Lib crossing our path; at least I hope so. Fifty Libs out tonight, all on the same track. I hope we don't bump one.

Ahh, that's nonsense. From England, they run a thousand planes into Germany. The fantastic thing about the sky is its incredible vastness. Especially over the empty Indian Ocean, I expect you could have a million-plane raid and not scrape a wing tip. Those are the realities. Nevertheless...

I miss having Phil in the front turret, a good look-out position. But the C.O. said, "To deliver even a three ton load as far as Bangkok, we have to save weight somewhere. We can't economize on petrol, so the nose gunner and one wireless op won't go. As we don't think night fighters would attack from the front, there is no ammo in the nose. Nor the beam guns. But you'll have four hundred rounds in the ball turret, six hundred in the rear, eight hundred for the mid-upper."

That's about normal. The rounds allotted to a turret each mission depend on the type of target, opposition expected, and the plane's position in the group. Tail-end Charlie in the formation will get the biggest ration. But maybe fighters... and no front gunner?

"Land ahead, Wal," from Smitty. "A peninsula coming in from the left."

"Likely Tavoy," from Bob. "If so, we're on track."

As a crew, we're now pretty well aware of each other's quirks. The guys know I worry a lot about mid-air collisions and running out of gas. Bob's big concern is hills higher than we are. He'll be calling to discuss it.

Crackle, here he is. "We're at five thousand feet, skip, right? If that was Tavoy, there's nothing higher ahead. But if it wasn't... if we got the wrong bay, there are several peaks, two about five-two, one that hits six thou. Should we be a little higher?"

Dammit, once over these hills, we'll let down again. Why waste petrol to climb then give away those extra feet in just minutes. Besides, deciding what height to fly is the pilot's job. I don't like even Bob telling me what to do!

Jeez, I'm crabby! More up-tight than usual. I do not like this skulking through the dark. We should stick to daytime missions; in the sunshine, you only worry about real danger, not things that aren't really there.

We're now over the coast, have climbed to 5,300, which satisfies Bob in part as Eddie assures him he could spot anything higher.

"Water below, skipper," reports Jonesy, in his turret tonight.

I'm familiar enough with the area's geography by now to know it's the Gulf of Siam. That's Pacific Ocean water down there, a bay sixty miles wide — a 'bight' — running up to Bangkok. That's where we are now.

Target in twenty minutes. Half of me says, "Let's get there, get it over with, one way or the other." The other half says, "What's the bloody rush?"

I'm reducing height. We were told, "Bomb between two and three thousand feet." I have no intention of going lower than necessary. Nobody's going to get above Peter, drop his load on us.

Bangkok is somewhere over on our port side. The plan is to cross the Bight of Bangkok, passing south of the city. Then we'll swing north, turn left again and cross the city on a westerly heading, already pointing towards home. It sounds a good routing.

Eddie's voice. "Big fires... on the left. Wow! Is that Bangkok?"

Omigawd! A red glow. Other squadrons have bombed, left it burning!

We're now about even with the city and the fires look even bigger, redder, uglier. Searchlights are probing the sky, there are explosions and flashing lights, both on the ground and in the air. It looks a conflagration, an inferno... the main street of Hell on a Saturday night!

We have to fly into that?

I can't keep my eyes off the fiery mess. And we have to look at it for a full 15 minutes while we do a big circle, get in position for the bomb run. What a lousy plan. I'd rather come upon it suddenly — as a surprise — rather than be mesmerized, terrified, have to stare at it so long.

We've swung north, a very short leg, and here's Bob again:

"The I.P. is right ahead. Turn to port... now. Smitty's on the 'sight.' Just a four minute run to the aiming point. You didn't want to be the first 215 kite across the target, nor the last. We're about dead on ETA... should be in the middle of the pack."

How the hell can he sound so calm? Has he not looked out his window — too busy with maps and protractors to see what's ahead?

Smitty's saying something. "Ready for bombing." I think that was it. "Our markers... the red markers... are straight ahead. Height three thousand, airspeed one-seven-five. Can you hold her steady?"

But I have other things on my mind. All those flashing lights... directly ahead now. So many! They must be the tracers. What's the usual? Every fifth shell a tracer, a coloured one mixed in so gunners can see where their fire is going? From all directions, little lights... brilliant red lights... streaking skyward in a straight line — zip, zip, zip, zip, zip — one after the other. Fast as lightning. You could think they're pretty... until you remember each bit of flashing colour is preceded by four shells able to knock a plane out of the air... and followed by four more.

Now we're into it. Into a fireworks show! Flashing lights screeching past our nose, another line going by my window. They're everywhere, thousands of them — a maelstrom of pyrotechnics, a barrage, an impenetrable curtain. We're sure to get hit.

And there must be A/A fire. You don't see the puffs at night — just the occasional glint, wisps of smoke drifting past the window.

I've never been so terrified, so close to panic. It's like having to cross a mine-field, wondering which step will be your last. Or made to walk through a pit of rattlesnakes, waiting to feel the first strike... feel the first pain. And there's nothing you can do. You can't dodge. There's no place to hide. You can only lumber along, hold your breath, wonder which shell will get you.

And now I see searchlights, dozens of them... hunting, probing, poking around the sky... searching for prey. Cheez, they've got one, a Lib, down to our left, coned by three lights. She's twisting and turning to escape — like a mouse cornered by a cat — but the lights are still on her. Will fighters come in to finish her off?

Only vaguely do I hear Smitty shouting, pleading for "right, right," I think... but his voice seems to come from far, far away. Besides, I'm busy. I'm concentrating, hard, on me! I have to keep steady, try to stay calm, keep my wits about me. Don't panic... don't go over the edge. But I do give a kick to the rudder pedal, sort of automatically.

Now I hear Smitty say, "Bombs gone."

Then let's get the hell out of here. We haven't been hit yet. Could our luck hold? Just a little longer? I push the nose down, but get a peek at the air speed gauge. Hell, we were at 200, not 175. That wouldn't put Smitty's bombs where he aimed them. But... right now... the thing that matters — get out of here. That's what we're doing. I'm pushing the nose down, picking up speed, concentrating on that. But why's Jock banging my arm now? Pointing at the airspeed gauge?

Cheez, almost 300. Wings don't like that. Gotta ease the throttles back... gently, don't rush it... level out. Hope we don't run up another Lib's backside. Check the altitude. We've levelled off but still doing 220. And down to 1,800 feet. I better start climbing.

There's time for a peek out the window. Only a few tracers. Now none. The sky is a beautiful black... no ugly, coloured lights. The ground is mostly dark too. We're out over open country, the city behind us.

Have we made it? Surprise! I didn't think we would, not a snowball's chance in Bengal! That was the scariest, worse than Insein. A lot worse. All those flashing lights. The curtain of tracers looked seamless, impossible to get through. But we did... without a scratch!

I'm almost overcome... relief, happiness, surprise. Roll Out The Barrel, let's sing and dance and have a party, a celebration. Three cheers for being alive. But you can keep that damned night bombing. Let me stay in the sunshine: no shadows, no ghosts, no mystery.

The gunners are still watching for fighters but they're unlikely now. We're going to be okay. And here's Bob with the course home.

"Fly three hundred for now, skip. We're to take the shortcut across central Burma again. I'll work out a course correction later. But you'll have to climb to get over the hills... at least seven thousand feet."

"Whatever you say, Bob."

"ETA Dhubalia... nine a.m... about seven hours."

Another seven hours! Well, what the hell, that's okay. Even that thought can't spoil the great mood I'm in.

MAR. 7

All 54 aircraft on that Bangkok job got home okay. A lot were dinged but we didn't lose a man. Amazing! Is it another result of the sky being so vast, the empty spaces between aircraft still a thousand times bigger than the planes themselves, big cracks for shells to slip through?

On the trip home, `George' quit on us. Manhandling the plane for the final six hours is desperately wearying. Worst is the hour before dawn, your energy level at its lowest, adrenaline drooping to a dribble of droplets.

Abdul and Smitty

For the hundredth time, I scan the eastern sky. Finally, is that a lighter smudge on the horizon? When I point, Jock turns to look, but shrugs. Well, maybe not. But minutes later, a certainty; the long night is going to end. And, miraculously, you come alive. As the sky gets brighter, so do you. The sun pops up to start a new day and you think you could join it, go another 14 hours. But the medicinal properties of the dawn are short-lived. Before the sun reaches mid-morning height — mid-morning heat — you're ready to collapse again. But by then you'll be home in bed.

Except that Joe picked up a radio message. "Fog at base; divert Digri."

"Five crews from your Squadron already here," the lorry driver said when we'd plopped down. "If you flew out of Digri with 215, Mr Frazer, you'll know a lot of the 159 captains here, won't you?"

Wrong. With those long mining jobs on 159, you can finish a tour fast. The fellows I knew are all gone, finished their tours or dead. Nobody I spoke to even remembered their names. Something else gone is the bottle of Coca Cola, its shelf empty. Nobody remembers it either.

It was mid-afternoon when we got home, and straight to our beds.

"Smitty, tea time! Abdul's here. Want to join me?"

Thin walls save steps. And we might as well sit together. Smitty's been morose, concerned about his mother. But, photos developed, the Bangkok op got a very good rating. We both think it's a great joke our own stick went right across a building. Maybe I should always be 25 mph faster than expected.

Smitty has a newspaper. The war news is very good now; everyone says the Germans are crumbling. But that's only marginally interesting to me. My real concerns are extremely self-centred and immediate. Such as, "What's the next trip Roy will have us on? How tough will it be?"

Officer's Mess

Longer term aims? "We're nearly finished here. Don't do anything stupid for the next few weeks."

One enjoyable aspect of squadron life is the lack of any spit-and-polish kind of discipline. There was enough of it during training days, obviously designed to knock the 'school boy' out of us in a hurry. But it's said that the closer you get to the front lines, the less you have to salute.

From an airman, it's not unusual to get a casual "sir" or a "mister," but I haven't had to return a salute for weeks. There's no marching about, no shouting of commands, no standing at attention. With individuals or groups ambling from their billets to or from their place of work, it looks more like a factory site than an air force base.

In her last letter, Jean asked, "Do you get to meet many Indians, been in any of their homes?"

The truth is, except for somebody like Abdul, we have little contact with the people of India. Military personnel live in a very separate strata, super-imposed on Indian society but not a part of it. I'm sorry but, no, I've never been in any of their homes.

It's time to get over to the Mess for dinner. Waiting outside for Smitty, I pass the time hunting for the Southern Cross. Usually it looks more like a diamond or a kite but tonight the sky's clear enough I can make out the dim star in the centre which finishes the design.

In the opposite direction is the North Star, so low on the horizon in these latitudes it can be hard to find if there's any ground haze.

And hey! There's Cassiopeia, the big 'W' in the sky. I wonder if Jean will see it tonight. Because it's my initial, we agreed it would be our point of contact. Even half a world apart, we could both see it and feel closer. Okay, that's dumb, not something you'd ever admit to any of the guys, but I think it's comforting.

I guess I'm feeling more lonesome than usual tonight.

CHAPTER 17

CALCUTTA CAPERS

MAR. 14, 1945

Bad news! We've lost three more Canadians — Ed Gilbert, Smokey Williams, and Mac Gardner. From enemy action? No, Eddie took the little single-engine Argus into Cal on some errand for the C.O. Just an hour into Cal, then right back after lunch. Mac and Smokey went along to keep him company — Eddie was a guy who always liked lots of company — or maybe just for the lark.

Did they perhaps do too much larking over lunch? Whatever, they were late getting back to Dum Dum airport, apparently picked the wrong

Eddie Gilbert, Mac Gardiner

196

rail line to follow back to Dhubalia. But there's little twilight in these latitudes; the sun dips below the horizon and it's like someone switched off all the lights. They ran out of gas, tried to land in the dark, didn't make it.

Today I had breakfast with Bill Waddington. He looked up from his fried eggs to ask, "When you and I came to 215, Wal, how many RCAF in the Mess?"

"Nine."

"Right. Not counting new arrivals, how many are left?"

"Two. Just us."

Bill took a long swig from his cup, finally looked up at me and said, "Keep your fingers crossed."

"Yeah, Bill... you too."

MAR. 17

"All turrets... a full load of ammo. The bomb load? Each aircraft has four one thousand-pounders, eight five hundred-pounders."

"Just a damn minute, m'ite," someone explodes behind me. You wouldn't holler at the WingCo in that tone, but it's only the Armament guy.

"That's eight thousand pounds. Last week, s'ime trip, the load was seventy-five hundred pounds. To compens'ite, petrol's been cut a hundred gallons. Thanks for nothing. But what'll that extra bomb do to our t'ike-off w'ight?"

Every week the tonnage we have to coax into the air goes up another notch. Scrape off the deck with 63,500 pounds, next trip it's 63,700. It's our biggest labour-management dispute. But the orders come from Group. The C.O. can only say, "Don't make any mistakes and you'll be alright."

Today: supply dumps at Rangoon. Down to undershorts, I'm waiting in line for take-off... always a nervous time, especially with added weight.

The first aircraft pulls onto the runway. Everybody moves up a notch. P-Peter was fifth in the row because we're leading the second box; now we're fourth... now third. Sand is swirling all about.

We're next. Okay, let's go. Pounding down the runway, I check on the plane ahead, ninety seconds ahead. Yes, he's airborne... climbing, looking good, and swinging slightly to port. That's what I've been preaching. I'll go a little to starboard, a slightly different path, separate Peter a bit more from the whirlwind kicked up by his engines.

Jock is calling out our airspeed, "One-ten... one-twelve."

It's increasing, but too slowly. The end of the runway is coming fast.

"One-thirteen."

Cheez! Peter needs help or we won't make it! Jam the throttles through the stops? That's a no-no, can damage engines. They could fail... sputter and quit. Maybe not today... maybe another trip, another crew.

Wham, it's done! Who wouldn't? All pilots do; I'm sure of it. They must... must do whatever is necessary at the moment to stay alive.

"One-eighteen...one-twenty."

The plane is throbbing, shaking, shivering. Peter's ready to jump... to leap for his life one more time.

On any take-off... any overloaded take-off... there's that critical second — immediately after "too soon" and just before "too late" — which is precisely the right time to pull the stick into your belly. On your first flights, you're not sure when that is. By this time, I know. For this flight, it's now! Not that there's any damn choice. We're out of runway! The wheels come off the pavement, but Peter hangs suspended — two feet above the concrete — uncertain whether to continue the struggle, or give up, accept the crash. No, we can't have that, have to keep climbing! The engines are bansheeing like creatures in torment. But they can't quit now.

Ahh, we're starting to climb. Small trees... I'm looking out at them, not up at them. Now they're below us. I can ease the throttles back, raise the undercart. A "bump... bump" as the wheels settle into place in the wings. We're going to make it. I remember to swing slightly to starboard.

Even with all planes in the air, getting the heavy-loaded beasts into formation is tricky. But today's plan sounds okay. Roy is to climb straight away to 1,000 feet, then start a long, slow climbing turn to port bringing him back across the airfield at 2,000. The rest of us will make progressively tighter turns as we climb, slide into place behind him.

We're into our climbing turn when Jock points up, says, "Cloud!"

Damn. But just fluffy thin stuff. Low stratus, not very thick. We burst through and are back in the sunshine. But where is everybody? Oh no! Have I lost the formation again! There are chunks of haze about, but we should see the other four kites. Or did they all stay below the cloud?

Whatever, we have the sky to ourselves, as if the only humans in creation. I'm out of my harness, starting to dress, when... a funny sight. The next plane has emerged from the mist below. One moment, nothing but cloud; next, a full grown Liberator has been spawned, suddenly popped out of the frothy white, an oversized tadpole swimming across the sky.

The cloud has now given birth to another, then a third. Soon seven Libs are following us, my biggest brood yet. But we better find the others; Roy was unhappy the last time I lost him. On the other hand, I have more followers today than he has. Couldn't I argue, "What the hell, Roy? Who lost who?"

Bob gives us a course to Comilla. And that's where we find Roy, his box circling with 99's twelve kites. He even waggles his wings to welcome us.

We're home now. The trip was routine. Except, for the first time, B29 Superfortresses joined us. Sort of... just three miles away. We bombed from 15,000 feet; they were at 30,000.

The custom is for Spitfires and planes of that genre to celebrate a return from a mission by 'shooting up' their airdrome. After recording a 'kill,' they'll even do a barrel-roll at tree-top level.

Can Libs match that? Hell, no. So what instead? Hah, we do steep turns! Spitfire jockeys would laugh out loud. But I do mean steep — each week steeper than before — the port wing pointed at the runway, loose articles rattling around the fuselage, crew all hanging on to something. We keep expecting the C.O. to object, but he hasn't yet. He knows we have to celebrate too.

MAR. 24

Calcutta for a week! I was in the Adj's office when he took the call.

"A course on Radio Range Beacons," he told me. "A vacancy and 215 has to fill it. You've been on the last two ops? Right, you're it."

A week off the station! But it's strange to be without the crew. For ten months, we've spent several hours together 'most every day.

I came into Cal with Rolly Templeton, an English bloke on 99 I knew in England. His name suits him because he's a roly-poly chap with a slightly over-fed look. It's just hard to see him as a war hero. But that's what he is. He was a fighter pilot in the Battle of Britain and if you'd like to be a 'somebody' in the RAF, that's the very best you can be.

He was also a hero to get us into the Grand Hotel. We both had reservations but the Indian desk clerk couldn't find them, pawed through his file of papers, muttering, "Ver' sad, sahibs; no room reserve."

Cheez, there'd be no rooms anywhere. But the five-rupee note Rolly slid onto the counter disappeared into the clerk's little brown hand in an instant. Surprise! Our reservation slips were right on top of the pile.

Our room has a big fan blowing up a small typhoon, had us wondering if we'd have to lash ourselves to the bed posts at night. But we won't need the mossie nets. Mosquitoes could never manoeuvre in that gale; they just don't have the horsepower.

After camp life, modern conveniences quite impress you. To wash up, just turn a tap. Best of all — the toilet! Tug a chain and a gush of water leaves everything clean as a whistle. I'd never even heard of this John Crapper who designed the contraption. With an invention that great, no wonder his name... both names... are so well known, right up there with Edison and Pasteur.

Rolly has a newspaper. The big headline: "Our troops take Mandalay, the threat to India definitely over."

We now hear that a major strategic fear a few months back was that the Japs might take India and hook up with the Germans in Africa to cut off our Arabian oil supply. That Imphal battle may have been very important.

There was also an account of the trip we did this week. The target was Na-nein, near Chumphon on the rail line that runs from Bangkok to Singapore. "The longest formation mission of the war," it said. "72 RAF and US planes attack Jap installations on Isthmus of Kra, 2400 miles round trip."

Doesn't that sound impressive, an armada of 72 war machines sweeping across the Indian Ocean to smite the foe? Actually, we went in separate groups — 12 aircraft each — a full half hour apart. Except for our own planes, I didn't see another aircraft all day.

But the distance wasn't exaggerated. I now believe it; the earth's surface is two-thirds water. Mile after mile of blue on blue, right to the horizon. And when you finally do get to that point, where one blue should meet the other, guess what... nothing ahead except another horizon. But the WingCo eventually turned us east, to the Isthmus.

What beaches! Miles of golden sand. And the most amazing thing — a girl was out walking... and she waved at us! But we continued inland, found Na-nien, gave the rail junction a pasting, and not a shot was fired at us.

The trip back... gas problems again. By leaving Jonesy and Mac at home, we'd brought 2,650 gallons, the big Imperial-measure kind; it seemed ample. But headwinds again. With Arthur, Jock and Bob all checking and rechecking the consumption logs, that left me free to sit and bite my nails. We eventually detoured over to Chittagong, spent the night there.

The course in Cal is going well enough. But we aren't expected to think very hard or long at a time and I checked they still have my name on file at the RCAF office, recently grown in size. "To accommodate all the crews now arriving from Vancouver," the new Liaison man said.

"You're the only Canadian in an RAF crew, eh? And all those different nationalities on 215. How do you get along together?"

He expected to hear of problems, but I insisted we meshed just great.

There was news of the Blackpool Four. Ted Willing has finished his tour, but remains in Cal. Bill Jackson is still with 355. And Phil Cloutier, my Montreal pal? Phil didn't make it back from a flight a month ago into Indo-China. Damn! Along with Louis Bisson, my buddy through training days, both my French-Canadian friends are now gone.

Talk of losses makes you realize how lucky we've been on 215 — only one crew lost on ops. Other squadrons have had worse luck, the latest being F/O Dean from 355 at Na-nien last week. The hush-hush squadrons, 357 and 358, have been having a very rough winter. Of the regular Lib outfits, the guys at 159 have lost seven crews. Minuscule compared to what's happening in Europe but, as someone put it, "just enough losses you don't get bored with the work."

A story out of 99 was hard to believe. They're into some plan whereby four non-flying people get leave in Britain; one officer and three others were chosen by lot. This Flt/Lt Plant had his name drawn, but gave up his spot to an airman whose mother was seriously ill. Isn't that right up there with Damon and Pythias, lovely proof there's still some brotherly love left in the world!

A big party at Canada House. It's possible there isn't one girl from my country in all of India but the organizers managed a good selection of English damsels and Anglos. Another fellow I haven't seen since Canada was there: big John Ross, easy to remember, in part because his father owns the Boston Bruins hockey team. He's still in the RCAF — 'USA' tabs on his shoulders, of course — still flying Spits.

Last night I had a date, a blind date.

Rolly knows a girl here in the FANYs, a nursing service, from his home-town in England. She could bring a friend — a blond, Rolly was told — and we might all go to the dinner dance at Firpos. Sure, sounded great.

At the hospital, Rolly's friend, Jane, a smashing brunette, showed up first. Then Doris came out of the elevator. She really was a blonde... but, omigawd, nearly three hundred pounds. Our cab driver, the scoundrel, took one look and demanded extra fare. What could I do? With Doris standing right there, could I get into a big argument about her avoirdupois?

And when the orchestra at Firpos came on to play, I told a bare-faced lie. I thought I had to; how do you waltz with a whale? I said I didn't know how to dance. It made for a long evening — after dinner, nothing but sit and talk, talk, talk — my feet just itching to get on the floor.

But what really crumpled me was Doris saying she didn't dance either. Then Rolly said he also would rather not; Jane was too good for him what with all the ballroom prizes she'd won in England!

Damn, damn, damn! If I'd kept my big mouth shut, I could have danced with the cute brunette all evening.

APR. 1

Calcutta is too hot, stinking, overcrowded. Chowringhee sidewalks are almost impassable. Horns honk incessantly; everyone shouts. You stand in line for everything... though I think the problem is the crowds, not the line-ups. People joke about the British penchant for queues, but at least they're orderly and fair. Could they even be evidence of a civilized society?

Indians don't believe in them, but their alternative is ugly. When a bus arrives at a stop here, a shoving match begins, a donnybrook of people pushing, elbowing, fighting for seats. The very old, the frail... they get

Cobra

pushed aside, have to hope there's a chance on the next bus.

At the railway station going back to camp, a typical scene: half out of the taxi, a dozen coolie porters have descended on you, shouting in your face, each demanding you choose him to carry your suitcase.

For one bag, who needs a porter? But refusing would bring horrendous arguments. So you point, choose one with your finger, which brings a rage of snarls from the others. Okay, so the coolie porters are desperate, maybe need your eight cents if they're to eat today, would almost kill for it. You think of that later. At the time you're just fed-up, snarling back, wondering again how much longer you'll have to stay in this gawdawful country.

At least in comparison, life on the squadron is serene. The crew said they'd had a quiet week off-duty, made jokes about missing me.

"With no one to take us on a wee adventure, we were bored stiff."

But the squadron was busy. A locomotive-shoot on the B.S.R. bagged wagons and several engines. Bill Waddington's crew had something else to report.

"At Milestone Eighty-two, we saw a hundred men in a fenced compound, standing close together, looking up."

"Yes," the I.O. said, "POWs there. Knock out a trestle, they rebuild it."

The poor devils! Camps placed near prime targets, sometimes right in the middle. And, let's face it, bombs do go astray. I've wondered what POWs think about that? Do the signs of our growing air strength — more and bigger planes and formations passing overhead — give them hope, make them cheer? Or do they curse the bombs dropping so close?

The other two ops were against supply dumps in Moulmein and Bangkok, the latter a big-budget affair with three USAAF squadrons, four RAF outfits, and sixty P51s. Surely the sight of 140 of our aircraft passing overhead would cheer any POWs they flew over.

Other squadrons had stories: 355 planes making individual runs on bridges on the B.S.R got jumped by fighters. Just three, but that's plenty when you're all alone. A Hamp made several passes at 'R.' Being at low level for the bomb run likely saved them. Mobility is a fighter's main advantage but much of that is lost if the quarry is right on the deck. The captain dove to ground level — to fifty feet — zigged and zagged and got away.

Aircraft 'L' fought off an Oscar three times at the bridge. Returning home, they were crossing the coast at 2,000 feet when the Jap attacked again. The Lib won; the ball gunner shot the attacker down.

Lesson: Japs don't like big formations, but don't get caught all alone.

The native boys killed a big snake this week just behind our basha — a cobra, seven feet. That happened to be the night I drew the short straw.

About ten of us decided to take in a Betty Grable picture. To get to the camp cinema over at Wing HQ, you can walk all around the perimeter track — two miles — or cut across the airdrome in half the time. But the short-cut is risky; the weather is balmy enough for snakes to be camping out.

So that only one in the group is at risk to step on a rattler, we walk single file. The fellow who pulls the short straw, who's at the front of the line, gets the torch to carry, and lots of advice.

"Come on, Wal, speed it up or we'll be late. And stop complaining. You always said you wanted to lead the squadron!"

With Roy in Calcutta, I'm in charge of 'B' Flight this morning. Guys keep coming in to ask about my week in Cal. What we're really doing, of course, is putting in time, waiting for the Orderly Room corporal to arrive.

"Here he is," someone shouts, and I join the crowd at the bulletin board. Daily Routine Orders aren't that important, but are there Battle Orders?

Yes, and we're on the list. "A/C 'P' — Flt/Lt Frazer" — with the other ten names listed. At least the full crew will be going. The big question is "what target?" but we won't be told that until Briefing. Smitty thinks it won't be a long one; extra petrol tanks aren't being put in the bomb-bays.

But already the first signs of tenseness, the first butterflies fluttering in my stomach. Later they'll turn into rodents, nibbling at my innards. Where are we going? What'll the target be?

We're back to our basha. With the noon-day heat getting fierce, the station has switched to 'summer hours' — 0600 to 1200. Admin people and ground crews have to go back to work — 1630 hours until 1800. Of course, they get Sunday afternoons off. But everyone celebrates Siesta. The entire camp is quiet, everyone staying as still and un-energetic as possible. The atmosphere presses down on you, hot and thick, and the buzzing of the cicada chorus seems muffled by the effort to get through the heavy air.

Letters today! Jean's, written a month ago, was headed 12345, with appropriate slash marks. A unique date. Smitty's reaction? "Numbers interest you that much? Perhaps the accounting field might be right for you."

There, I've just finished my log book to March 31. Total op hours — 217. We're getting there. But it's time to catch the transport to the briefing room, find out what the target is. I hope it's not a tough one!

We're back. Smitty's guess about a short trip was wrong; it's Siam again — railway repair shops at Keng Goi, northeast of Bangkok — the usual four RAF squadrons. Another long one. As an experiment, we'll fly in a 'gaggle' — in a cluster, but no set alignment. With monsoons nearly upon us, a gaggle may help us squeeze individually through small gaps in the clouds. Also, it's supposed to be easier on gas.

"Might be no opposition at all," the I.O. said. "You'll by-pass bigger cities, and our photo reconnaissance plane didn't spot a single gun position in the town. Of course, they might just be well camouflaged. We don't expect Jap fighters, but of course we can't be sure of that either."

That's the trouble. You never, never know.

The petrol? The gaggle is supposed to save so much juice we're going all the way on just the wing tanks. No reserve at all.

The tightness in my gut is even worse than usual. I'll have trouble sleeping again tonight. All the usual thoughts: gun batteries, Jap fighters, slave camps... plus empty gas tanks, no reserve at all.

CHAPTER 18

A CHANGE OF SCENE

APR. 11, 1945

Our trip to Keng Goi rated a full four stars, our own bombs splattering workshops and godowns. And we did have enough gas to get home.

Petrol consumption is now checked closely at 231 Group, the C.O. reporting after formation trips on each aircraft's 'air miles per gallon.' The average is about 1.1, a bit more on long flights. But gaggles are indeed more efficient. Everyone did better. And Peter? Best of all — an A.M.G. of 1.25.

That shocked everybody. "Did you smuggle extra petrol drums aboard?" "Did you find a short-cut home in the dark?"

But I think we've finally learned to fly 'on the step.'

Then another screen job, with Fl/Sgt Dineen who's taking over Cameron's crew. Hey, we're really babying new crews nowadays. On our first op, we were just handed the keys to Peter and told, "Follow those other guys."

It was another formation trip to the Rangoon supply dumps. Over the target, I did what most crew members do — nothing! That absolutely has to be the worst, far too much time to stare at the flak, count the puffs, wonder if they're getting our height.

"A/A fire was fairly light," I was told at de-briefing. Hell, the bursts were all around us, front and back and on both sides, every damn gunner down there trying to be a hero, get himself a Lib for his trophy case. When I saw puffs directly above, I figured out that the shells to get there must have gone right through the formation. That's when I sat very still, fists clenched and holding my breath, waiting for the explosion to happen.

It didn't. We just flew home.

With so few RCAF in the Mess, very pleasing to me was the arrival of four officers wearing 'Canada' badges. Two joined me for a get-acquainted visit.

Royal Canadian Air Force

De-briefing: Art Brown's Crew

"Not many RCAF here, eh?" from Russ Scriver. "Lots on other squadrons now, pouring out from 5 OTU near Vancouver. We weren't in the first course there, but earlier crews came by boat. We flew out, were likely the first to reach India."

"No, didn't fly our own plane," from Jack Insull, the double wings on his shirt showing he'd be one of the pilots. "In a Transport Command Lib. Our skipper, Art Brown, flew second pilot; I filled in sometimes. Yeah, saw a lot of the world... Montreal to Gander, then the Azores, Morocco, Tripoli, Cairo, Iraq, Karachi. Eight days. Down to Bombay, a long train trip to Calcutta, got to 355 Squadron the end of November."

"November? I thought you'd just arrived."

"No, no, did ops there for three months," says Scriver, the bombardier. "Then to 159 where Art became Flight Commander. Four more ops. Then got orders to come here. Art was an instructor in Canada; I think they send us wherever they need an experienced captain."

So that's it! Brown will be taking Beadon's place.

Windy Watters, the navigator, joins us. A skinny fellow, he seems likable enough, maybe even intelligent, though that's certainly not important in the Air Force. But Windy? Why would such a quiet fellow be called that? Ahh, yes, guys are no more likely to call him Wendell than they are to call me Wallace.

At dinner, I meet Art Brown, the captain. I'm so glad to see the new arrivals that I appoint myself chairman of the welcoming committee, making sure they don't pay for drinks their first night in the Mess. I have help from Bill Waddington, also Joe Reid, a bomb-aimer just arrived last week.

"You say you don't have enough ball players here to challenge other squadrons," Scriver reminds me. "There'll be enough now. Our NCOs play, and we'd have a good pitcher. Joe Reid was on our team at Boundary Bay. He's very good... used to play in tournaments all around Ontario."

I've only met Reid once so have a closer look. He's been in some kind of scrape, but I don't know what. A big fellow, he sports an over-size black moustache, certainly has a sparkle in his eye. And when the singing starts, he has a song to contribute. The rest

Joe Reid

of us come in on the chorus while he does the verses in a weird German accent, the lyrics very funny though not what you'd sing for your grand-mother.

The new guys are certainly going to liven up this place.

We take laughs wherever we can find them. The C.O. passed around a 'thank you' letter received from one of the contractors allowed to provide services in the camp. It was a good effort except that the writer had apparently copied from the wrong page of the text-book. It began: "Dear Sir (or Madam)"... and ended, "Your loving husband (wife)".

Other developments: I no longer pay to go to the cinema, and I'm now licensed to drive station lorries. In a way, the two are connected.

To use Motor Transport vehicles, you need a license, have to pass a test. I applied, and the sergeant at the M.T. Section tried to teach me to double-clutch. Several stripped gears later, he threw up his hands but signed the paper anyway.

When guys suggest at dinner there's a good movie at the flicks, that we should all go except it's too hot to walk, I say, "No, not me, not tonight."

They always reply, "If you drive, we'll buy your ticket."

APR.17

Damn, damn, damn! Everyone's in shock, mad as hell!

It's crazy! We're coming off Libs, won't be a bomber outfit at all... are being switched to transport work. We're to join something called the Combat Cargo Task Force. Instead of Libs, 215 will be flying DC3 Dakotas.

The news came so suddenly, I think even the C.O. was stunned. He made the announcement at a big meeting. Next day, two Daks arrived. More kites, plus instructors, have been coming in all week, the sky full of the strange two-engine birds as guys practise take-offs and landings. We've had lectures on their fuel and hydraulics systems, also matters unique to the job... such as how to make sure your load is securely tied down.

I've flown a few circuits-and-bumps, and solo'd today. They're easy to fly. As a small truck to carry cargo, they'd be fine. But compared with big B24s, they're light, flimsy, and — I swear this is true — the wings flap. It's like changing from a Cadillac to a Model-T. Instead of sailing off to faraway places in the Queen of the Skies, we'll be flying the Pack Horse of the Hills, dodging tree tops to deliver groceries. Anyway, that's what Lib pilots think.

An Air Commodore who came to the big meeting said he'd fought to keep us in 231 Group and was sorry to lose us. "However, the exigencies of the Burma campaign are such that the supply and servicing of our troops rapidly advancing on Rangoon has become a higher priority."

The P-Peter gang will be split up. DC3s require only a navigator, radio man, two pilots. The rest will be re-assigned to other captains, other crews, other squadrons. We're very unhappy. Especially when so close to finishing our tours. I now have 238 hours; another five trips could get us to 300.

"Why waste all that four-engine experience in the bombing business, start from scratch to learn a new aircraft, a new job?"

I cornered the C.O. in the Mess to give him the benefit of my thinking, but it only drew a shrug. Sindall would have little say in the matter. In fact, he'll be leaving the squadron; also Beadon and Roy Williams. Maybe our three senior men becoming tour-ex at the same time is the real reason our outfit was chosen for the switch-over.

People with DC3 experience will lead the new 215, and we'll be moving to a place called Tulihal in the Imphal area. The Dakota instructors are from bases near there, one pilot from my country.

"From 435, an RCAF outfit," he said. "All units with 400 numbers are Canadian. Yes, I know Tulihal. Quite near us. Sure, some permanent buildings on the site — abandoned horse stables, I think. Oh yes, I expect you'll be living in tents. Amenities? No, I don't believe there's much there, nothing at all in fact. Of course, to take in a movie, you could come over to 435 any time you want."

He told me something about DC3 operations. The flights are usually short, but several a day. They sometimes still deliver supplies by flying over a drop area and kicking the cargo boxes out, but most trips are now made to landing strips in central Burma, often with very short take-off and landing distances. They take supplies and fresh troops in, bring men out for rest leave or medical attention. Flying over disputed territory at low level, they chance taking a hit from light flak or even machine guns. Or running into a hill in foul weather.

How could they do that to a Liberator crew?

APR. 24

Surprise, surprise! We're back on Libs!

Just Art Brown's crew and us; everyone else is still changing to Dakotas. Brownie and I complained the most, must have convinced someone to let us continue on B24s. So we've been sent to join 356 Squadron at Salboni. That's where we are now. We flew down four days ago, getting out of Dhubalia quick before someone changed his mind again.

We even brought P-Peter with us, a dowry to our new outfit. But you can have only one 'P' per squadron. Painters have been at work so we now have the 356 insignia on the tail — a white 'X' on each black rudder — and where there used to be a 'P' there's now a big black 'D.'

She's D-for-Dog, or Donald, depending on which system you use. Not that she seems to mind; she just sits, silent and uncomplaining. But 'D-for-Donald' will take some getting used to.

And there's been a change in the crew. Each man had the choice — come with me or stay with 215, see what happens. Everyone opted to stay together except Smitty, terribly anxious to get back to England to look after his mum. Being a bomb-aimer without a crew might offer some hope of that happening.

I think his chances are very slight, but he's entitled to try. We all wished him the best of luck. In wartime, "goodbye" is a dog-eared word.

His replacement — we brought him from 215 — is Joe Reid, the ball player, life-of-the-party guy. "Great to be back in a crew," Joe says.

The Mess gave us a great send-off. It's jammed now: tour-ex guys waiting for orders, Lib crews who are switching to Dakotas, the excess gunners and others still there, and new DC3 personnel arriving daily.

Sometimes the time is just right for a party. The six of us leaving for Salboni got it started. The corollary to the rule that you drink 'on the house' the night you arrive is that you stand everyone a round when you leave. A half dozen glasses of tipple-juice per man is a good start towards a major carouse. The party got very noisy, very happy.

When Tommy, our piano player, got his fingers liquored up, we were off on another boozy bout of baritone belting... our complete repertoire of all the old Brit favourites I've come to like so much. We went On Ilkley Moor without hats, All went Down the Strand, cheered the Troopship Now

Leaving Bombay, invited Honey to Have A Mmmph on us, helped the Sally Ann Girl Carry Her Flag. The Brits have great songs, tunes to have fun with, and singing parties have provided the best moments I've known in this country.

A parade of fellows came by all evening to shake hands, exchange "good lucks," and insist I have one on them although, hey, that isn't the usual custom. I got both woozy and emotional. I have no wish to go to Tulihal with them but, dammit, it's not easy saying goodbye to the Adj, Roy Williams, Bill Waddington, and a whole slew of absolutely the greatest guys.

"Civilians in uniform, just till the war's over," someone wrote. Yeah, I don't know of one `career officer' on the whole squadron. Another magazine article questioned, "Do wars make men more callous and unfeeling?" Well, not for the people we have here.

The scotches kept accumulating on the table in front of me. Yeah, that's what I drink now. Not sure how I got to like the stuff, but it happened. Guess I got used to them. Cheez, thirty scotch-and-sodas and I still had another party to go to. But Taffy bottled them for me to carry.

The bash with the ground crew was well underway, but my contribution was welcomed. Again, toasts to the "best damn... in the whole damn..." — filling in the blanks as appropriate.

Isn't it normal practice for a fighter plane on special occasions to 'buzz' an airdrome — zoom across it with a combination of maximum speed and minimum altitude? I don't know if 'special occasion' is defined anywhere but, surely, leaving your squadron should qualify. And if a Spitfire is entitled, why not a Lib? We followed Art Brown's plane to the runway and watched him take off, climb away, and set course for Salbani. That's okay if you're a Squadron Leader, been on the station just two weeks. But I thought we'd earned the right to signal our 'au revoir' in a more definitive way.

When the field is flat and with few obstacles, you can skim fairly low. Joe Reid swears he saw people ducking.

"If any of those guys with his head at his ankles was the C.O., you may not even be a corporal by the time we get to Salboni."

Not so. A great welcome. "Glad to have two more experienced crews," the WingCo said. Sparks is his name, a small man in his thirties with a black moustache, thin but wide. I haven't had a C.O. who said "eh" since I had my wings pinned on.

"Only a few RCAF here when we started ops last September," one chap said. "Lots now. This is still an RAF squadron; all the admin and other ground staff are Brits, but three-quarters of the air crews in the Mess are now Canadian."

Most captains are older than me... ex-instructors... whereas the others are usually younger. They seem a good bunch.

I share a room with Joe. It's pretty bare but we have a fan! The previous occupants had hidden it under a charpoy. But I'm missing Abdul. To come with me, he demanded another increase in stipend. You get fed up with labour disputes every month so I fired him. Maybe that was dumb. All we could find here was Sammy who is quite useless. Joe says we should pay him in peanuts.

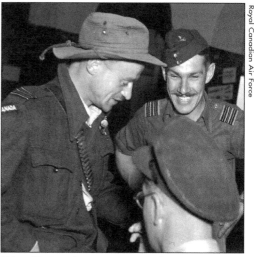

WingCO Beagle, WingCO Sparks

I've been on this drome before, of course, at 355 across the field. That was our first stop in Bengal after Kolar. With moves to Jessore, Amarda Road, Digri, Dhubalia, and now back to Salboni, we've had the grand tour.

"I was here too," Joe says. "355 was my first squadron."

Hey, am I finally going to get his story?

"From Halifax we took the slow route out here, boat all the way. Coming through Suez, there was this fantastic sight of the Italian navy — battleships and everything. So I took a few snapshots, not to get printed right away, but to keep till after the war. But somehow they got mixed up with other pictures I was getting developed. Wow! Two Military Police showed up and shipped me off to Bombay under guard for a Court Martial. I was there six weeks."

"Yeah? What happened? Did they lock you up?"

"Naw, they decided I was no enemy spy, just stupid. So they told me I'd be shot if I did anything that dumb again, and shipped me back to Calcutta. But my crew had a new bomb-aimer by then so I was sent to 215."

Which was my good luck. I'm enjoying Joe. He's a bubbly, happy kind of guy with a great sense of humour. He's also pretty bright, can talk about a lot of things. And he has a picture on the wall of his girl friend, a most lovely-looking young lady. I have a theory that you can tell a lot about a guy just by seeing a picture of his girl.

While we were messing about with the DC3s, 356 did four ops, twice more to the Rangoon supply dumps and twice to Siam. One was a successful trip to Bangkok to smash canal locks. Which seems a shame, however, when you hear that the waterways have such colourful names as the "Prosperous Revenues Canal" and the "Comfortable Kings Way."

Eight planes left Salboni, seven came back. Flt/Lt Newman's plane was hit, crashed into one of the canals.

The speed the 14th Army is advancing caused a problem. A mission the RAF planned to soften up Jap defences at Toungoo, just 150 miles north of Rangoon, had to be changed; a tank column had already taken the town. The bomb loads were dumped instead on Rangoon. Gun batteries there are still dangerous; F/O Gibbs, an Aussie pilot on 99, was hit, didn't make it back.

An ugly rumour is circulating. The Adjutant on one of the squadrons is saying that crews can forget about being released after doing 300 hours, that we could be kept on the job indefinitely. But I don't believe it. They'd never change the tour requirements at this stage, would they?

We're to find out tomorrow if Joe is any good on a bomb-sight. I'm hoping it won't be a rough target.

It's time to go to the Briefing but I'm waiting for him to finish his push-ups and knee-bends, can hear him grunting out on the back porch. I think he's crazy, that it's much too hot for that kind of nonsense.

Myself, I'm not too big on this exercise stuff. Joe's a great guy, makes a very enjoyable room-mate, but we'd get along even better if he'd stop pestering me all the time to join him.

MAY 1

My first week in this Air Force, in early `42, was spent in barracks. Two hundred of us, recruits all, were then taken out for some exercise and oxygen, a long route march in crisp Toronto winter air.

Okay, I thought, anytime now we'll start shouting that "sound off" thing or sing the Lilli Marlene song, like the soldiers in newsreels and movies. Hell, no! For two hours, the only sound was the measured beat... the crunch, crunch, crunch... of four hundred big boots in crusty snow.

I thought war and martial music went hand in hand but I've heard a brass band only twice in three years. The drums go bang and the cymbals clang but rarely; modern war is fought mostly 'a cappella.'

But when scared half to death, wouldn't some heroic music buck you up? Instead, being in an aircraft is mostly like being in a morgue; except for the engine noise, not a sound other than grunted comments.

Until today! The damnedest thing. I heard the overture just beginning. But there was no music playing. It was all in my head!

We'd pulled out of the Dispersal, joined the line-up on the taxi strip waiting to move forward... propellers twirling, but slowly, as if the engines too were ruminating on what might lie ahead. It was almost dawn. I think a string of big bombers, dimly seen in the half light, lined up and ready to go is... well, at least a bit dramatic.

By this time, as soon as we've left their care, we usually see our ground crew scurrying about, hurrying to clean up the site, anxious to catch the lorry back to their breakfasts. But not today; this morning they were all lined up, facing us, standing at attention! At the next Dispersal we passed, and the next, the same thing: six or seven men standing in a row — not saluting or anything dumb like that, but lined up side by side — like a row of sailors on a ship leaving port.

Ahh, they've been told to do it; that must be it. But it does look nice. Wouldn't it be great if it was spontaneous, a gesture perhaps even saying, "Gentlemen, you who are about to leave on a voyage that could be hazardous, we who remain behind salute you and wish you luck."

Yeah, it's always nice to feel appreciated, and we sure don't get much of that here. Not that you'd expect anything more from guys in the Mess; flying missions is just a routine job all your friends do.

Anyway, that's when the music started. I could feel my heart beating a little faster. A rousing tune... maybe Pomp and Circumstance... it made you wish you could stand up, swing your arms, march up and down the aircraft.

We'd taken off, were well into the sky before the volume faded.

A very historic day, of course; a combined operation with the British Army, Navy and the USAAF to re-take Rangoon. Our job is to demolish gun positions so our troops can storm the beaches tomorrow.

This is our third trip with 356. Assigned to 'A' Flight under Art Brown, we must have retained some of the seniority built up at 215 because we were leaders of a box on a 'daylight' to Rangoon. Then a rare night attack, again to the Rangoon dumps. On both trips, opposition was slight. What interested the I.O. were reports of fires burning throughout the city. What does it mean?

"A Lib right above us, skip. Don't think he sees us," from Eddie.

That might be; nobody's using ball turrets today although Jonesy is on a beam gun. "Okay, Ed. I see him. Yeah, too close; I'll move over."

In formation flying, you at least know where everyone's supposed to be. But today's a gaggle, fifty aircraft charging around clouds, every kite for itself, lots of sudden swerves to one side or the other. With the cowboys flying planes these days, you could get clipped from any direction.

Rangoon is on an estuary leading south to the Bay of Bengal. Several miles wide, there's plenty of room for landing craft to penetrate close to the city. But batteries of artillery are lined up on Elephant Point to complicate any invasion attempt. Our job is to knock out those guns.

The coast line has appeared on the left. "Elephant Point straight ahead, Wal," Joe says. "Cloud's bad. Briefing was to bomb at thirty-five hundred, but some planes have dropped to two thousand to get under the cloud. Do you want to go lower too?"

"Not bloody likely, not unless there's no alternative."

"We're to make two runs so let's try the first stick from this height. Yes, I see the gun batteries... our group's to take the third one."

We miss to the right. But six more 500-pounders to drop. We're circling to port to come back in for the second run. I hate that. I remember being taught we should all have precepts to guide us through life. These days I have one main rule to live by: You speed across a target, you drop your load, you get the hell out of there. No dummy runs, no go-arounds.

But that's what we're doing — several dozen bombers milling about, like circuits-and-bumps time at Elementary Flying School. But it's essential we knock out those guns. Even one battery pumping shells into the landing barges would make a terrible mess.

This time our bombs hit right alongside the gun site, wipe it out.

Starting home, I'm still thinking about that music. Bizarre! What brought it on? For a few minutes it made me feel high-spirited, almost courageous. But is that smart? Could too much of that music get you feeling fearless, heroic, maybe even make you foolhardy? In fact, could that be what it's supposed to do? Hey, I don't want to fantasize like that ever again!

MAY 8

We've taken Rangoon. No problem; the Japs had gone.

On May 2nd — Invasion Day — more aircraft went back to attack the city's defences, and saw our troops going ashore. Surprise, no opposition! The Nips had smashed and burnt docks and buildings, then left. But why abandon Burma's main city after putting up such a battle for Mandalay?

A map explains it. The Gulf of Martaban slices into Burma right up to Pegu, separating Rangoon from Moulmein over towards Siam. With the 14th Army closing in on Pegu, the Japs at Rangoon risked being cut off from their overland escape route to the east. They'd left in a hurry.

A recce plane flew at low level over the main POW camp in the city, and brought back photographs. On the roofs of their huts, prisoners had painted messages such as "Japs Gone," and "Extract Digit."

Dakotas have been flying food and doctors into the camps, bringing POWs out. Several were guys previously listed as 'missing,' no word of them since. And one was the 215 gunner who bailed out in mistake. Villagers had accepted his 'help-me' money but still turned him in to the Japs. He'd had his face smashed, been treated very badly, but was still alive, supposed to be okay.

But one of 355's captains on the op, Sq/Ldr DeSouza, sent a message, "Returning to base, fire in Number Four, unable to maintain height." Then an S.O.S.

A Navy launch patrolling in the area got to where the plane had ditched, but picked up only two survivors. What makes it especially shocking is that a passenger in the aircraft was Wing Commander Nicholson, DFC and VC — the only Fighter Command pilot in this war to be awarded the Victoria Cross. And he was just along as an observer!

After bombing at Rangoon, each crew had to find its own way home. The weather worsened, black scudding cloud almost to the deck. As the terrain west of Rangoon is flat, we decided to go that way, barrelling along at under 300 feet, in and out of rain. But there were things to see: little farm plots with small buildings, modest but neat. I saw a farmer in a wide hat standing behind his bullock, just looking up. Maybe he'd never seen a flying machine so close before. The villages all had a temple, no doubt with a fat Buddha sitting cross-legged and serene and...

"Skippah... the road ahead. Big lorry... can we fire?"

Cheez, what to say? Think fast or we'll be past it. Big truck... would a farmer own it? No, has to be Japanese, or working for 'em.

"Okay... get it!"

The usual clatter and stink. The guys have had little to shoot at lately, took it out on the lorry. It only lasted seconds, then the shouts.

"We got it... blew it up. Men jumping out... diving for the ditch? Yeah, wearing uniforms. No, didn't see we hit any... but we blew up the lorry!"

In this big war, it was a trivial incident, but I worried some. It's the first time we've actually fired at people, at anyone close enough to see. Dammit, was I right? Or were they just peasants?

But the I.O. at base reassured me. "Oh, there are still pockets of Japs left behind. If it was a big lorry, they weren't Burmese."

Of course the important news all over the world is that yesterday was V-E Day; Hitler is dead, the Germans have surrendered. The radio tells of huge celebrations at home, dancing in the streets.

But no tremendous excitement here. Not a big surprise, of course, only a matter of 'when' for several weeks. Or had the European battle become 'their' war, to read about in the papers, whereas the conflict of main concern to us — as a matter of pure and selfish self-interest — is the one with the Japs. The main importance of V-E Day is that it could bring V-J Day closer.

Nevertheless, Sparky declared yesterday a 'stand-down' to celebrate. The party in the Mess promised to be a big shindig, but turned out to be a fairly tame affair — at least compared with the riotous bash-ups that were a regular occurrence on our last station. At 215, any excuse for a party was good enough; I'm realizing it was a very happy squadron.

Did its international aspect contribute to that? Maybe living with guys from different parts of the world adds a bit of ketchup to life. And did everybody, aware of our varied backgrounds, make a special effort to be congenial? Whatever... it certainly worked.

CHAPTER 19

SUICIDE OR BUST

MAY 12, 1945

"Wal, I know you don't care much for screen jobs, but that's what you've got," Brownie said, "with Flt/Lt McMaster, just arrived here. An all-RCAF crew... their first trip."

Jeez, first trip! I talked to Phil McMaster in the Mess; he's quiet, good-looking, very much a gentleman type. Not that such things matter a damn when all you're trying to assess is whether he looks competent to get an over-loaded aircraft off the ground with you in it.

Take-off was just after midnight, and the darkness makes any take-off several shades trickier. McMaster was obviously nervous as we strapped ourselves in and started the pre-flight checks. That's when I blew my top.

Do I still resent flying instructors, remembering all the times they chewed me out during training? Perhaps it was my disgust at having to baby-sit another screen trip. Or maybe I'm just getting cantankerous.

Part of the warm-up procedure is to give engines a run-up. But he forgot to set the brakes. When he gave #3 a burst of throttle, the plane surged forward, almost beheaded the airman in front.

That's when I started to shout. How could anyone be so careless?

Well, anyone can forget things when he's on his first mission no matter how many instructor hours he's logged. I shouldn't have shouted. I apologized right away, and I was sincere about that. It was also important to get him calmed down — fast —before he started the take-off.

But the lift-off and climb were flawless. The navigator, with Bob Done along as his mentor, gave us the course to Moulmein. The bomb-bay held a load of fragmentation clusters to drop on Japs escaping from Burma. Until this point we've been trying to stop them from entering Burma; now we're trying to keep them from leaving.

It was a clear moonlit night with good weather promised all the way. There are no Jap planes over the Indian Ocean, and 'George' was behaving well.

"You've flown two thousand hours, Phil, so what do you need of me?"
He agreed, so I curled up and slept till dawn.

To be so relaxed on a mission surprises me. Catnaps with Jock Govan at the wheel are one thing, but this was all night... with a guy I hardly know. Have I become a fatalist? Do I think that things are going to happen in a certain way, no matter what, so why not relax and accept what fate provides?

We talk about such things in the Mess. When you're keenly aware you are never that far from getting the chop, questions of luck and fate are a lot on your mind. Maybe we're still thinking of that chap with the Victoria Cross who 'bought it' while flying as a passenger. Guys say, "It was in the cards," or, "His number just came up."

But surely no one believes anything as foolish as that.

But sometimes bad things happen, sometimes they don't, and we wonder why. If flak hits just one aircraft in a group, why that particular plane? When we don't know the reason, a quick answer, a simplistic answer, is just that "The shell had his name on it" — as if somehow pre-destined.

To me, that's dumb. If you're flipping coins, you could also ask, "Why sometimes heads, sometimes tails?" Is that pre-destined too? Surely it lands one way or the other completely by happenstance, by random chance. But if so, if one's fate is to some extent controllable, shouldn't you concentrate on increasing your chances.

Then why the hell did I sleep all the way to Moulmein? Why didn't I stay awake — attentive, vigilant — doing everything possible to improve the odds?

Apathy! That's what it's called.

We're warned that apathy — a lethargic indifference — is a dangerous, insidious malady. But you can reach the point where you just get fed up with the struggle to stay alive — all the ditching drills, compass swings, air tests, the interminable concerns about not killing yourself. You can get to the stage where you say, "To hell with it; if it happens, it happens. I don't give a damn any more."

Yes, a dangerous attitude, but I'll get over it.

The sun woke me over the Gulf of Martaban. Our 12 Libs and the 355 planes made individual runs on the military camp from 5,000 feet. Flak didn't knock anybody down. Cec Shannon, the bomb-aimer, placed our stick across the railway station where troops were quartered, likely woke them with a bang.

"Should I take over?" I ask Phil when we're back over the sea. "You could have a rest."

"No, I'll take us home... don't need any help."

He's still peeved at that blast I gave him, I expect. Anyway, that's what I hoped he'd say. I felt a little guilty, swore I'd regain my ardour for our next trip, but went back to sleep. When you can get ten hours of op time, and sleep for eight of them, that's my kind of mission.

MAY 14

It's a suicide job, that's what! We're on our way to attack the Jap Navy. No, not all of it, not a lot of it, but still too much.

Down in the Bay of Bengal, south of Ceylon, are the Andaman Islands. Owned by India, occupied by the Nips, they lie in the sun just a few miles off the Equator. Port Blair has one of the best harbours in Asia.

Reconnaissance planes spotted an enemy naval force in the Indian Ocean — a cruiser of the Nachi class, four destroyers, a supply ship. Both Salboni squadrons had been waiting on standby until the Intelligence boffins figured out just where the ships were headed. Now we know; they're going into Port Blair and we're on our way to intercept them there.

It's not often we get the Group Captain over from Wing HQ to speak at a briefing. Clearly, this is not just another routine mission.

"It is extremely important," he said, "an absolute imperative that we get that cruiser. Troopships and freighters are now rushing men and supplies to India. Letting the Nachi with its big guns loose in these waters would be like releasing a hungry bass into a minnow tank."

We're used to pep talks, get one before each mission, but this one seemed overdone. As he went on and on, the real message filtered through: sinking that warship was well worth the sacrifice of a few bombers.

The Bombing Leader shook me even more. First he detailed the bomb load: each plane was to pack a dozen 500-pounders. Bombardiers got pictures of the cruiser. Then he added, "Ah, yes, bombing height will be at five thou."

What the hell! For such a target, that's too low. That recce course I took in Canada — I learned a bit about naval vessels —and 5,000 feet is too damn low. "Any large warship," a lecturer said, "battleship or cruiser... basically is nothing but a floating gun platform."

The Nachi will bristle with armament, gun barrels pointing upwards and outwards like the quills on a porcupine, spewing venom like a thousand rattle-snakes. Destroyers and shore batteries firing too. Jeez! At 10,000 feet it would be too dicey. Lumbering overhead at only half that...!

Were other guys as shocked as I was? I couldn't tell. Faces were grim, impassive, tight-lipped. That's what you try for; keep your lips closed, jaw clamped, eyes blank, and your fear isn't as likely to show.

We at least have good weather, just bumpy from the midday heat. Because of that, we're in a very loose formation. The planes from our sister squadron are almost out of sight but the WingCo in 356's lead plane is just ahead.

218

Good old Sparky. He's been doing his share of ops lately, could have skipped this one, sent one of the Flight Commanders instead. But he's right here with us. Everyone going has noted that, appreciates it.

We're over water now, the target another four hours. It's not going to be that long a mission. We should be home about midnight if we... damn, I was trying not to think about it, about the big 'if.' But the thought brings back, stronger than ever, that icy sensation in my belly. The same rodent — a mouse escaped from an ice box — is back in my stomach, chewing at my guts. The pain isn't intense, just a cold, gnawing ache that won't stop.

But should it affect my breathing? Ever since Briefing, I've been short of breath, as if running uphill. I have perspiration on my forehead and my lungs won't fill up. When there's something to say to the crew, I have to wait, save up enough air, or it would sound terrible.

There's something else going around in my head — a verse, Tennyson, I think. How did it go? I haven't heard it since High School.

"Into the jaws of death, into the mouth of Hell, Rode the Six Hundred; Cannon to right and left, volleyed and thundered."

Something like that. And isn't there a bit about, "Their's not to reason why, their's but to do and die."

But the dumbest line went, "Forward the Light Brigade, was there a man dismayed?"

What was the poem called? Such stupid lines. "Was there a man dismayed?" On a suicide charge, they'd all be shaking in their boots.

Or, were men more courageous then? The Crimean War — a hundred years ago, a different age. Were troops braver in that era, more willing to give their lives for king and country? Even further back: Napoleon's men, Greeks fighting Trojans? Didn't they fear death too? History books seem to suggest men died smiling in olden days but, no, I don't trust stories like that.

Jock taps my arm; he points at himself, then the steering column. I give him a thumb up. It's good policy to change drivers every hour.

The Andaman Islands — who gives a damn about them? Although the I.O. was certainly doing his best to drum up interest. "... over two hundred, large and small, in a group two hundred miles north to south, but never more than thirty miles wide." He went on about how the British arrived in the 1700s to start a penal colony, stuff like that. But when he said "cannibals," I tuned back in.

"Yes, an unusual race, descendants of pygmy stock, extremely ferocious... a bad reputation for massacring shipwrecked sailors. Whether or not they actually savour human flesh is not certain, but the rumours have persisted for centuries. Should you perchance find yourself in their midst..."

As if I needed that to think about too.

"The Charge of the Light Brigade," that's what the poem was called.

And, hey, was the incident so different from what we're doing today! Isn't this a charge we're making too, on bombers instead of horses? Guns on those ships are certainly going to be thundering. Even the numbers are roughly comparable. Instead of six hundred men, about half that. And aren't we just following orders? Were we given any real opportunity to object, to "reason why"?

"Into the Valley of Death." Well, people don't say corny things like that any more. And no poem will be written about today's charge. It's no different from similar things happening all over the world these days.

Another thing. Important. All my life I've had good luck. Has it finally turned bad on me?

What's this, what's going on? I haven't fallen asleep again, have I? Why's Joe Barlow pounding my shoulder?

I swing around and his mouth comes to my ear, shouting. But I can't make it out. Anyway, how could he possibly speak clearly when his mouth's in that shape. Joe has a big grin at most times, but right now it's so broad, so wide, I can't see either end. What's so damn funny?

Base? Is he saying base?

I point to his mike, pull my head-set over my ears, quick as I can.

"Pilot to crew. I think Joe has news for us."

Joe's voice, gleeful and excited. "Return to base," he's saying. "Wireless message. 'All aircraft return to base.' That was it. No details, no explanation. Just 'return to base.'"

Who cares why? We're going home!

Already the formation is starting a big sweeping turn. I feel ecstatic. Nobody in the group will end up tonight in some Andaman stew pot.

My luck... it's still holding good!

MAY 18

The Jap cruiser had skipped, that's why we were recalled. A recce plane flew down, found the harbour at Port Blair empty. Three huzzas for that.

But no big 'still alive' celebration. "The Navy is out looking for those ships," Sparky told us. "We're to stay on standby in case they're located."

Then a report that the Navy had intercepted the Jap force south of the Andamans, got some hits on the Nachi. Planes later spotted it limping towards Singapore, obviously in distress. The Indian Ocean belongs to us again.

But Tojo still has Port Blair. We went back yesterday, independently.

Even without the naval ships, A/A fire was fierce. The aircraft of 355's F/O Totham, on his first op, was hit. Smoke pouring from an engine, they

Royal Air Force

Port Blair Jetties

were seen to turn, bomb the target on the way down, but slowly lose height and crash into the harbour.

We had cumulus problems too, but bombed through gaps. Joe swears he hit the jetties, but we didn't get photos. No pictures, no brass ring.

Refreshments were flowing freely in the Mess as the day's adventures were discussed, recounted, reviewed and analyzed — not unlike the way golfers sit around, discuss their putts. There was discussion about the flak, the small boats in the harbour, a fighter which circled above but didn't attack. But most of the talk was about F/O Totham's crew. Even hit and in bad trouble, they put their load on the target before hitting the water. That's hero stuff, the kind of courage people talk about, wonder about.

But am I getting more callous about losses? Particularly when it's guys I don't know, do I really shed that many tears? Or do I mostly just think, "Hey, that's too bad, I'm sorry, but mostly I'm glad it wasn't us."

Yeah, maybe war does make you more callous.

A big party last night because today's a holiday; second instalment of our two days off to celebrate V-E Day, with an extra two-bottle issue of

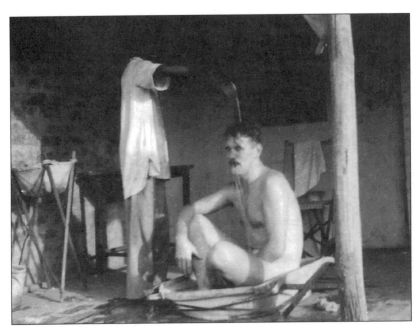

Boudoir Scene, Joe Reid

beer. Our usual six bottle pittance does of course get supplemented by quantities of gin and scotch. Truth is, some lads supplement quite a lot, even to excess.

"Do guys drink like that because they really like the stuff, or do they just think it's a swashbuckling thing to do?" someone pondered.

A whole day off is a treat. Here we go back to the drome after siesta, usually just to sit on our fannies. Are stories I heard in England correct? Are RCAF-led squadrons more likely to operate 'by the book' than RAF stations?

From my charpoy, the view out the open doorway is an un-warlike scene. Green canvas tubs are stacked behind buildings, sheets hang from poles to air out or dry. White-uniformed bearers are fussing at housekeeping chores, nobody moving very quickly in the heavy heat. Not that the damn war is ever far from your mind. I've been thinking about the new bombing technique we're to practise tomorrow — dive-bombing!

It sounds a crack-pot idea for big bombers, but our low-level attacks on targets such as bridges haven't been too effective. The USAAF is to send us some special low-level bomb-sights, but they haven't arrived yet so I suppose it makes sense to try something different. But dive-bombing?

"I finished the book," Joe says." I can re-read Damon Runyan stories a dozen times. Time for the game? How are your feet?"

I've been soaking my ankles; those flying boots really do pinch.

We play volleyball most afternoons. It's both fun and exercise, and on those days Joe doesn't bug me to join him in his damn knee bends and push-ups.

222

"Half an hour? I'll go see Cec Shannon," Joe says. "He's feeling rotten... a fever or something. The Doc doesn't know what."

Okay, that'll give me time to finish these letters. They'd be done except we had a parade of visitors all morning. I especially liked Tim's account of the bearer who came by his billet looking for a job.

"He handed me a chitti, his all-important Letter of Reference. It read: 'To Whom It May Concern — This is to introduce Khasi Habib who is a scoundrel. When I fired him, he still insisted he was entitled to a reference. I wish to state that he is a lazy, slovenly rascal. Hiring him would be a big mistake. Sincerely...'

Author, Joe Reid

And with that, the man was trying to get a job!

One rumour has been confirmed. Our tour has been extended. The new rule: No longer than twelve months on a squadron, no more than one monsoon season, but 400 hours. Damn! I almost get to 300 and they raise it another hundred.

Oh, oh, where'd the sun go? Clouds have rolled in. We're going to have a shower, the late afternoon watering a harbinger of imminent monsoons. Rain starts to pelt down just as Joe comes sprinting into the room.

"There goes the volleyball game," he says, "but we'll do exercises instead. C'mon, get up. We'll start with 'running on the spot.' Ready?"

Damn!

MAY 22

What stinking weather!

"You may run into low stratus over the Bay," the Met man said, "but nothing serious. It should clear by the time you reach the Isthmus."

But for an hour we've been enveloped in soggy greyness, moist and thick. The colour varies, going from dark to darker as we plough in or out of rain squalls, visibility nil in every direction.

But the gunners in nose and tail — the turrets manned today — can see water by peering straight down. So can Joe on the bomb-sight, but they're complaining again it's too misty, too dark, that we'll have to go lower still.

But, dammit, we're down to 200 feet. We reduced height to 500 when we first hit these clouds, have been dropping further down every few minutes.

As usual, Bob's worried about islands higher than we are. But, if we climb up, we'd lose touch with Mother Ocean.

"Got to keep those waves in sight," is what I say. "That's our best insurance against splashing into them. Go up, then sooner or later you have to come back down, the cloud perhaps right on the deck. You'd have to let down, down through the pea soup without knowing where the surface was. Over land, you'd plough into a hill top. Even over water, you could be under the waves before you saw them. No, we have to keep the sea in sight."

We've made the turn south of Burma and are getting close to the Kra, hoping we see the Isthmus before we run into it.

"We'll have enough warning, room to turn or climb," Joe says. "There are wide beaches along the coast; the hills were at least a mile back."

Jock agrees, in part. "Aye, that's what we saw. But we won't hit the coast at the same place. Therrre might be cliffs right to the waterrr."

Both were here two days ago, substituting with Ralph Weymouth's crew on the trip to Chumphon. Today we're going after a railroad bridge just south of there. The Malay Peninsula is a 15-hour trip anyway but it'll seem twice that if the weather stays like this.

Jock is flying. I'm just sitting here, mostly wondering what we should do now. I do a lot of that. The rain had stopped for a time, but is pelting down again, the wipers swishing back and forth, back and forth, doing their level best to keep the windshield clear. It's a frustrating job; they take a swipe, but it's immediately covered again with another thousand droplets.

We could abort the mission. That's one option. We could scrub the trip, head back to base.

But does the weather justify that? It never rains forever. Maybe the cloud will lift at the coast as Cloudy Joe predicted. And if we scrubbed the op, would we be the only crew to do so? What if the other kites all make it to the target and we're the only ones to turn back? Yes, we better keep going for a few minutes yet. I'll see what Bob thinks, if he knows where we are.

"Skip, I haven't seen land... haven't had a pin-point or a fix for over five hours. In this stuff, not even a drift reading. I don't know where we are. According to my dead reckoning — that's all I have — we'll hit the coast in twenty minutes. Especially as we're approaching from an angle. I could be out an hour either way."

Bob sounds frustrated, even cranky, which is not like him. But I can't blame him. Navigating in conditions like this is a terrible job and...

"What the hell was that?" A wisp, the slightest suggestion of a darker colour... a shadow, nothing more... just went by my window. Close!

"Anybody see that... see what it was?" But I shouldn't be shouting.

"I saw something, skippah," from Phil. "Just passed us on the port side, going the other way. Just a flick... could've been another aircraft."

"Harrumph." It's Arthur's deep, certain voice. "I'm at the beam hatch. It was an airplane, a Liberator. Had to be... it was so big. Can't really say I saw it... just a blur, but big... had to be a Liberator."

That's what I think too. Another Lib, aborting the op and going home. Some dumb S.O.B. of a captain, turned around and heading for base, flying right into on-coming traffic. How stupid can you get?

And yet... what else could he do? He wanted to stay in sight of the water too. And there's no highway out here, no road to stay off of. And with maybe no more than forty aircraft within five hundred miles, the chances of a collision — of even seeing another plane — must be one in a billion.

It's now past the time Bob expected to reach the Isthmus. Am I still shaky from that near miss? I've about decided we should turn and go home. We've never before failed to get to our target, but this weather's impossible.

And we now know we wouldn't be the only crew to give up.

I'm reaching for my intercom switch when I hear Phil's voice. "Clouds may be breaking up, skippah. I can see two hundred yards ahead."

Saints be praised. The rain has stopped, the visibility half a mile now. Still solid cloud above, but the ceiling has lifted. We climb to 500 feet, just under the cloud layer. I'm breathing easier again.

And there's the coastline. We swing south to follow along it until Joe and Bob figure out where we are.

Bob's soft accent. "Joe's got us a pin-point. We're north of where we should be. You can carry on south for a few minutes, but how are we to get across the Isthmus?"

A good question. I can now see some distance inland. There's a flat stretch along the water's edge, but further back are big hills going right up into the clouds; the map shows one going to 2,500 feet. Climb back up into the cloud and fly over the top? No, I won't do that.

"I don't know. Any ideas?"

"One possibility. Pretty chancy According to the map, the biggest hills are on this side of the Isthmus. A little river goes through them; we might follow that. The stream goes about halfway across to a small town in the middle. Then the land seems to level out. There's a road from there to the other coast, leads right into Chumphon."

"Where's that peak that goes to twenty-five hundred?"

"Well, it'd be close. It looks to be right beside the river, starboard side.

It'd be dicey. With this cloud, you'd only see the bottom of it."

Hell, we'd be flying into a sort of tunnel — hills on either side, the cloud as the ceiling. We'd try to follow the river, then the road. But how sharply would they twist and turn. Could 'Donald' turn as quickly? Would the valley be too narrow, the hills closing in from either side.

It sounds crazy. And yet... we've come all this way.

Also, dammit, it's a challenge. And isn't there rivalry among crews? Of course there is. If only a few planes make it to the target today, we'd want to be one of them. And now... being one of the senior crews... could we have rookies getting to that bridge if we turned back?

Also, isn't today's challenge much like a game, one that certainly beats Parchesi? Our task is to reach that bridge. There's some danger involved, but if we do it, we'll have won the match. There'd be satisfaction in that.

I question Jock... hands out, palms turned up. He gives an exaggerated shrug. He's leaving the decision to me. I know by now the others will too.

"Pilot to crew. We'll have a go at following that river. The Kra's narrow here so just a short run, less than twenty minutes... maybe no problem at all. But if it is... if hills close in on us... we might have to get the hell out of there fast, jettison the bombs, start climbing. Be ready for that. Phil, keep checking the terrain ahead... warn me about hills or sharp turns."

We're into the tunnel now. It's scary to feel you've flown into a box, a long narrow box with jagged sides. But the weather's not too bad, a 'cloudy-bright' setting if I had my Brownie. The boys have no trouble seeing the little river down below.

"Here's the dicey part, skip," from Bob. "The mountain's on the right."

But all I can see is jagged granite next to our wing tip, disappearing into the clouds. I'm steering very, very carefully, and cursing a Lib's wing for sticking out so damn far.

Phil's guiding us, his instructions, "Turn left ahead... straighten out now," easy enough to follow. Good, we're past the mountain. Now the urgency in his, "turn right... quick... now sharp left," tells us the river's gone into a little dance of zigs and zags, twisting and turning, but nothing so convulsive we can't stay above it.

In minutes, the valley seems to widen and straighten out. Phil is saying, "Here's your town, Bob, down in a valley... and a road going east. The cloud's higher now, right to the coast. And smoke ahead? Maybe Chumphon?"

The fires are still smoldering from the op two days ago. But we by-pass the city, follow the railway south, come to TF 104, a tiny bridge over the Ta-ko River. This'll be interesting. Four crews were briefed to bomb at 3,000 feet but we're in the foursome trying out the dive bombing technique... or continuing our training. We dropped three practice bombs at Salbani and missed every time.

"There it is. Not supposed to be any flak so let's do a dummy run." Joe sounds relaxed. "Not very big, eh?... Hey, it's already been hit! It looks crooked... yes, it's still standing, but the southern end's been dislodged, three feet out of alignment."

"Yeah... well, what now? Hit it again or look for something else?"

"Was never told what to do about half-bashed bridges. But it could be fixed. Let's knock it in the water."

Which is okay with me; no guns fired at us on the dummy run. Let's try this dive-bombing. I'd sure like to get a bridge for my log book.

We're at 1,200 feet, the clouds well above us but leaking rain again. Joe wants to approach from the south at an angle to the bridge even though it'll mean a cross-wind. He also wants to make two runs, but I have to veto that. It could be a rough trip home. We'll save some gas for that.

Joe's directing me along the rail line. I can't see underneath.

"Okay, Wal, we're almost there, right in line with the bridge. Get ready... ready... start your dive... go!

I push the nose down. Hard. Flaps down twenty degrees to reduce speed. We're not pointed straight at the ground but it's not a shallow descent either. The landscape is spread out in front of me like a map laid on a table. Our thirty tons are aimed right at it. I see the railroad tracks right in the centre of the map, but... where's the bridge?

Where in hell's the bridge? It's gotta be underneath. I should see it — at least the far end — but it must be under us. Have we left it too late, didn't start the dive early enough?

Jam the stick forward... still no bridge. Push the nose down some more... we'll have to go steeper yet. Okay, okay, there it is now... the far end of the main span. Except... for a bomber... ridiculous... we're diving almost straight down... left it too late. Can we still hit it? Then... can we pull out?

"Height eight hundred, speed two-ten," Jock's calling out. "Height seven hundred, speed two-twenty."

Dammit, too fast. Ease back on the throttles. But gawdamighty, I hope I don't forget to push them forward again when we level out!

"Height six hundred, speed two-twenty, holding," from Jock. "At this angle... you'll have to level out beforre thrree hundrrred."

"Wal... we're sliding to port. Right, right... or we'll miss!

Everything's happening too fast. Not only am I flying this crate, I'm supposed to aim it... at the end of the bridge... the trajectory of the bombs then supposed to have the stick start at one end, run right across it. All I have to do is keep us straight on the aiming point, keep the nose from bobbing up and down, stop the yawing from side to side. But the air is bumpy, the rain

Royal Air Force

Near miss (Frazer Crew)

is pelting, the crosswind is trying to push us to the left.

And Joe won't stop. "Right, right. We'll miss. Right, right!"

But Jock was correct. "Drop the damn bombs," I shout. "Let 'em go. I havta stop the dive, level out."

I hear Joe's voice, "Well, okay... bombs away!"

I pull the control column into my gut, can feel Jock helping. There's a lot of 'G' but the nose comes up and we're levelling out, still some air under us. And, yes, I do remember to advance the throttles again.

"Speed one-eighty... height one-fifty. You betterrr climb back up."

We're waiting for the bombs to go bang, the time delay 11 seconds.

"Fourrrth... fifth." Jim is counting off the explosions. "Gnahh... you missed. Close, verrr close, but they all missed... everrry one."

"Dammit," from Joe. "Range was good, the whole stick right beside the bridge, but ten yards to port. But thousand-pounders shake the ground, would weaken the pillars, do some damage."

Damn! All this far and we miss it. I didn't want to weaken the bloody bridge, I wanted to level it. And it was all my fault. On the dive, I just couldn't keep Peter's nose straight on the target.

We're halfway home now. The cloud has broken up and there's no problem getting across the Kra. It just seems an especially long trip home when you've bolluxed the job. I'm disgusted with myself.

But leaving the bridge, we came upon two trains. The gunners raked them, set several wagons afire. At the coast we passed over a small tanker and put some slugs into it. But then the ship started pooping shells in our direction — got some hits on us —so I said, "To hell with this," and we came on home.

At least we have another 15 1/2 hours to put in our log books. But what will I say in the remarks column?

I suppose, "Bad weather, bombed Ta-ko railway bridge; missed."

CHAPTER 20

PRAYERS AND SUNSETS

MAY 26, 1945

"Don't forget your salt tables," from a perspiring Met man. "Official reading today — a hundred and fourteen Fahrenheit."

Our 72-hour pass was wasted. Calcutta is out-of-bounds because of a cholera epidemic but too hot anyway. So three days in front of the fan, stripped to the skin, venturing out only for showers or victuals.

Except once. I showed Motor Transport the driver's license I got at 215, neglected to mention any trouble with double-clutching, so can now requisition a vehicle for any valid war-winning purpose. What surely qualified was taking the crew to the all-ranks swimming pool down at Kharagpur.

That's also where we change trains coming from Cal.

"But at night, don't leave the station area," we were warned.

The city's a hotbed of Indian nationalists. And I haven't forgotten Ted Viens from home who came to India with the RCAF, went on leave, and was never heard from again. But eleven guys in broad daylight, what's the worry?

Behind us in op hours, Joe Reid's trying to do extra trips to catch up. With Cec Shannon back in sick-bay, he's been filling in with McMaster's crew. Two missions have been scrubbed but there's something on tomorrow. We have to get him back for a four o'clock briefing.

The swimming pool was great. A major feature is the adjacency of the Army hospital, and not just because of its medical facilities.

"Famous for sightings of off-duty nurses," Joe rhapsodized. "With luck, one might even spot a grouping of them — a bevy, a brood, a covey — frolicking and splashing around water, twittering and chirping gaily... in summer months commonly seen after the moulting season, after the shedding of heavy winter plumage. Timid and skittish if approached too closely, too suddenly, but highly entertaining to view even from a distance."

Great luck, a full dozen of the colourful young things appeared simultaneously, all in bathing attire with no excess plumage whatsoever. We stayed late, barely got Joe back for the briefing.

A real wing-ding party in the Mess Saturday night; maybe I misjudged these guys. The joint was really jumping as we helped two RAF crews celebrate the completion of their duty tours on the squadron. To become 'tour-expired' must be one of the biggest things in anybody's life. They'll go to non-combat jobs for several months; with the way the war is going now, it's unlikely they'll ever have to fly another mission.

What a day! They can now think about the future with the delicious optimism that they have one. That's what we all covet — a future.

The newspaper headline about our Chumphon trip said, "Equivalent in length to a flight London to Leningrad and back."

Of our eight planes, four got to the target. Chuck Schmoyer's crew got most of the kudos, their bombs hitting the bridge close enough to twist it. Bob Badley bombed level from 2,500 feet and Art Brown dive-bombed; we were the second closest, though there's no prize for that. But there were handshakes just for getting to the target at all, enough to make it very difficult to keep my smile from getting excessively wide.

A small fib when I enlisted has caught up with me. Instead of putting "clerk-bookkeeper" as my job, I wrote "accountant." A harmless exagger-ation. But the Adj dumped the Mess books on me saying he needs an accountant to "get them in balance"— whatever that means. Cheez, rows and columns of rupees and annas up and down and everywhere. Where do you even start? Maybe I need a crash course on those lessons under my bed — or persuade the Adj to re-open my file, change the 'previous-job' entry to "piled cement blocks."

We're due for leave in June... if we want to take it. It'll be just Joe and myself; the others have decided they'll stay in camp. Yeah, travel in this country is both uncomfortable and expensive. But can you miss seeing at least one of the Hill Stations, and the Taj Mahal?

Another reason. Maybe we should cram in more ops before the monsoons get even worse, but everything's in flux here... talk of new crews arriving, other changes coming. And those tour-ex RAF guys had only a few hours more than me. Should I disappear for a while? Maybe even come back to find we're finished?

MAY 28

Joe's dead! And Phil McMaster and seven others — the whole crew — killed over Moulmein last night. Their luck ran out, they "bought it," they "went for a Burton," they "went for a shit"... take your pick. Use a corn-ball euphemism if that makes you feel better, or a crudity if that does a better job of expressing your shock, your disgust.

"Missing in action" is the official word, but how can it be called that when other crews saw the aircraft crash, smoke rising from the carcass?

Five officers, four sergeants — all young guys far from home — killed over a jerk town nobody ever heard of. Nine lives snuffed out, and one was Joe, a superior guy, one of the best I've ever met. I feel sick.

The Mess is a sombre place after you've lost friends. The usual games — dice, cribbage, darts, gin rummy and bridge —others in low conversation. But no laughter. I talked to Cec Shannon, whose place Joe had taken. You can imagine his thoughts: a mixture of relief, sorrow, and guilt.

I'm in the Mess again, a little argument going on at the next table.

"That Ernie Pyle guy. Absolute nonsense."

The outburst was by Nicky, directed at this lad recently arrived. We're all feeling indignation at losing buddies, not sure who to aim our anger at. And many find this particular fellow hard to like. Most bases have at least one guy badly bitten by the religion bug, often someone not that knowledgeable on most topics but convinced that in the easy field of theology, he has all the answers. We also had one on 215, and he fascinated Howard Johns.

"The chap's certitude is amazing, and he doesn't perceive there's the slightest arrogance involved. The Great Mystery of the Universe, reduced to a few rudimentary tenets. Yet he's shockingly uninformed in religious thought, of the teachings of Buddha and others where so much of the Christian thinking originated... has never heard of Zoroaster or Spinoza. Incredible."

We're not a very religious group, I expect, though it's a topic not much discussed. But the Protestant padre is always complaining he can't get men out to Sunday services. And yet, when another crew takes Peter, we'll often find a St Christopher medal, or a rabbit's foot, left hanging in the cockpit.

Maybe guys figure, "They may not do any good, but can't do any harm."

Neither Jock nor I have any faith in the ability of good luck charms to deflect a speeding bullet. However, if magic amulets will comfort others in the crew, they should carry them.

The argument we heard had started when the chap remarked, "There are no atheists in fox-holes," a quote popularized by this Pyle fellow, a war correspondent. It's become quite famous — in religious circles, anyway — a dictum almost to be printed on a banner and waved.

"Ridiculous," Nicky said. "How many fox-holes was this Pyle ever in? Never in mine. Yes, I've been in a few. No, not on the ground; mine were in the air. With bullets flying, one hole is much like another. I was surely as terrified in mine as any soldier in his, but it did not make a believer out of me. I've seen nothing in this war to make me think the Creator gives a damn about people, would ever come to my rescue. Don't rabid believers sometimes get killed too? How can anyone believe such nonsense?"

But everyone's entitled to his opinion. I just don't think this laddie should try so hard to push his views at others. We should just ignore him.

But I did let him irk me last night. We were talking about the unfairness of life, why one crew would get the chop while others went without a scratch. We weren't coming up with very good answers. Maybe there aren't any.

If you ask a padre about life's aberrations — obscenities such as a baby born deformed, a child dying of polio, earthquakes, famines, floods and other Acts of God — he'll mumble, "Ah, the Lord moves in mysterious ways."

But that's just ducking the question... no answer at all! After nearly two thousand years — how many millions of man-hours spent studying such conundrums — is that the best our preachers can come up with?

I remember another of Howard John's comments. "Everyone knows what's said to be the oldest profession. That may be wrong; I expect that priests were in business long before prostitutes."

But that isn't what started the kerfuffle last night. It was our resident religioso remarking that he personally had no fear of being killed because his family — his entire family — prayed for his safety each day, every day without fail. It takes a moment for that to sink in. If prayer would save his hide, what about those who died? Was he saying that Joe Reid and Brodie and so many others would still be alive if only their parents, family and friends had prayed harder?

A ghastly thought! Not that the question of prayer isn't a fascinating one. Does it have any effect at all? A lot of people would like to know, would like a proper scientific study made to prove whether it did or didn't.

Would it be so difficult? And wouldn't war years be a good time for it? Maybe select the names of a thousand servicemen, half who survived, half who died. Then look into the family backgrounds of each, checking which had been prayed for, how long and how hard. When these assessments had been correlated, the figures could be published. Then we'd know.

But surely some such study has already been made by Church scholars to prove that prayer is effective. If not, wouldn't you wonder why?

I asked the padre today if he had any ideas on the matter. He just mumbled. I miss the old Adj at 215; you could always get thoughts from him. Someone asked if he believed in God.

"Hmmm, I trust you're sophisticated enough to know it requires more than a simple Yes or No answer. For example, which God do you mean? There are hundreds of religions, countless gods. Even in our own faith, it's been said that one hundred Christians can have a hundred different concepts of the Supreme Being. But for a quick answer, I'd say that, yes, I believe in God, although my God might be quite different from yours.

"Do I consider myself a Christian? Well, that would also depend on your definition. I suppose I am... at least as far as Jesus' teachings on most ethical matters are concerned. But the theology is pretty simplistic."

"About the Universe, Howard — what it's all about, questions like that. You must have theories."

"Theories? Oh, no. Speculations, I suppose. Such fascinating riddles! But answers? Have I told you about my terrier? A smart dog, he can figure out a lot of things. For example, he understands the geography of our neighbourhood, even of areas some distance away. But I don't think he has any mental picture of Britain, could never conceptualize Europe, or planets whirling in space. They're just beyond his mental capacity.

"Could Man be like that, the Universe too immense, too overwhelmingly complex for our tiny brains? As yet, anyway. We may learn in time. But it might help if we first rid ourselves of ancient superstitions."

Yeah, I guess the old Adj really was a free-thinker.

MAY 30

Again, it's Siam. Another long one, another 14 hours. Our target is a big merchant ship at Sattahip across the Bight of Bangkok.

"Cloud over the Kra," the Met man said. "Tops to twenty thou, sitting on the mountains and filling the valleys. You won't fly under them this time.

"And have you seen the newspaper account of the B24 which tried a short-cut through cumulus last week? It entered a cloud at eight thousand, got sucked into a down-draft, was chucked out fifty feet over the water."

After an op yesterday, our ground crews could get only five crates ready for today, another gaggle. But Peter was late getting away — a brake pedal wouldn't release — so the other four are ahead of us, out of sight. Other squadrons went earlier so no sign of them either.

Just an eight-man crew. We left Phil, Eddie and Mac in their charpoys, but Jonesy is in the front turret. Though the target's a naval base, the I.O. thought there'd be no fighters. I hope he's right, especially with empty turrets top and bottom.

The replacement on the bomb-sight is Jim Hamilton from Jack Gilles' crew. An English chap I know only slightly, he looks capable. Close-mouthed during briefing, though, maybe unhappy at drawing the extra duty.

"Clouds ahead," from Jonesy in the nose. "Big ones, a solid bank."

"Okay, we'll have to climb. Everybody on oxygen."

Nobody will have to be coaxed, certainly no one who had that demonstration during training days. Eight at a time, we sat in a special room — a decompression tank, really — given pencil and paper and a column of figures to add. Easy! Then air was withdrawn to simulate the lower oxygen level in the atmosphere at 15,000 feet. The Doc stayed with us — the only one hooked up to the good 'O' stuff — and handed out more figures to be added up.

Whoopy, Doc! No diff-ee-cul-ty... everybody laughing and giggling and horsing around as we handed in our answers. That's what we were told, that we'd acted like imbeciles. We didn't remember that.

When oxygen had been pumped back into the room, the columns we'd added were given back for checking... and every one was wrong! Despite our supreme self-confidence, we weren't able to add ten numbers together. Convincing evidence that at fifteen thou, without oxygen, our judgement — our ability to calculate or reason — had failed us.

"Same effect as alcohol in the blood," the M.O. said.

Liquor does that too? Is that why drunks act so stupid?

"To ten thousand feet, most can function quite well. At twelve, for a few minutes. At twenty thousand, get on oxygen quickly or lose consciousness."

We're at 11,000 feet, still climbing, the engines groaning, cursing me in their own language. But I know what they're saying. "If that S.O.B. keeps pushing us like this, we know how to settle his hash. We'll gorge on his gas as if he had petrol to burn... like there's no tonight!"

Now the clouds are all around us — big burgeoning, bubbling behemoths, tops a mile — two miles — above us. We're inching past them the way you'd creep by a bull elephant asleep in the grass. But some clouds are smaller; we can skim over the top. It's no trouble finding the passes between the peaks.

Jonesy, enjoying himself, is directing us through the gaps. After twenty minutes, "I see water, must be across the Kra."

We're letting down now, throttles pulled back to placate the engines.

"Heading zero-eight-five," Bob instructs. "Across the Gulf of Siam... twenty-two minutes."

"Bomb-aimer to pilot. I'm on the `sight,' Captain."

But what I'm already thinking about is the trip home... getting through those clouds in the dark. It's almost six now, the sea's surface murky. By the time we get back to the Isthmus, will it be pitch-black? We could pick our way through the clouds in daylight, but at night?

Jonesy's squeaky, high-tension voice. "Aircraft, the port side, skipper. Libs... two of them... going the opposite direction. Must be going home. Too far to tell what Squadron."

From Bob, "Must be our 356 guys; the other squadrons were here earlier."

"Hamilton again, Captain. Coming into the harbour now. It's huge. If you turn to port, we can follow the coastline till we come to something."

Royal Air Force

'S for Sugar' — 356 Squadron

"More Libs, skipper. Ten o'clock. Two more... also going home."

That's four planes, four out of five. And we're the fifth. We won't have to worry about a collision today. But maybe I'd prefer some company. What a long, long way from base to be so all alone.

Here's Jonesy; I'd know his voice anywhere. "Town ahead... right in front... sheds and docks and ships. Look out! Here comes the flak."

Dammit, how can such a ratty place throw up so much stuff, the puffs all around us. I'm sitting rigid; my hands move... hands and feet... but only enough to fly the plane. Otherwise I'm a statue, bolt upright at the front of my seat, as far forward as the harness will allow, braced for the explosion. I'm thinking of Phil McMaster getting it. And cursing that we're the last plane here today, no more a surprise to the gunners than another sunrise.

Again, it doesn't happen. We're not hit. Already, we're past the flak. I feel my spine starting to relax, my posterior wriggling back into my seat.

Am I more nervous than usual today? I've heard tour-ex guys say, "The closer we got to our end-of-tour goal, the more we worried that the big prize might be snatched away." But, no, I'm not like that. How could I be more scared now when I was a hundred percent terrified from the beginning?

Hamilton reminds me we still haven't finished our job. "No large ship there, Captain. Small boats only. And two destroyers. The big ship's either been sunk, or left port. Do we go back in for the navy ships?"

Damn, go back into that flak! I guess we've no choice. But the intercom brings Arthur's voice from the beam window.

236

"A ship... out in the harbour. Could that be it?"

It is. We've come out to check. Hamilton is certain. "Two funnels, high bridge. Fits the description. When bombers showed up, it must've cast off... rather be a moving target than tied to the dock."

But what I'm thinking is... it won't be protected by the shore batteries or the destroyers' guns. Only it's own pea shooters. We're now circling our prey, studying it, like red Indians around a wagon train. It certainly looks big enough to hit. Maybe the other planes didn't spot it.

The ship certainly sees us, is popping up shells though they aren't coming close. The water is calm and I can see the ship's wake, see how it's been changing directions every few seconds. So what do we do now?

"We have nine bombs," Hamilton says, "I'd like just one first."

Bomb-aimers always want sighters. Well, I suppose so. The late-day air is soft as whipped cream as we make our run on a 270 heading, the ship heading in about the same direction. We're sort of chasing it. The bomb drops.

"An undershoot," Hamilton reports. "Fifty yards short, but right on line. If we'd dropped the whole stick, they'd have straddled her. Settings must be okay. Never tried to hit a moving target before," he went on, very talkative for him, I expect. "It was zigging, but I guessed which way it would go next. But I mightn't be lucky every time. Can we do two more runs?"

Circling for the next attack, I get a good look at the ship and its wake. With streaks going in all directions, it's zig-zagging like a beetle on a pond. But the funnels' shadows on the water are longer than the funnels themselves. The sun? It's just above the horizon, ready to take its final big show-biz dive. I'll have to be a kill-joy again.

"Sorry. We have to get out of here fast. One stick... all or nothing."

Truth is, I'm completely confident we're going to get ourselves a ship anyway — a big one. With smooth air, bomb-sight settings correct, little gunfire and a good bomb-aimer, I can feel it in my bones.

We're on the run-up, bomb doors wide. I've heard lots of "left, right, left" shouts in the past year but today it's, "Right, right, he's turning on me! Right, right, right!"

Never have I concentrated harder on keeping height and airspeed bang on, nose and wing tips level as the bombs are released. Such a long wait for the results. I'm more impatient than usual; this is a target worth hitting.

"Missed!" Hamilton says. "Close... very close, but a miss. It was turning, turning faster than we could, and I missed it... ten, twenty yards to port. Eight big splashes... no ship."

Jim confirms it. "The ship was turrrning, but you just bloody missed it."

I feel as if ice water had been dumped on my head.

But no time for post-mortems. Without waiting for Bob to give a course, I've swung west, nose up and throttles forward, pointing at where the sun is slipping below the clouds. Not an easy-on-the-gas climb, either. The four props are swirling as fast as they can. But enough? Maybe a little more power can be squeezed from the Pratt and Whitneys. I adjust the pitch, force the throttles a bit forward. At my shoulder, Arthur winces. Okay, I don't like to overtax engines either but... right now we have to chance it.

Because what will we do when the light's gone?

The clouds are still piled up over the Kra, their silhouettes easily seen from here — but there's no moon tonight. It'd be suicide to blunder across in the dark, right into the centre of a seething cu-nim. The only alternative? Climb over the top... two, three miles higher, superchargers blasting. We've never been that high. Anyway, it would take forever; we don't have gas for it. We have to get across before the light's gone.

But we also need height. We're doing dog-legs, trying to wheedle a little more altitude before we reach the cloud bank. We're there now, but only at 10,500. I was hoping for twelve. Should we circle back, climb some more? But then it would surely be too dark.

Right in front is one of the monsters, an ebony giant of solid black. At least I think so. It's hard to tell one black from another. Which way to go?

Jock points. "Therrre's some rrred showing on the rrright." He's peering out his window. "I think we should go that dirrrection."

He's right. Definitely a bit of red. Not large, not bright... but red! Hey, is that how we do it — follow the pink? If there's colour at all, there can't be cloud there, right? It must be clear, an opening, a passage-way.

We're following the sunset. It's working great. Everyone's involved, peering out windows, hunting for bits of crimson.

It's like a game. The colour is fading... very quickly, no more than a washed-out almost-pink now, but it's enough to show the way. We're half-way over the peninsula already. There'll be enough glimmer to get us across.

Disaster! Our beacon's disappeared, like a candle snuffed out. What happened? Where's the light? Everything's black. It has to be one of those cumulus directly in front, right in front of the nose. Cheez, what do I do now? The truth is, I've no idea. Except... we can't go straight ahead! What I do is swing to port, jam the throttles forward, start to climb. But there's nothing but black in that direction too. What will we blunder into? We're flying blind, waiting for a cloud to grab us, a down-draft or an up-draft to bat us like a ping pong ball.

It's Jonesy's high squeak. "Colour. I see colour." Almost screeching. "Not much, but I think so. Two o'clock."

I careen to the right, afraid we might lose it. Yes... there it is... just the faintest flicker — not solid black, a dark grey. It's enough, a pin-prick of light. Beautiful! But the air is bumpier; are we scraping the side of something?

But now the air is smooth again. The hint of colour is even dimmer, but wider. There's no more sunset, but no more cloud either. We're over the sea, and okay. Bob will get us home from here.

I'm quite confident of that, would bet my life on it. Come to think of it... I suppose it's something I've bet my life on lots of times. Literally!

JUNE 10

Hey, hey! It seems we sank that merchant ship after all. Somebody did! We're claiming a big share of it.

Several aircraft attacked the ship, but there wasn't one hit on the twisting, squirming target. But nobody's near-misses were more near than ours. Bombs that close can apparently loosen rivets, let sea water trickle in through a thousand tiny leaks. A recce plane reported the ship sinking, and Mac has painted half a ship on Peter's trophy panel.

"What's up, Fraz... given up the flying business?" I'm being asked. We haven't been on an op since the Sattahip job. But I did go to one briefing — to a place called Phnom Penh. Crazy! Too far... we'd never get back. I figured out that with any tail wind at all we'd have a better chance of going straight on to the Philippines. But the mission was postponed, then scrubbed.

The weather's been awful. There's to be a 'Burma Star' campaign medal for those who serve in SEAC. "Should be called the Monsoon Medal," we say.

Lots of new crews pouring in. "Net increase in May — eighty-four bods, of which sixty are RCAF," the Adj reported. Great! Any one could be my replacement.

My new room-mate? Cec Shannon, the fellow Joe Reid was filling in for. Now Cec has Joe's charpoy. Isn't there irony in that?

A surprise visitor last night — Smitty! His hopes of a posting to England didn't work out and he's now with a crew at 355 across the field. Seemed in good spirits. Muttering about the weather though; it was his crew that got in the newspaper, spewed out of that cu-nim 50 feet above the water.

He had news of 215. "Yes, the squadron did move to this Tulihal place. The temperature in the hills is better than Bengal, but the camp was dreadful, the only buildings former stables... full of flies and excrement."

Even worse were the flying conditions, a daily ration of cloud and rain, runways washed out, planes bogged down in mud. Starting May 7th, flying two or three times a day, they still did over a thousand flights by month's end.

They've lost two crews — one from running into a mountain, the other suspiciously like an aircraft that had been overloaded.

"I talked to Bill Waddington," Smitty told me. "He flew back to Salbani for something, said you'd never recognize 215 now... a very different outfit. Living conditions were bad, though the RCAF on 435 had been a big help. They've been working hard but he said they were enjoying it. At least, everyone was complaining about having to move again."

"Again! Where to now?"

"Bill said north of Lahore, almost to the Khyber, a place called Basal. He's finished his ops so won't be going. But "training with glider crews" they'd been told. Some people were to take a jump-master course, which would mean parachutists. See what you missed?"

Yeah, coming to Salbani was lucky.

Those mess books have really thrown me. But Jock heard me moaning, said he'd have a look if I wished. Great! He's halfway to becoming a professional accountant. I was very happy to dump the ledgers on his bed.

"Lucky" Jordan was in for a chat; late afternoon is the social hour here too. An RAF chap I met in England, he's one of the more entertaining men here. He's called "Lucky" because that's what he is, although "Fearless" would be suitable too. His DFC ribbon is for his escapade in November.

The target was Bangkok, a night raid. The trip didn't begin well for him because of start-up problems. He reached the target twenty minutes after the others had left, bombed, then headed for home. An hour later, someone noticed that... oh, oh... all the bombs were still hanging on the racks!

What did Jordan do? He returned to Bangkok and bombed again — all alone, two hours after his first run. That was the fearless part. The "lucky" came from having just enough petrol to make it to Chittagong. Nit-pickers argue that his caper was half lion-hearted, half bird-brained, but I give him the benefit of the doubt, especially as he treats it all as a big joke.

So I start my leave tomorrow. In this stinking heat, and with everything overcrowded, getting there won't be a barrel of fun. I don't even have reservations; Brownie's guys couldn't find anything for me. But surely... just one guy. Yes, with Joe gone, I'll have to go alone. There are those who think I'm bird-brained too.

But I have to see the Taj Mahal.

CHAPTER 21

HIMALAYAN HIGH

JUNE 16, 1945

The Taj... just a mile to go!

Do you know how to ride a roller coaster, both hands gripping the bar in front? Then you're ready for taxis in this country.

What a trip to get here. Train tickets fouled up, I had to go to Delhi, a hundred miles too far, then back to Agra. The month of June, just pre-monsoon, is said to be the hottest month. I'm able to vouch that Delhi thermometers can reach the 115 mark quite easily, no sweat at all. For homo sapiens, shirts will be sticking to skin like wet wallpaper to plaster.

But, great luck! Good old Robbie, my railwayman friend, is now at the Delhi station and he squeezed me onto a crowded train back to Agra. Also, he threw enough of his ample weight around — both physical and official — to arrange a hotel room. Reputed to be world famous, celebrities visiting the Taj in peacetime would have stayed here. Glancing through a very old guest book, one name I saw was "Samuel Clemens." Hey, did Mark Twain sleep in my bed?

As everyone in the civilized world knows, the only proper time for your first viewing of the Taj Mahal is at night under a glorious full moon. But what if you arrive two weeks early?

And would it be too 'Irish' to say, "The best thing about travelling alone is that you nearly always find someone to team up with?"

I had breakfast with a young English army doctor. Ian something — full names aren't important for short friendships — is visiting the Taj today, going on to Naini Tal tomorrow, also with no room lined up. It was an easy decision to join forces.

"Must be the Agra Fort," Doc says, pointing with his chin at a high red wall beside the road. He's holding on with both hands too.

I'm more aware of the terrible slum we're passing through, within a mile of the Taj! Has it been planned this way? To emphasize a lighter

Author's photo — Taj Mahal

colour, I've heard that a painter will put dark hues alongside; a musician will stress a quiet passage by sandwiching it between booming bits. Has this area been left so squalid to heighten the beauty of what we're about to see?

We're coming up to a gate now. The taxi is slowing... this must be it. Anticipation is oozing out my pores.

But will it be a disappointment? Hasn't it been called "the most perfect structure ever built"? Well, we'll see about that. I'd heard so much about Niagara Falls that, when I got there, I thought, "Is that all there is?"

We're at the entrance.

Omigawd! It's beautiful... exquisite! I'm sputtering to refill my lungs. It's not that I'm startled by something unexpected. We've all seen pictures: a huge silvery dome rising out of the square under-structure; slim, delicate towers at each corner stretching just as high as they possibly can. It's magnificent, a loveliness potent enough to make your knees buckle. You just want to stand and bathe in its... in what? In its elegance?

Because after the first flush of wonder, you find yourself querying just where the beauty comes from. What are its elements? What miracle of architectural sorcery has conjured up such a vision? I suppose many artists and architects have attempted to explain it. Or is perfection hard to analyze?

Over two hundred feet high, the structure is larger thanI expected, but that's likely not important. My guess, should anyone ask, is that its loveliness comes from just two elementary, uncomplicated factors: perfect symmetry and a sublime simplicity. Somehow those two elements have been arranged to present a vision of consummate calm and tranquility.

The building — if that's what you call it — sits well back from the main gate, silent and alone. Crowds are now trudging towards it, looking from here like slow-moving insects. But the edifice is indifferent to their presence... unconcerned, serene, oblivious to anything else in the Universe.

"Let's go this way," the Doc says. Two walks lead up to the complex, a long ribbon of water between them... a nice touch as it looks cool and deep and the structure is reflected in its calm surface. But the water, I now see, is not six feet deep and crystal clear; it's one inch deep and muddy. We've discovered one trick the Taj builder has played on us.

But that's the only flaw we find. We've circled the four towers, on the look-out for other artfulness, and the place looks completely legit. Some of the marble, close up, may not look as shiny white as from afar, but you have to remember it's three hundred years old.

One surprise — which doesn't show up on most photographs — is that the Taj sits on the edge of a cliff. Just behind it, the terrain drops sharply down to a wide river bed. The Jumna River is experiencing a severe shortage of liquidity, but monsoon rains will soon remedy that.

"Seen enough?" from the Doc. The noon sun is close to a boil.

I suppose so. We've tramped around the grounds to check the view from all angles, took our shoes off to visit the tombs. We also read the inscriptions describing how it had all been built by some old Maharajah to honour his favourite wife, the one who died in child-birth after giving him 14 children. What a monument to a guy's lady!

"Okay, Doc. Let's go." An afternoon at the hotel swimming pool will be pleasant, then dinner before we catch the midnight train to Naini Tal.

But you have to stop before leaving to take a final snap-shot, a long final look. I'll never be back. And I think you get the very best view right from the main gate. Exquisite!

But was it worth the trouble? Three days to get here, as many to get home... just to see a fancy tomb. Maybe I'm crazy. At home we once stood in a long line-up for some special movie; one couple didn't wait, said they wouldn't have stood that long to watch Creation itself.

But I think that's wrong. I'm glad I came. Long after I've forgotten the discomfort, I'll remember what I saw today. In one lifetime, how many chances do you get to see really great beauty, partake of a piece of perfection? When the opportunity arises, it's worth some degree of nuisance.

Unless, of course, we believe that comfort is all we should live for. No, I don't think that. Seeing something like the Taj is worth a great deal of inconvenience. Maybe any price you have to pay?

The little meter-gauge train pulled out of Agra at midnight and headed north towards what people here call "the hills." Hah, that's British understatement; the hills are the Himalayas with peaks five miles high.

At sunrise, 150 miles later, we reach Bareilly. Then on to Kathgodam — the end of the line with nothing ahead but big, sharp peaks.

"Every persons to depart train," the conductor shouts. Alongside is an ancient bus with a "Naini Tal" sign on it. Great! Except that standing in front are two MPs checking papers. Reservations are what they want to see.

"Sorry, sirs, if you haven't a room confirmed, we can't let you go on. They don't really have accommodation for all who do have bookings."

Cheez, what now? This village has little but mud huts.

"One slight possibility," the corporal is musing, "another hill station, smaller but quite nice, twenty miles further on. It's called Ranikhet. Usually full-up too, but I could phone, see if there's any chance."

Hot damn! They can take us... a spare room in somebody's home, twin beds, meals at a nearby hotel. Except, dammit, the bus has just pulled away, nothing to be seen except a swirl of dust following it up a steep grade.

"Bloody hell," the corporal says. "He's never left that fast before."

Lines on his forehead show he's thinking hard, never a time to interrupt.

"The only other hope... that old lorry. It's going to Ranikhet. Has a full load of fruit though; you'd have to sit up with the cargo. The vehicle looks rickety but the driver does the run every day. He'd get you there... and I don't know any other way. Shall I ask if he'll take two passengers?"

He will, for ten rupees a head, but only on a first-come basis. As all the watermelons, bananas and other fruit got there first, even filling the passenger side of the cab, the best seats have all been taken.

"On top," the driver points.

Even perched on orange crates, it's a marvellous ride, three hours of it. Up... up... up... the old truck rattles and shudders, mostly in second gear. But the scenery is magnificent. With much doubling back, you can often look down and see where you'd been a half hour earlier.

But the main feature isn't the scenery, nor the change in vegetation from parched straw-coloured grass to the lush green forests of the foothills. And it's not just lower temperatures, though dropping three degrees each thousand feet makes a marvellous difference. Something surpasses even that.

"Most remarkable," Ian says, "is the relief to the olfactory senses."

Translated, he means this part of India doesn't stink so bad. In cities, the stench is fierce. The heat and too much wholesale sweating? Doc says it's more the lack of concern about the disposal of garbage, a paucity of street cleaners combined with "a plethora of cattle and other animals."

From the Doc I'm learning a lot of new words. "Plethora," he explains, means "a whole lot."

Whatever, you're aware of something in the air that's subtly different. What is it? Our noses are quivering like rabbits sniffing a cabbage patch.

Of course — pine trees! A plethora of them!

A fantastic fragrance. For the first time in months, I'm breathing not just from necessity. Is it another example of taking something for granted, not appreciating it until you've lost it? On this trip, I've seen the Taj and smelled pine scent again. I'm not sure which has impressed me more.

The road leads us into Ranikhet at dusk. The driver stops in front of a building with "Visitor Centre" over the door, presumably run by volunteers because the lady who comes out is no clerk. I suppose the sight of two of the King's Officers climbing down from the fruit truck — materializing out of the mangoes, a plethora of them — is funny enough. She thinks it's hilarious.

"My, my," she chortles. "What a novel way to get here. Yes, they phoned through you'd be arriving late. Crowd into my little Austin and I'll drive you to your billet; boys will bring your bags directly. You'll be with Mrs Poole. I'm sure you'll be very comfortable."

JUNE 28

For a quiet vacation, Ranikhet was perfect. With big trees, shady lanes winding through them, and high peaks all about, the place was like a resort town in the Adirondacks or Laurentians. And at 6,OOO feet, marvellously cool. We even used a blanket at night.

Streets were stacked like shelves in a pantry. Mrs Poole's nice old house had three storeys, her top floor leading onto the high street. Four servants had the bottom area. Our second-floor room reached by an outside stairway to the lane below; with a separate entrance, we could come and go as we pleased.

Not that bumping into Mrs Poole was at all distressing. For a married lady with two children at school, very attractive. She spends the hottest months at Ranikhet; her husband, a Lieutenant-Colonel stationed down on the plains, gets up for a visit only occasionally.

The hotel meals were poor so we took memberships at the Officers' Mess. But mostly we were at "the Club" — the social centre for the white population of the town. A big outdoor patio was a fine spot to sit and take the breeze. One pastime was to try spotting Himalayan peaks through telescopes anchored on the parapet. One clear day, I think I saw Mt Trisull — 23,OOO feet. Of course, at fifty miles, the wish to see might be father to the viewing.

Ranikhet Hill Station

The Doc was great company and the days raced by with tennis, golf and long strolls just to savour the mountain air. We even went riding, though horses aren't really my vehicle of choice even when the terrain is horizontal.

"Trail ver' easy," the stable boy lied.

I should have known that Himalayan paths would be mostly perpendicular. But my big mare surely had mountain goat in her lineage. She'll remember me though; fingernail marks on the neck take time to heal.

Most evenings were quiet — billiards, bridge and darts at the Club. But Mildred Poole threw a party Saturday night, starting at her home. The Scotch I contributed was treated with reverence, measured out with great care. It was a stand-up supper, then over to the Club. Such a variety of people, permanent residents and some visitors. Not one brown face in the group, though. Half were civilians, maybe "bearing the white man's burden." I expected they'd be stuffy, but they were a jolly, friendly group. Perhaps they found a Colonial lad a curious novelty.

Away behind in fox-trots, I was on my feet for every number, danced with every lady there. For a mother, a landlady at that, Mildred could certainly make her feet fly. Leaving home two years ago, would I have believed I'd end up in India, jiving with mothers and grey-haired grannies... and enjoying it?

Yes, to live in India, Ranikhet would be my first choice.

But vacations end. I boarded the old bus Monday morning, fog thick on the ground. This is Hindu country. With visibility zero on the hair-pin bends, and sheer drops of a half-mile if the driver should miss a turn, it seemed appropriate to murmur Vishnu's name occasionally.

Three days later, I'm still on the way home, but our train should be in Calcutta in another hour.

We're not crowded, only six Air Force types in the largest compartment. The train's slowing down again for another station, another big crowd of would-be passengers massed on the platform. As usual, there's no line-up, no queue. It's another mob scene, people pushing and shoving to get to the edge of the platform, fighting to give themselves the best possible chance of finding a spot on the train.

But they've no hope. I was out on the platform a few stops back where the station was much less jammed. Every coach was bulging with humanity, sweating body against sweating body. On the roof of each car, a hundred crouched. Also on the little steps leading up to the engine, the coal car, each coach — clinging to anything that'd give them a foot-hold or a hand-hold.

The poor devils, they must be desperate to get wherever they're going.

The train jolts to a stop. The crowd pushes forward, the air full of what sound like Hindu curses. They're pressing right up against the side of every car — our coach too — looking for something to hang on to.

What's this! A face at one of our windows — a young man's face, curly black hair — looking right in. Somehow he's managed to clamber up, or been boosted, to reach that height. He's saying something, pointing his finger.

I think he wants... he wants to come in, come right through the window into our compartment... right in here!

That's shocking! Absolutely! Indians never ride in First Class. Well, I suppose they could, a rich one might, but I've never seen it. And he wouldn't have a ticket. But it's more than that. By all custom, First Class is reserved for whites! Natives can't just barge in like that. Maybe I'm not sure it's fair — I guess I never thought about it — but that's the way it is. He can't come in here!

And yet... the lad's face is pleasant. Bright-eyed and clean. Could we make an exception, maybe for even a few more like him if they don't smell too bad. Just for the hour into Cal. But, if you let some in, how would you stop the others? There'd be fifty of them; we'd be swamped.

Jeez, that's done it! The decision's been made for all of us, made by a husky English guy. He decided for everybody because he smacked the kid. The Indian with the curly hair was trying to squirm through the window and the RAF guy hit him, so hard the kid was knocked backwards, blood spurting from his nose. He'd have toppled right to the platform if people hadn't caught him.

Hey, that's really done it! The crowd has turned into an angry mob, an enraged horde... shouting at us, furious, shaking their fists and screaming. The incident has triggered something and they want blood; you wouldn't go out on the platform now. I'll be glad when we start moving again. Until then, we're safe enough; our doors are all locked.

Jeez...! They're coming after us! What the hell! Twenty or thirty, more behind them, charging our coach... climbing up the outside, trying to come through the windows after us — through the open windows, all at the same time. We have to stop them! We can't let them inside now... not in the mood they're in. It could be a massacre. Now it's a fight. We're pummelling them, any face or arm or leg that comes to a window... trying to pry fingers off the sills, trying to close the windows.

"There's a leg. Push it out."

"Gimme a hand; got two of them here."

"Look out, he's got a knife." Omigawd, we *are* fighting for our lives!

"Watch that door, don't let them reach in, don't let them unlock it."

Yes, that's right, that's our weak point. If they could force a door... if a few got in, they'll all get in. We'll be finished, our throats cut. The door has a window, a small one. An arm is reaching in, groping for the lock release. He's almost found it. I kick... hard. Even above the tumult I can hear a yelp as the hand is withdrawn. Now there's a face at the window, looking straight in at me. Not a nice face, not a friendly face. The eyes look wild, full of hate. I try to punch it. Oh... no! Hands have grabbed my wrist. In panic, I pull it, twist it, wrestle it back inside. But a man can't come through that window, not the small opening in the door... only an arm and it's a long reach. But it's a shorter reach through the big window beside the door. They've figured that out. An arm stretches in, reaching for the lock, hunting for it, and I kick. Another arm, another kick. Everybody's shouting. Another groping arm, and I kick again.

I couldn't guess how long this goes on. Maybe, in true sixty-second minutes, it hasn't been that many. I just know I'm getting so very hot, so very, very weary. I'm not even sure who it is who's wearing my clothes.

Is it me? I suppose it must be, from the neck down anyway, because my feet and wrists and arms are aching. But it doesn't feel like me at all, not the person I'm used to being.

Like the bell at the end of a round of boxing, the train whistle signals the end of the skirmish. Now the train is lurching forward.

That's finished it. Our attackers are dropping back to the platform. There's a final barrage of stones smashing the windows we'd managed to close, more shouts and curses. But we're pulling out of the city. We're okay now.

JULY 4

Back to Salboni at dawn, I first heard the rumours — about another move — on the lorry that meets trains. Yes, the Jap retreat into Siam has meant long, long trips. If we were closer to the enemy, trips would be shorter, cloud banks fewer, bomb loads bigger

"The Mandalay area," the driver assured me, "helping the Yanks ferry supplies over the Hump into China. I'm sure of it."

But at breakfast no one knew anything for sure. And, big disappointment, not a word about any crews going 'tour-ex.'

I did get stories about interesting missions. A combined op was against the biggest bridge the Japs have built on the Burma-Siam railroad, POWs used as slave labour, of course. The bridge was over the Kwai near Kanchanaburi, "kwai" being the Siamese word for river.

Using 'Master Bomber' technique, Yank B24s and Libs from 159 circled above to bomb gun positions, draw A/A fire and direct traffic. Aircraft from 355 went in low after ground defences. With gun batteries thus distracted, others attacked from low level. Les Evans, our RAF Flight Commander, led 356 against the secondary by-pass bridge and left it broken in three places.

But 159 aircraft, led by Sq/Ldr Watson, got the big prize. Going after the main bridge at less than 400 feet, they placed sticks right across the main span, knocking it in the water.

I've met this Tommy Watson, an RCAF-er. Quite a wartime career! The boys on 159 say you can sometimes get him talking a little. A fighter pilot in England, his Hurricane squadron was ordered out East — by boat via South Africa — to bolster the defences at Singapore. Still in the Atlantic, they got news of Pearl Harbor.

Leaving the ship, the pilots scrambled across North Africa, practised short take-offs and landings and boarded HMS Indomitable, an aircraft carrier on its way to the Far East. Reaching Sumatra, they flew their Hurricanes into Singapore as Jap artillery shells were falling on the airfield. There were skirmishes with Jap fighters and bombers, but the fortress surrendered days later; a few surviving aircraft got away just in time.

Watson's been called "the last man out of Singapore."

They retreated to Sumatra, then Java, the Nips in pursuit. Tom eventually made it to Australia with adventures all the way. My favourite is of the time in Java he got shot down behind Jap lines. Trying to walk back to his base, he came upon retreating Dutch cavalry with extra horses, but their commanders all dead. They just assumed an unattached officer would join them, take command. For two days, Tom led a cavalry unit.

He flew with the Australian Air Force, eventually got sent back to Canada to the Boundary Bay place. Returning to India as a Lib captain, Tom knocks down that big bridge on the Kwai.

On another effort, 356 started off on one mission, were re-directed to go after a 10,000-ton tanker spotted in the Gulf of Siam. The weather was so bad that four planes turned back, but WingCo Sparks and two others got there. John McNabb's crew, Brad Bradshaw on the bomb-sight, laid a string right across the ship. "We could see the crew jumping overboard," the boys said.

"Atrocious weather," everyone reports. Eight kites went to hammer Japs near Moulmein. Five reached the target, two turned back. F/O Ross climbed into the clouds, disappeared. The kite was later found, crashed into a hill top.

As for possible moves, the P-Peter guys were disgusted that, from the Officers' Mess, I couldn't bring them any better rumours than they already have. Maybe not as good. Bob has a wild one; one of his navigator pals had talked to a friend from 99.

"The Dhubalia group believes they'll be moving to the Cocos Islands," Bob says. "I checked the Atlas. They're just a speck in the ocean, three thousand miles south of here, only eleven hundred from Australia. Closest land would be Sumatra and Java — six hundred miles — so all those Dutch islands would be in bombing range. Singapore too. There's some sense to it. What do you think?"

I think it's ridiculous. Hope so, anyway. If we're to move anywhere, I want it to be closer to home, not 3,000 miles further away.

JULY 10

O' day of days! We've done it! The whole crew... we've completed our missions. We're tour-expired... finished!

And what does that mean? It just means we're through with being shot at, through with plodding through skies bumpy with cloud or flak, worrying about Jap fighters pouncing, watching the sun come up and wondering if we'll see it set. That's all behind us now! Permanently? Well, if the Japanese hold out long enough, we could be called back for more missions, but I won't even think of that today. I just feel too damn good... as if I'd just hit a home run, scored the winning goal in overtime, sunk a hole-in-one!

No! Better than any of those, or all combined. It's as if I'd been handed a box, gift-wrapped with pretty ribbons. The card would say, "Enclosed, please find your life. The Air Force thanks you for the use of it, the loan of it, but you may now have it back. Very soon, you can start to do with it whatever you wish — have a normal life, maybe even live to a ripe old age."

Who ever received a gift better than that?

The C.O. told me last night to come to his office this morning and bring my log book. "Certified that Flt/Lt W. W. Frazer has completed one operational tour on Liberator aircraft." That's exactly what he wrote!

There's other stuff, not important: "Total operational sorties —

35; total op hours — 340." Under "Assessment of Ability as Heavy Bomber pilot," he put "above average"! How about that! But then he muttered, "I figure a pilot has to be rated above average just for managing not to kill himself long enough to complete a tour of ops."

The reason for being released? The Squadron really is moving. Only needing a few missions to go tour-ex anyway, it wasn't worth taking us. And, yes, it's those Cocos Islands! 356 will join 99 there while 159 and 355 stay in Bengal to continue the war from here.

Leaving the WingCo's office, I know I have to get letters off to tell Jean and the folks they can stop worrying about me. But even that has to wait. In fact, I'm already in a trot by the time I exit the C.O's door, heading for the crew's basha, stopping only to pick up the Scotch I've been saving.

The guys are all waiting. They've also acquired some gin in case my summons to the WingCo's office meant what they hoped. I don't even have to tell them my news; they can see it in my face fifty yards away.

Yippee!

I used to consider the P-Peter gang a fairly serious, sober bunch. Over Jap territory, yes, but not here, not today. I'm sure the whoops and hollers can be heard all over camp. Not that anybody will complain. Most will guess the reason for such a mid-day party. They'll be saying, "Yeah, the Frazer crew... they're tour-ex today. What a bloody racket they're making."

But no one will question our right.

JULY 16

No problem finding a chair in the Mess now, not since the boat party left. The place will soon be empty; all the aircraft leave in just two days. An overnight stop in Ceylon, then a very long flight over the Indian Ocean. The Cocos Islands are only five square miles total, a tiny speck in all that sea. Each crew will hope its navigator doesn't have an off day.

The rest of us? We now think we'll get a posting back to England.

"When? I don't know when," the Adjutant grumbled. "Whenever your name appears on the Boat List, that's when. How should I know when troopships will be available? But if you want a guess, I'd say two or three months."

Art Brown's crew has been added to the tour-ex group. "Yes, taken off the Cocos list," Art tells me. "Maybe because we have nearly three hundred hours now."

"When you get to the UK, you'll still have a long wait," we're told. "There's a huge bottleneck in Britain, thousands waiting for transport to the States, Canada, other places. The wait could be months."

For guys just bustin' to get home, that's terrible. But at least there's a formula to decide who in the UK will get on a boat first. Everyone gets a Repatriation Number — the lower the better. Add two points for each month of the war until you enlisted, plus a point for each month thereafter you stayed in Canada. For example, troops rushed to Britain in September '39 would have a Repat Number of O. But some guys here go as high as 12O. I get a 7O which is fairly low, maybe why I consider the system quite fair.

We did two short errands in P-Peter this week. In case we don't get another chance, we give her a little pat on the nose after each trip.

When it's goodbye time, you have a party. It was a big affair, NCO's included. The WingCo made a short speech.

"Tonight's gathering is to salute those who have recently completed a tour of operations on this squadron. My congratulations. Also, it marks the end of 356's operations in India and the beginning of new adventures."

But I happen to know of another reason for the bash, especially the free liquor; Jock Govan had a hand in it. While I was on leave, he had worked on the Mess books, had them all balanced up.

"But look at this," Jock showed me. "Your bar is making a forrrtune."

I trotted the books right over to Bradshaw who is Mess Secretary now.

"All balanced up," I told him. "My co-pilot's a genius. And look at this. Did you know the bar is making this much money?"

"I knew that," Brad said. "That's why we're having buckshee booze."

With two hundred guys milling about in a room designed to hold not half that many, it becomes a crush. When drinks are gratis, the liquor flows like water, the harried bar staff not caring whether they pour two ounces or six. Soon you have a room over-crowded with guys in various stages of tipsiness, shouting and singing. The area in front of the bar becomes a war zone of elbows and shoulders and bodies trying to squeeze through, the floor slippery as drinks don't quite make it on the return trip to the tables.

The Peter crew had another very 'toasty' evening. We saluted everybody

— ourselves, front turret to rear, not forgetting Smitty and Joe Reid — plus the ground crew, Flight Commanders, the WingCo, right to the very top.

The past weeks have been tough on my resolve to reduce my liquor intake. By night's end, I was having trouble with toasts to people with difficult names — guys like Loory Mowbutton, and Winnon Churshill.

But the biggest salutes of all? They went to good ol' P-Peter, no matter what ridicklush name they called her here. A super wind-up party!

AUG. 7

We're on the Boat List! Next stop — Bombay! No particular ship; we just have to get our fannies over there fast.

Magic Carpet — won't take off

Group did find a chore for us, a two-week stint at 158 Staging Post at Alipore. The job was trundling people and supplies around India, flying a Mark 3 Lib at least three years old. It nearly killed us one day.

No, I don't agree it was entirely my own fault. At the Alipore airfield in Cal, we loaded boxes for Madras. As usual, there were airmen hoping for a ride; a six hour flip looks good when the alternative is three days by train.

"Sure, climb aboard," I told about 15 of them. I suppose I was playing the big shot, being a good guy. But then three more showed up, and then four. And then another two. It's hard to say, "Sorry, that's enough."

"D'ye ken we could be rearrrr-end heavy," Jock warned me.

If so, that's serious. Aircraft weight has to be properly distributed.

"Well, we had twenty-three men from Chitters the other day," I countered. Having agreed to take them, how could I tell them I'd changed my mind?

"That's trrrue," Jock persisted, "but today we have all those crrrates in the tail end." Sometimes Jock's unfailing logic gets a little tiresome.

"Okay, okay. No more, but we won't kick any of them off."

So as many as possible were jammed on the flight deck, more shoulder to shoulder on the cat-walk, which left only a few smaller guys to sit away back on the damn boxes. We tried to adjust the trim tabs to compensate for the centre of gravity being back near the tail, and managed to take off... though I admit it's traditional for the rear end to leave the runway more or less coincidentally with the front.

But then the old tub wouldn't climb. True, her posterior was dragging, but P-Peter would have handled it without everyone getting so excited. Even with the throttles forward, our rate of climb was negligible. And then — straight ahead, appearing out of the smog — three huge industrial smokestacks lined up in a row directly across our path.

Considering the strange angle at which we were hanging in the air, it was no time to experiment with a big turn. So I pushed the throttles through the stops and we inched a little higher, a little higher, the engines shrieking. And we slid right over the middle stack — the smallest one — clearing it comfortably, no real problem at all except of course for the smoke and everyone coughing.

And, hey, we finally touched down in Burma, three times at Akyab. But I've still never seen a Jap; they all left weeks ago.

On our flight to Lahore, Bob did some very sloppy navigating, got us miles off course. We found ourselves over a city that looked familiar. To me, anyway; the others had never been there. It resembled Agra, but we had to circle several times to be sure. I can now report that the Taj looks very nice from overhead too.

We're now back at 356, but it's like a ghost town in a Wild West movie. We're still in our basha though Messes have been closed. But we have a lorry, so can shuttle over to 355 for meals. Mostly we just talk, read and sleep.

But only until we can get some train reservations to Bombay.

I'm spending most of these last days with the crew. Sharing such a variety of experiences — about 14 months now — provided most of the elements needed for a great camaraderie. The other ingredient? I guess you also had to like one another. By some fortunate fluke, it seems we melded together very, very well.

A great experience. I'm glad they let me be their skipper.

AUG 14

What the hell's an "atomic device"?

We got no news at all on the train. Since pulling into Bombay today, "A-bomb" is all we've heard. The Yanks have dropped two on Japan. Some new kind of bomb, it can wipe out a whole city. Might it even shorten the war?

"Six o'clock news in the Mess," Cec Shannon says, "in five minutes."

The Frazer Crew — au revoir

But I'll finish unpacking. And in the trunk I see the carved trinket box Mac gave me. It gets me wondering how the guys are doing back at Salboni. If the crew were still together, we'd have another officer; Bob is now Pilot Officer Done. I bequeathed him my lamp, fan and tool-box. And it was a big pleasure to take him into the Mess, introduce him around. Then Smitty came over from 355 with the big news that he too has finished his tour.

Next day, my orders to leave — on the midnight train into Cal. Everything was a rush, no time for lengthy goodbyes. But the crew all came around for final handshakes, bringing the news they are definitely being split up. Jock, Arthur and Bob are going into Burma to spray mosquitoes with some miracle new insecticide called DDT. The others will head off in different directions.

Though away from home longer than any, I still feel guilty to be leaving them. The time came; a hard moment! We agreed we'd all keep good memories of our little adventures together.

Have you ever tried living for four days on a park bench? Seats provided Third Class patrons of Indian railroads are neither that comfortable, nor as roomy. As usual, our reservations got fouled up. Art Brown got berths for his crew, leaving half of us behind — without tickets, and me in charge.

"No First Class for a week? But we have to get to Bombay, could miss

Another Stop — 4 days to Bombay

our damn boat. Third Class? Yes, okay, it'll have to do. Give me ten tickets."

Every bench was jammed; kit bags filled the space between. Overcrowded by day, a shambles at night! But did anyone complain? Ha, they bitched non-stop for four days, most of it directed at me.

We chugged into Bombay at tea time, were told the monsoons had preceded us by two weeks; yesterday's rainfall was ten inches. Combine that with gale-force winds and you get a horizontal rain that laughs at raincoats.

But what's the racket? Guys just came in the door, shouting. Everybody down that way is yelling. What are they saying? Can I be hearing it right?

"The war's over! The Japs have surrendered... just came over the radio."

Hey, hey! It's actually happened. The war's over. Hallelujah!"

CHAPTER 22

BLESS `EM ALL

AUG. 21, 1945

> "There's a troop-ship now lea-ving Bom-bayyy,
> Bound for old Bligh-ty's shore,
> Hea-vi-ly la-den with time ex-pired men,
> Bound for the land they a-dooore..."

The band has blasted into "Bless 'em All" once again. It's been playing the same tune, verse and chorus, over and over for an hour. Not that anyone's complaining; it's not often you can feel a song has been written just for you, just for this special occasion in your life.

Now another group has picked up the words:

> "There's ma-ny an air-man now ser-ving his time,
> There's ma-ny a man sign-ing on.
> You'll get no pro-mo-tion, this side of the o-cean,
> So cheer up m' lads, bless 'em all!"

The *Durban Castle* is another P & O ship... should mean a good trip. And, hey, the gangway's being put in position. Won't be long now!

Our group includes Art Brown and his guys, and Shannon, and more I know. We were lucky, only had to wait in Worli a week. The Maple Leaf Club was a good place to get news. Yes, 215 had trained for the dropping of parachutists, and taught glider pilots. Now they're based at Hmawbi, just outside Rangoon.

I asked if anyone knew of Johnny King, my Poona tent-mate. "King, RCAF navigator? Sorry, but I think he was killed on 358."

At the bazaar, is it more foolish to buy from a sharpie in a fez — risk paying gold prices for brass — or get nothing and maybe miss big bargains? I chanced the purchase of a black sapphire pendant for Jean, some silks and ivory carvings for the folks.

"Great weather in the Cocos; always a breeze off the sea."

A plane brought back the first news. Three 99 planes flew the first mission on August 1st, attacking a ship off the Java coast. The 356 guys then joined 99 in dropping supplies to resistance forces on Sumatra and Malaya.

"C'mon, Fraz, let's go!"

Yeah! Our line has started to move, the first guys climbing the steps. We're leaving India! But first: a little ceremony. Everybody's doing it. Before boarding, you kick your feet against something solid. More properly, you take off both shoes and bang them together. That's what I'm doing now.

Slap!

You have shaken the dust of India from your feet! Now pull the shoes back on. The band is playing again. Here we go. Bless us all!

SEP. 15

The lights are on again in England!

And how can a city be kept so clean, the streets not used as garbage dumps, the sidewalks free of slop. Best of all is the air — not only smelling sweet, but cool and crisp and invigorating. It's wonderful to feel fully alive again; last night we walked the streets of Bournemouth for hours.

The voyage was okay, though 25 days on a crowded ship is quite enough.

A BBC broadcast had an item on Siam. "The railway system is a shambles," the commentator said, "bridges down, trestles and track smashed, locomotives and freight trucks out of commission. Thai officials don't know how or when they can get it operating again."

Should we be proud of that? I suppose so. You feel sorry for the Siamese, but it was what we were sent to do and the job got done.

We passed Gibraltar in the middle of the night. I've now missed seeing it from both directions. There was Canadian talk there of pointing our revolvers and taking control of the ship. Instead of turning north to England, we'd make the captain sail straight on to Halifax. But the Brits wouldn't agree, swore they'd fight us. So much for wartime friendship and co-operation.

In the chilly Bay of Biscay, Air Force types all switched to 'blues.' A lot of sweaty khaki, ready for the laundry anyway, got pitched into the Atlantic. At Liverpool — 18 months after leaving there — a military band played, appropriately, "Smoke Gets in Your Eyes."

I like Bournemouth, know it fairly well as I spent six weeks here back in '43. How long ago that now seems.

Back in Bournemouth

We parade for roll call each morning; otherwise our time's our own. Located in a resort city, room and board provided, and with adequate spending money even without any more India Allowance, you have to admit this isn't too hard to take. But some other time; not right now. I just want a boat crossing the Atlantic.

OCT. 15

Another month, still sitting in Bournemouth, no boat yet. We're getting restless, fractious... no doubt why a Group Captain came to talk.

"The delay," he said, "is because ships have been diverted to the Far East to bring home men who were prisoners of the Japanese."

Well... okay then. The reports we heard of the brutal treatment of POWs were apparently not exaggerated. The Japs were bad, Korean guards even worse. On the Burma-Siam Railroad alone, 60,000 Asians and 20,000 whites — mostly Brits, Aussies and Dutch — died on the job. For minor transgressions, men were beheaded. Okay, okay, we'll wait. Bring the survivors home.

Then we learned that, for ships still plying the Atlantic, Repat Numbers are being ignored. Another meeting, a big squabble. Junior officers don't usually get into shouting matches with Top Brass, but can they wash me out at this stage?

The closer you get to home fires, wives or girl friends, the more impatient you become. Another reason: there's concern there are only so many jobs to be had. Will the last home be out of luck? Discussing what we'll do for a living is a very large question. But we now have details on options our government is offering. The Rehabilitation Credits, based on years of service, are generous. My 46 months are worth $2,OOO.

I'm still thinking about Accounting, a five year apprenticeship program with a firm of auditors. Beginning salary: $4O a month. You can't start much lower than that. But the government will supplement it, bring it up to $1OO. With increases in pay, my Credits should last four years.

But can you ask a girl to marry you on that? She'd have to work, could earn another $75 without reducing my stipend. But only $175 for two?

Another good question. "How hard will it be to change to civilian life? Will servicemen have trouble settling down to a more routine existence?"

"We don't think so," the Counsellor said. "Most men already gone to civilian jobs say the transition has been painless. When you take off your uniform, it's like closing a door behind you, stepping into a new life with new and exciting challenges to whet your interest. Some say their wartime experiences already are remembered only as bizarre events that must have occurred in a previous existence, or in a dream."

So a quiet month. Medical and dental checks, revolvers and flying stuff turned in, medals drawn. In RAF parlance, a real award — such as a DFC — is called a 'gong.' But not many of those in India; we just got campaign medals. My admiration for British humour was not diminished to hear that these are called, not gongs, but 'tinkles.'

After a week in London, the mail rack had 47 letters in my slot. Mom's trying to find shirts and socks for me, but they're scarce everywhere. Dad is trying to get the heater fixed in my '34 Chev. It's almost winter.

And Jean says she's waiting. All I need is a boat!

NOV. 11

Maybe because of that big fight with the Brass, Repat Numbers are now back in use. So I have a ship — the *Queen Elizabeth*! I'm to get to Southampton two days early on the 'advance party,' whatever that means.

And our Squadron guys arrived back from the Cocos. What an adventure! Only a few bombing jobs before the Japs gave up, then trips to drop leaflets to make sure everyone knew the war was over. That was followed by supply drops of food and medicine in Malaya, Sumatra and Java.

The weather was terrible, likely the reason four crews were lost. From 99 Squadron, one RAF crew flew to Palembang, another to Singapore. In each case they reached their destination, then disappeared. From 356, Roy McLeod's RCAF crew and John Watts' RAF gang did supply drops to Malaya, but didn't return. What makes the news even sadder is that all four crews were lost after August 15th — after the war was supposed to be over!

Bournemouth was like old-home-week. Al Bishop, who was a clerk at RCAF HQ in Ottawa, is now Adjutant here. He bought me dinner at the

Waiting for a boat
Author, Art Brown, Cec Shannon

Permanent Staff Mess and plied me with liquor. "I've never yet seen you properly inebriated," he complained. Which I guess is a terrible reputation to take home.

One officer there, wits addled by liquids of some sort, was trying to be poetic. "We're the lucky ones," he kept repeating, "the fortunate few, the survivors of this enormous conflict, congregating here from many parts of the world for the final dash to the finish line."

But not many care for fancy talk like that.

Newspapers use phrases like "returning heroes." The term's embarrassing. If 'hero' implies exceptional courage — doing something risky above and beyond the call of duty — there may have been a few, but not many. I don't think a man is being heroic just because he does something — even in dangerous circumstances — when he has no alternative. Like thousands, I just did what I had to do — cursed and hated it, but did it because the job had to be done. Never once did I feel even slightly heroic... though often the opposite.

One bit of advice from fellows already home is surprising. "If you think family and friends are just waiting to hear all about your big adventures, forget it. No one's interested. All they want to discuss is the future."

And I thought I had several stories worth the telling. Try writing them down some day? Naw, too much work.

But one of the gang at school had an ancient uncle who'd been in the Boer War. How his eyes would light up when he told us of those old battles — long marches, the Zulus, horses hauling artillery! Oh, the horses!

Such an archaic kind of warfare — quaint, quite beyond our ken. But he spoke not of momentous matters written in history books, but of the little things seen by someone who'd been there, had been involved. He should have written them down.

Is it possible this war will seem old-fashioned some day? Even quaint?

This afternoon, I have letters to write, but they'll be the last of this war. They've all been numbered, and the one to the folks is number 155 since leaving Canada — about one a week. To Jean, it's 198. But she's the champ; her last to me was number 352.

And it has the answer I want. If I decide to start the accounting course, she'll still marry me, share starvation rations for several years.

To which I say, "Hurrah, Yippee, and R.O.T.B... 'Roll On That Boat.'"

NOV. 19, 1945

We've had the coast of Nova Scotia in sight for an hour now.

It's a cold, misty morning. You can't make out any topographical features yet but there's a big crowd on deck trying... and I'm one of them.

A sailor came by, said we'll dock in Halifax in thirty minutes. That started a buzz. It hasn't stopped, hasn't faded away even yet.

The crossing took just five days, the Queen E charging into heavy seas as if really trying to get us home fast. But I've spent most of the trip below the water line. 'Advance Party' meant being 'Deck Officer — E Deck Aft.' No one told me, but I think my job was just to be there in case anybody needed something. Lots of good discussions, one airman with an interesting point.

"Do you realize that with German and Jap air power disbanded, the RCAF is now the fourth largest Air Force in the world?"

Hey, maybe so. And as so many RCAF flew in RAF squadrons where the ground crews were Brits, could we have been the highest anywhere in percentage of the population who were aircrew members?

On 'E' Deck, too, much of the conversation is about jobs. We'll get a month of disembarkation leave before being discharged... will have to use the time to find someone who'll hire us.

I did leave my post below decks a few times. Big money was changing hands, poker and crap games all over the lounge. My thought was to let a hundred bucks ride for a few passes of the dice just to see if I had a lucky streak in me, but the room was so jammed I couldn't get near a game.

The closest I got to poker was standing room behind one of the players. He wasn't doing well. But in this hand — draw poker, nothing wild — he picked up two pairs, kept the aces, discarded the sevens. The three cards he drew included two more sevens. Bad luck. With all the betting, two pairs wouldn't win. My interest shifted elsewhere.

Then I noticed my lad hadn't folded; he was raising the bets. When he showed his hand — four nice sevens — he'd won a very nice pot.

Question! By some freak, had there actually been a half-dozen sevens in that particular deck... or had he finagled the discards. But, as Confucius say, "Kibitzer keep mouth shut."

I can see Halifax now. We're almost there. And the sun is coming out!

It'll take several hours to unload the ship. Then directly to a train for a non-stop, two-day trip to an RCAF station near Montreal. There's to be no big fuss, no welcoming ceremonies, certainly no speeches... just a day for some paperwork. Then another three hours on the train and I'll be home — on my own for thirty days before getting the final big handshake from the RCAF.

We're right in the port area now. Lots of flags with a Union Jack in the corner but, as usual, I can't tell which is Canadian and which means it's a British merchant ship. When the hell will we get our own flag, one we can recognize!

I'm so excited I've started to tingle.

We've slowed right down. There's such a crowd it's hard to see. But, hey! What's that commotion ahead... on that dock on our left?

It looks like people... a big crowd... two, three thousand, maybe more. And they're all waving, waving their arms and their hats in the air. I think they're cheering.

Yes, I can hear them now. They're all shouting and hooraying like crazy. Welcoming us home. Not me, of course. I know that... but someone special to each one. But couldn't some of the greeting, some of the cheers — a bit of it anyway — apply to all of us. Yes, I think that's possible. Hey, isn't that beautiful!

And now, fellows on the ship — guys all around me — are cheering back. They're all yelling and hurrahing too, shouting at the top of their lungs. And waving their arms. Acting like they were nuts.

And, and... hell, yes... me too! I'm doing the same damn thing. I just noticed. I'm shouting my own head off!

But that's not all. Not the worst of it. It's ridiculous, but I need a handkerchief. For Pete's sake, I'm a grown man, 24 years of age, a war veteran even. How the hell can a war vet have big tears running down his cheeks?

If they don't stop, I'll have to wipe my face in front of all these guys!

But I can't help it. They won't stop. I feel overwhelmed, weak-kneed, completely choked up.

I'm going home! I'm going to get there! I'm going to make it home!

Epilogue

Wally Frazer did start accountancy training in January, 1946 and received his C.A. designation in 1950. Married to Jean in July of '46, they happily have two sons and a daughter.

With a partner, and one employee, a professional practice was opened in Ottawa in 1959 under the name Frazer and Otton, Chartered

Accountants. Wally retired in 1982 by which time the firm's staff had increased to, "Oh, about the equal of two Liberator crews."

Jean and Wally now spend the summer months at a quiet lakefront summer home near Perth, Ontario; the winters in Florida are more hectic. Both enjoy travelling (though never yet to India), take University courses, play some golf, like lots of socializing with friends. She also enjoys gardening and crafts while his interests include singing with a men's chorus, a couple of stage appearances, some painting of pictures, and a little writing now and then.

Author   Jean

Two P-Peter reunions have been held in England. Several of the original crew members not located for the first gathering had been traced by the time of the second so that Wally has had a visit with each. But advancing age is becoming a problem; Arthur Cooper, Joe Barlow, Stan Jones and Eddie Hill are now deceased.

"But we did all manage to live to what was, at least relatively, a 'ripe old age'," Wally says. "In 1944, we'd have all settled for that."

Crew Reunion – 1970
Govan, Author, Cooper,
Howse, Jones, Slight,
McIlwaine, Barlow

"Will you now start another book," he was asked.

"No way. Not full-sized anyway. It was fun to do but, hey, I never guessed it'd be such a lot of work. But tell readers that if they have any questions or comments, I'd be glad to hear from them. The address: RR5, Perth, Ont., K7H 3C7."

For more copies of

A TREPID AVIATOR — BOMBAY TO BANGKOK

send $17.95 plus $3.00 for GST, shipping and handling to:
GENERAL STORE PUBLISHING HOUSE
1 Main Street, Burnstown, Ontario
Canada, K0J 1G0

Korea Volunteer	$17.95
Past Tense — Charlie's Story	$14.95
Choco to A.I.F.	$14.95
Valour On Juno Beach	$14.95
Black Crosses Off My Wingtip	$14.95
The Ridge	$14.95
Trepid Aviator	$14.95
The Wing And The Arrow	$14.95
In The Line Of Duty	$39.95
Mud and Blood	$14.95
Ordinary Heroes	$14.95
One Of The Many	$14.95
Fifty Years After	$14.95
The Canadian Peacekeeper	$12.95
The Surly Bonds Of Earth	$12.95
The Memory Of All That	$14.95
No Time Off For Good Behaviour	$14.95
To The Green Fields Beyond	$14.95
Time Remembered	$14.95

For each copy include $3.00 to cover GST, shipping and handling.
Make cheque or money order payable to:

GENERAL STORE PUBLISHING HOUSE
1 Main Street, Burnstown, Ontario
Canada, K0J 1G0